EVALUATING AND TREATING FAMILIES:
THE M^CMASTER APPROACH

EVALUATING AND TREATING FAMILIES: THE MᶜMASTER APPROACH

Christine E. Ryan
Nathan B. Epstein
Gabor I. Keitner
Ivan W. Miller
Duane S. Bishop

Routledge
Taylor & Francis Group

NEW YORK AND HOVE

Published in 2005 by
Routledge
Taylor & Francis Group
270 Madison Avenue
New York, NY 10016

Published in Great Britain by
Routledge
Taylor & Francis Group
27 Church Road
Hove, East Sussex BN3 2FA

Printed in the United States of America on acid-free paper
10 9 8 7 6 5 4 3 2 1

International Standard Book Number-10: 0-415-95157-7 (Hardcover) 0-415-95158-5 (Softcover)
International Standard Book Number-13: 978-0-415-95157-9 (Hardcover) 978-0-415-95158-6 (Softcover)
Library of Congress Card Number 2004023339

Library of Congress Cataloging-in-Publication Data

Evaluating and treating families : the McMaster approach / Christine E. Ryan ... [et al.].
    p. cm.
  Includes bibliographical references and index.
  ISBN 0-415-95157-7 (hardback) -- ISBN 0-415-95158-5 (pbk.)
    1. Family psychotherapy--Technique. 2. Family psychotherapy--Methodology. 3. Family assessment. [DNLM: 1. Family Therapy--methods. 2. Models, Psychological. WM 430.5.F2 E92 2005] I. Ryan, Christine E., 1950- II. Title.

RC488.5.E937 2005
616.89'156--dc22   2004023339

Taylor & Francis Group
is the Academic Division of T&F Informa plc.

Visit the Taylor & Francis Web site at
http://www.taylorandfrancis.com

and the Routledge Web site at
http://www.routledgementalhealth.com

Contents

Tables and Figures

Acknowledgments

When compiling the writings and research that make up the McMaster approach it was quite striking to note how many people have actually contributed to the clinical, teaching, and research work that has gone on over the past several decades. We purposefully did not delineate specific contributions of each researcher because we wanted to keep the focus on the McMaster approach to assessing and treating families. Nonetheless, we do want to acknowledge many colleagues and friends who have helped to make this book possible—whether the contributions were made in the early days of setting up training programs, doing clinical work, and participating in research studies—or in more recent times when we concentrated on developing assessments, teaching manuals, and testing our treatment model. We also would like to thank those who read numerous drafts, made insightful comments, reviewed several versions of the manuscript, bibliographies, instruments, and manuals.

In Montreal, key figures who worked on the McMaster model included Bill Westley, Vivian Rakoff, John Sigal, Herta Guttman, and Roslyn Spector. Josh Levy and Isaac Rebner helped with the clinical work while at McGill University. Dorothy Horn started with us in Montreal and moved to McMaster where she became centrally involved in the training program with Sol Levin, Jock Cleghorn, and Jack Byles. When we moved to Brown University, Larry Baldwin was a key player in helping to develop key McMaster instruments and manuals while Ron Evans focused on the area of physical illnesses and family functioning.

Those at Brown University who helped with feedback on the book include Dave Solomon, Rich Archambault, Joan Kelley, Curt LaFrance, Sandy Kazura, Alison Heru, and Walter Brown. Lisa Cronan, Sarah Forlasto, Roselee

Rego, and Kirsten Johnson provided much help with manuscript preparation, assembling the bibliographies searching out references and helping us meet many deadlines.

To all, we express heartfelt thanks and look forward to continuing our work with families.

Introduction

Much of family therapy being practiced today can be categorized as structural, strategic, behavioral, problem-solving, narrative, generalized psychodynamic, postmodern, or mixtures and amalgams of some or most of them.[1] It is clear that if any of these approaches were effective most of the time we would hear of no other suggested models for the treatment of families. With over 2,000 family therapy training programs operating in the United States and other countries around the world, the field of family therapy includes a wide array of health professionals from a variety of backgrounds and disciplines and with a variety of experience. New journals focusing on family therapy appear on a regular basis and also reflect an expanding field.

The renewed attention given to learning, understanding, and practicing family therapy has many sources. One is the increased focus on changes in the family and family composition, and the hypothesized effects of these changes. Another may be the increase in violence in the home and school and its association with the family environment. Whatever the reason for this new interest, a prerequisite for conducting good family therapy includes using an advanced treatment model that has internal consistency and demonstrated effectiveness. The McMaster model meets these criteria. In addition, the McMaster approach to family therapy is noted for the solid theoretical base that underlies the model and the comprehensive and collaborative therapeutic process between the therapist and family members. The parallel research and teaching components that have been developed in concert with the clinical model have contributed to its widespread use.

In this book we do not offer a review of current schools of family therapy, nor do we critique different approaches to studying and treating families. Introductory textbooks and literature reviews address the variety of theoretical models underlying clinical work with families and generally are useful for presenting the strengths and weaknesses of different approaches. It is all too common for practitioners to choose bits and pieces from different models and to set off in various directions to do therapeutic battle. While the motivation may be honorable, the result is often chaotic or ineffective. We believe there is no justification for an undisciplined approach to treating family problems. Consequently, one of our fundamental beliefs is the importance of clarity and consistency in the framework used by therapists when treating families. Professionals working with families need a model that provides an understanding of family functioning and one that guides their treatment. The McMaster approach provides a conceptual framework for assessing and diagnosing family functioning, and for treating families.

The McMaster Model of Family Functioning (MMFF) originally referred to the theoretical basis of how a family functions. The model was developed after years of working with a variety of family types who described a myriad of family problems. The therapy that derived from this model, the Problem Centered Systems Therapy of the Family (PCSTF) was referred to as the treatment model. In writing this book we use the term "McMaster approach" to encompass the model, methods of evaluation and treatment of families, and our underlying philosophical framework.

Purpose

Our motive for writing this book was threefold. First, our clinical, research, and teaching program has generated a large number of books, articles, monographs, and manuals addressing various theoretical and clinical aspects and research findings based on the MMFF. We are often asked if our work is available in one volume that includes all aspects of the McMaster approach: (1) how the original model was conceived and developed; (2) how the theoretical, assessment, and treatment components of the model are used and linked to one another; and (3) how our clinical and research findings help us develop further lines of investigation.

Second, we have noticed that as others have used the MMFF and PCSTF, the original concepts and ideas oftentimes become either diluted or misrepresented. We felt that if we describe the model in detail, trace its development, and explicitly show the linkages between the model and treatment approach, assessments, and applications, practitioners will have a more unified picture and be better able to apply the concepts, and, hopefully, the model more faithfully.

Finally, it has become increasingly clear that pharmacotherapy alone is often not sufficient, and sometimes not appropriate, to address the issues and problems presented by patients with a psychiatric or medical illness. A ceiling effect may operate for treating patients with medication only or it may be that medication is not warranted for a variety of reasons (e.g., patients unable to tolerate medication, less severe symptomatology, presenting problem is a family issue). Family therapy is one treatment option that a therapist can use either as an adjunctive treatment or as the main therapeutic offering to help patients and their family members.

However family therapy is used, it is essential for the treatment model to have explicit stages and clearly defined steps so that the treatment process is successful. Teaching programs often emphasize a survey of theories and practices as an approach to treating families in lieu of providing an in-depth knowledge and understanding of at least one method of family therapy. Students may be able to link different goals or techniques with a family therapy model, but they are still unable to evaluate a family's functioning, much less initiate and conduct family therapy. The end result is often a hodgepodge of ideas and ill-formed strategies that help neither the therapist nor the family. The McMaster approach provides a solid framework for eliciting information from families, obtaining accurate assessment to determine diagnoses, and for setting up a workable treatment plan. In addition, the model has been developed as a time-limited therapy, a fortuitous circumstance given the mandates that have recently been established by the current health care reimbursement climate.

Audience

This book is addressed to students, interns, experienced therapists, trainers, and family researchers. Because we try to reach as wide an audience as possible, the McMaster approach has been taught to social workers, psychiatric nurses, family therapists, pastoral counselors, family physicians, pediatricians, psychologists, and psychiatrists in a variety of clinical settings and with a variety of presenting problems. Further, since the original developers were practicing clinicians with a keen interest in research, they realized that the model had to be of use to both clinicians and researchers. For those who are interested in learning (and teaching) the McMaster approach, we hope this book becomes a useful tool. The components of the model—including family assessment, family treatment, and family research—form an integrated system. We have developed the model, however, so that each of these components may also be used independently.

Outline

We have tried to make the plan of this book as systematic as the model it explains. Throughout the book we give examples of clinical aspects of family problems and provide summaries based on case studies or family sessions that highlight the McMaster approach to a presenting problem. Any reference to clinical cases has been carefully reviewed and edited to conceal specific circumstances of a case and to disguise names, places, and situations so that families and individuals cannot be identified. Since our clinical work spans four decades we were able to describe a composite of family problems when we provided examples of how the assessment and treatment might work.

The book is divided into two parts. Part I includes a description of the history and development of the model, treatment, training process, assessments, and research. Details of the specific content of the chapters are noted below. Part II includes the instruments and assessment tools that we have developed when using the McMaster approach and a section listing related articles from researchers not associated with our program.

Chapter 1 traces the origins of the MMFF and places it in historical context. We show how the model evolved from earlier psychiatric theories and how we integrated these ideas with observations drawn from our own clinical and research experience. This chapter also introduces the originator of the McMaster approach, Nathan Epstein, and the development of his ideas. Chapter 2 provides an in-depth description of the MMFF by laying out the meaning and concepts associated with each family dimension and summarizing variations expected within a normal family. Chapter 3 presents the Problem Centered Systems Therapy of the Family (PCSTF), the treatment approach that is based on the MMFF, and includes specific steps to follow when using the McMaster approach in family therapy. Chapter 4 is a blueprint for establishing a training program to teach the PCSTF. Based on our experience in developing programs, we discuss key concepts, issues, and concerns to be aware of when setting up a training program.

In chapter 5 we focus on the instruments we have developed based on the model, including a self-report assessment, a clinician rated scale, and a structured interview for the beginning therapist or paraprofessional. We give examples of case studies for each of the assessments to show how they can be used as clinical, research, and teaching tools. Chapter 6 is a review of our research findings presented over the past several decades, an outline of our current research efforts, new directions we are planning for the future, and research gaps that we have not addressed in our work. In chapter 7 we answer questions that we receive periodically about the model, our instruments, research findings, teaching methods, and clinical issues. These questions originate from trainees in our program, attendees at conferences or workshops, or correspondence with researchers and translators of our instruments and assessments.

We believe that our model is useful for clinical and research purposes and represents a contribution to the field of behavioral sciences in general and to family treatment in particular. In writing this book, our goal was to present a useful, practical, and comprehensive guide for assessing and treating families. We hope that we have done so.

PART **I**

CHAPTER 1

Development and Historical Background

The conceptual beginnings of the McMaster Model of Family Functioning (MMFF) originated at McGill University in Montreal, Canada more than 50 years ago. Under the direction of Nathan Epstein, a team of clinicians and researchers began their work in family therapy by focusing on two major areas: (1) research with nonclinical families and (2) research on the process and outcome of conducting family therapy. A nonclinical family refers to a family whose members have no diagnosed psychiatric illness. The family may or may not be healthy and may have good or poor family functioning.

The model that was conceptualized and tested from the mid 1950s through the 1970s, first at McGill and then at McMaster University in Hamilton, Ontario was refined, elaborated upon, and completed at Brown University in Providence, Rhode Island where Epstein had relocated and created the Family Research Program. The prototype for some instruments and manuals (i.e., the Family Assessment Device and the *Problem Centered Systems Therapy of the Family* (*PCSTF*)) had begun at McMaster and became finalized and ready for distribution after the team moved to Brown. Other measures used to assess family functioning (the McMaster Clinical Rating Scale and the McMaster Structured Interview of Family Functioning) were more fully developed at Brown. Today, members and associates of the Family Research Program continue to teach and study this model, and to use it daily for clinical as well as research purposes.

We thought that a useful way to introduce the McMaster approach to working with families was to present a brief historical background of the conceptual beginnings of the McMaster model. The easiest way to do so

3

was to introduce the developer of the model and to discuss the specific schools of thought that influenced him and from which the model emerged.

Nathan Epstein, founder of the Family Research Program and the main developer of the model, first received training as an adult and a child psychiatrist. He underwent additional training in psychoanalysis, a highly valued component of every psychiatrist's repertoire during the 1950s and 1960s. Throughout his training, Epstein worked in the area of child psychiatry, seeing children, adolescents, and families. Epstein was interested in understanding a child's development—how he or she thought and behaved—not because he wanted to treat children, but because he wanted to better understand the thinking and development of the adults he treated. The training he received, his work with children and their families, and the ideas he was exposed to led to a change in Epstein's thinking and focus. Ultimately, the shift in direction resulted in a body of work that included the development of the McMaster model for assessing and treating families, the establishment of an interdisciplinary team of researchers who focused on family issues, and the creation of a training program for clinicians and therapists.

Although Epstein led the effort in developing the McMaster approach, many individual clinicians and researchers played key roles in designing the model, treatment, instruments, training, and research. Whether their contributions assisted the programs at McGill University, McMaster University, or here at Brown University, the work would not have progressed without their hard work, clinical insight, and research knowledge. In this chapter we first trace Epstein's development as a clinician and researcher, for it exemplifies how to intertwine clinical experience with research findings. We then highlight the unique features of the McMaster model, show how the clinical, teaching, and research components developed in concert, and introduce the philosophy and thinking which serve as the underpinning of the model and guide our approach in evaluating and treating families.

Early Training

By the early 1950s, workers in child psychiatry had begun to connect the role of the mother to the behavior of the child. Some therapists noted that other family members also had an effect on the identified patient. Nathan Ackerman, in particular, began to develop his ideas on working with the total family group in psychotherapy—a radical idea at the time.[2] Ackerman was drawn to families and the family environment through work with his own young patients. He reasoned that, since the family was the focus in a child's development, it did not make sense to expect a child to change in isolation from other family members.[2,3] By the time Epstein underwent training with him, Ackerman was already engaged in formulating family theories and family therapy techniques as a more effective way of understanding and treating patients.[2] The process he used had the significant actors in the patient's life attend the therapy session, thereby making it easier for the therapist to tease out family interactions that led to the behavior being treated.

Other leaders in the field of psychiatry and human development who were based at Columbia University also had an impact on Epstein's early thinking. Abram Kardiner, a pioneer in cultural psychiatry, examined the interplay between culture, economics, history, and social patterns and practices as they affect individual and group behavior.[4] Two other noteworthy figures who stimulated further thought were Sandor Rado, whose work centered on adaptational psychodynamics[5] and David Levy who taught research methodology and the process of integrating research findings with an understanding of human behavior.[6] The interplay between the theoretical ideas he was exposed to and the clinical work he was engaged in led Epstein to the same realization that Ackerman had arrived at, that is, that he could not help children unless he worked with their families. He realized that if he just focused on the child, the treatment was not effective. He was convinced that, unless he saw the family, his understanding of the clinical issues were lacking. He decided to stop treating children unless the family was present.

Once Epstein determined to include the family in treatment, he began to experiment with different ways of involving family members and patients in the course of conducting therapy. He tried several approaches: (1) seeing the mother and child patient in play therapy; (2) having both parents in for occasional sessions, with or without the child or adolescent patient present; (3) having mothers participate in activity-group therapy with children and seeing the mothers in a separate weekly group without the children; (4) seeing both spouses together when only one of them was the presenting patient; and (5) bringing in different members of the individual patient's family at various times during the course of the patient's therapy. As time went on, the approach that was used most frequently and seen, at least clinically, as most effective was one in which all members were seen together for conjoint family therapy regardless of the presenting problem.

Theoretical Foundation

During these early years, the basic conceptual model that therapists used when working with families was intrapsychic while the therapeutic approach was psychoanalytic.[7] For example, family interaction patterns that were thought responsible for the intrapsychic and behavioral pathologies in the identified patient were observed, stimulated, inferred, and interpreted. Then analytic concepts were used to interpret behavior seen in family meetings.

The concepts might include role projection, displacement, incorporation and projection of part objects, oedipal strivings, sibling rivalry, denial, and affective repression. The primarily analytic approach changed gradually to one that focused more on interactional aspects of intrafamilial behavior. Therapists began to emphasize the importance of releasing affect underlying the presumed and significant family interactions and the associated intrapsychic conflicts and fantasies. The primary objective remained that of easing the intrapsychic conflicts of the identified patient that were inferred to result in the pathological symptoms or behavior for which treatment was undertaken.[8]

When Epstein returned to McGill after his training at Columbia, he and several colleagues began a series of family studies. The first studies involved nonclinical families and overlapped with later studies that focused on families with an identified patient. Whether family cases were nonclinical or clinical, the primary function of the family was conceived as providing an environment for the psychosocial development and maintenance of its members. Over time Epstein and his colleagues came to believe that the family *as a system* was more powerful than intrapsychic factors in determining the behavior of individual family members. This insight, which came out of the series of small research studies, led to a fundamental shift in his approach to family therapy.

In practice, the shift from viewing therapy as primarily a psychoanalytic-interactional mode to a systems mode was difficult at best. In the family systems approach the family is looked at as the factor to be evaluated; it is the family that is centrally involved in the difficulty and in the behavior being examined. The 15 years of training and experience that Epstein and colleagues had undergone had to be modified and a new approach had to be developed. The new approach was controversial, for it questioned previous assumptions of treating patients and families and because it made use of research data to alter clinical practice. Now, the idea of evidenced-based treatment is much in vogue, but in earlier periods the link between clinical practice and research findings was tenuous. During the transition period, before the new method was fully developed and established, there was a natural tendency for Epstein to slip back into a primarily psychoanalytic approach when conducting therapy. Today Epstein may consciously decide to use a psychoanalytic approach to generate another viewpoint that furthers understanding or therapeutic progress.

Approaches to Family Therapy

As noted, Epstein's psychoanalytic training had resulted in a strong interest in the interaction between personality and the surrounding environment.[9]

Given his additional training with Ackerman, Epstein paid increasing attention to the family as an important aspect of an individual's environment. Not surprisingly, therapists viewed the family from very different perspectives. At least three important conceptual approaches marked the early advances in the field of family therapy and set the stage for later model development. The approaches included: (1) an individual psychodynamic model, (2) an interaction model, and (3) a systems model. Epstein's thinking about these models evolved over time and included some overlap. The three models and examples are described below, roughly as occurring in three sequential phases.[7]

Phase 1

Individual Psychodynamic Model

The conceptual orientation which Epstein used in phase one of his clinical work with families was based on an *individual psychodynamic model* in which therapists saw the family as a backdrop for understanding the intrapsychic conflicts of the identified patient. The primary focus of the therapeutic work was on the patient; the family was seen only as the context in which the individual psychodynamic processes and structures were worked out. Significant family members were referred to and even seen on occasion, but the focus always remained on the individual.

Example:

Donald, 7 years old, was referred for treatment because of a severe crippling anxiety. The boy was involved in a strong symbiotic relationship with his mother. Examination revealed that the anxiety was related to extreme separation anxiety. He displayed a school phobia, but only as one aspect of his unwillingness to ever let his mother out of sight. The mother contributed strongly to the maintenance of this symbiotic relationship as a means of fulfilling her own intrapsychic needs.

Therapy focused on the boy, primarily in the form of individual play therapy sessions. Epstein occasionally spoke to the mother and received reports from her on the patient between sessions. During these brief meetings, he encouraged her to extricate herself from this over-intense relationship and to develop a healthier stance with her son. Epstein saw the father only after many months and only because the mother indicated some unhappiness in her relationship with him. Epstein saw the father alone and dealt with some of his intrapsychic problems on a rather superficial basis. He never saw the couple nor any other family member together. The patient and the mother gave reports of the family to the therapist, but these were not dealt with in detail nor used to any great extent in the treatment of the identified patient.

After several years of regular visits, the patient was relatively free of anxiety and had a close, warm relationship with his mother, yet both seemed to allow for autonomous functioning.

Epstein's intrapsychic orientation was so strong during this period of his career that treatment focused on the identified patient (with some supportive work done individually with both parents), despite the fact that family pathology indicated couple and family therapy might be helpful. *Recognition of the impact that family members had on each other (including, but not limited to the patient) would later become a key concept in the McMaster model.*

Phase 2

Interactional Model
The *interactional phase* of Epstein's work is distinct from the previous phase despite some overlap in both the temporal and conceptual sense. Interactions between several family members (usually two) are observed and interpreted to members during therapy sessions. The interactions are usually related to the intrapsychic processes of the interacting members, but they do not have the same degree of detail, frequency, and intensity as does the intrapsychic phase. The assumption underlying the interactional therapeutic approach is similar to that of the previous phase—the psychopathology is centered in the intrapsychic structure of the identified patient and one or more family members. Interaction between family members is observed and used as a means of unlocking the intrapsychic pathological processes.

Example:

The presenting problem was a married man in his late 20s who complained of impotence. Psychodynamic investigation revealed that this man had severe conflicts in his relationship with women and in coping with his aggression. He was the youngest of a family that included many sisters and a mother who overwhelmed him with loving attention. According to the patient's description, the women were loving but powerful. He was a pleasant, smiling, ingratiating individual; as long as he repressed all anger and negative response he was showered by protective love. The price he paid for this happy state of affairs was almost complete impounding of his rage and aggressive responses. His dreams and fantasies of women, however, revealed the extent of his fear and rage toward them. He saw them as devouring, dangerous, and overwhelming.

Epstein treated the patient and his wife in couple's therapy. Examination of the spouse revealed a severely disturbed woman who experienced a traumatized and deprived infancy and childhood. This woman did not merely hate men—she hated everyone indiscriminately. The rage she carried inside her was limitless.

Treatment focused on the interactions of the couple with each other in the here and now—in the sessions and at home between sessions. The man overcame his impotence, but this was replaced by her frigidity. It took months of weekly sessions to get the couple stabilized in a relatively satisfactory relationship. The therapeutic focus was on how they could change their interactional pattern from one of mutual destruction, which reinforced their respective intrapsychic conflicts, to one of mutual support, which was a means of minimizing the intrapsychic pathology. Once the relationship was stabilized for several months, Epstein terminated treatment. Both were encouraged to recontact Epstein if they felt the need. In fact, they periodically contacted Epstein over the years whenever they had difficulties in their relationship with each other, their children, or in their lives outside the family.

In this example, Epstein always focused the therapy on the interactional level of the couple. The approach yielded reasonable results. *Three factors from this phase of Epstein's work reappear as integral parts of the McMaster model. They are: (1) an emphasis on the here-and-now, (2) use of the strengths of family members as active ingredients in the therapy process, and (3) an openness and active encouragement by the therapist for family members to return if further work is needed or other problems arise.*

Phase 3

Systems Model
In the *systems phase* of Epstein's work, the family is viewed as an open system. Structure, organization, and transactional patterns displayed by the family system are seen as the important variables that determine the behavior of family members. Changes from within or without that affect the family system affect the behavior of all members of the system. In treating families, the focus is on the disturbances in the system from the standpoint of its structure, organization, or transactional patterns. The intrapsychic processes of members of the system are of secondary importance. The implicit assumption is that if the system variables are in good working order, then the

individual's behavior will be favorably influenced as will the intrapsychic processes of these individuals.

Example:

This case was referred by a family physician who had attempted for some time to help the family solve their problem. The presenting issue was that the husband's mother lived with the family for the previous four years, causing constant friction between the wife and the mother-in-law. The situation also created dissension between the husband and the wife and a general unpleasant tension in the entire family. The whole family was seen in consultation—husband, wife, mother-in-law, and three teen-aged sons.

Clinical evaluation suggested the following family dynamics. The wife was frustrated in her attempts to get love and attention from the mother-in-law. The mother-in-law was aware of the wife's needs and enjoyed the power allocated to her. The wife was angry at the mother-in-law and attacked the husband for not standing up to his mother and demanding that she be nicer to his wife. The husband felt caught in the crossfire between his wife and his mother.

The children reported constant tension in the home and very little communication. Rather, there seemed to be an unhappy silent with-drawal on the part of the three adults. The husband suggested that he may be the cause of the trouble because he was not giving as much of himself to his wife as he should. This remark by the husband led the discussion to one of the central issues in the family, namely, that the wife was not getting enough gratification from her husband. Since her children were becoming more independent and since she could not derive support from them, she looked to an alternate source, her mother-in-law. The result was constant tension with the mother-in-law becoming a scapegoat.

Therapy focused on opening up the family system by dealing with the whole family unit.

Emphasis was placed on improving communication patterns within the system, and encouraging the husband and wife to develop their own relationship toward a more open and giving level. The wife was encouraged to demand more of what she felt she wanted from her husband and the husband was encouraged to open up to his wife and to discuss the conflicts he was feeling between his wife and his mother. The family responded well with only a few sessions of therapy. No intrapsychic probing was done during this family case.

Rather than address the intrapsychic conflicts of individual family members, Epstein focused instead on the structure, organization, and transactional patterns displayed by the family. *Specific system variables that he examined were power allocation, division of labor, patterns of intrafamilial affective expression and involvement, and communication channels. These factors appear again, albeit in a refined form, in the McMaster model.*

Synthesis of Ideas

Although there is obvious overlap in the theoretical and therapeutic approaches discussed above, the examples presented show how the emphasis differs in understanding the behavioral problems and, therefore, in the approach taken to treat the families. By this time, Epstein had finished his training at Columbia and had returned to Montreal where he continued his work combining clinical, teaching, and research in the area of family studies. Because a common belief in the 1950s and 1960s was that families were responsible for psychopathology in individual members, the focus in his own training was to recognize and name the pathology. A corollary of this thinking was often ignored. That is, if the family was responsible for psychopathology in individual members, then the family should be responsible for healthy behavior as well. Epstein recognized the value of working with family strengths and incorporated this idea into his thinking as well as into his clinical practice.[10]

His research studies also caused him to question what he did clinically and what he was led to believe both through the theoretical work that he had been trained in and through pronouncements of leaders in the field. One tenet that raised questions was the belief that if parents were emotionally healthy and showed no pathology, then their children would be healthy and show no pathology. Another strongly held conviction in the field was that parents who did not have a healthy sexual relationship would not be able to have a good functioning family. Both his clinical and his research work suggested otherwise. Also, as he observed, many parents were diagnosed with severe psychiatric illness or emotional problems, yet their children were fine. In contrast, some unhealthy children came from families that appeared very healthy in their functioning and, in fact, had healthy functioning siblings. It became apparent that there was a dissonance between the findings from his research studies and the ongoing family therapy that he and his colleagues were practicing in the clinic.

As he continued to treat families using the theories in which he was trained, Epstein realized that some of the underlying theoretical premises conflicted with what he observed and found in his research. He reasoned that if the research findings were valid, then some aspects of the theoretical approach were based on false premises. He and his colleagues went back to the data to check and recheck. Convinced that the data were accurate, he then retraced the clinical assumptions that he and his colleagues held. The process led to a rethinking of their clinical work. For Epstein personally, it led to a marked change in his own therapeutic orientation.[1]

Epstein became attracted to the systems approach and, with his colleagues, began to build a model for understanding and treating families. They borrowed major ideas from systems theory, but broadened its theoretical focus. A particularly attractive advantage for using the systems approach was that it allowed for the retention of Freudian and developmental theoretical positions that had not been invalidated by their research findings. In addition, some behavioral components that seemed promising and applicable to family work were built into the model. The result was eclectic in that concepts and theories that were particularly relevant to families in the clinic were incorporated into the model. Yet the model was structured in the sense that a framework was clearly delineated, concepts defined, and a therapeutic approach made as pragmatic as possible. Learning from past experience, Epstein and colleagues ensured that the model was testable.[9]

In the process of building a new model based on systems theory, the clinical/research team learned to sharpen their thinking, redefine concepts that were unclear, and rework therapeutic approaches to family treatment. The full extent of this exciting and challenging work, and the subsequent change in the therapeutic approach to family assessment and treatment, ultimately resulted in the development of the MMFF and the PCSTF, the building blocks of the McMaster approach.

The McMaster Approach and Other Family Therapies

The McMaster model is one variation of a family systems model.[1, 11] It is clear that Epstein and colleagues incorporated components from other models, perspectives, and theories as they built a new model. To place the McMaster model in a context vis-à-vis other family therapies or systems approaches, we provide a guide that cuts across several theoretical perspectives. These perspectives/therapies may include systems models, the psychodynamic and interactional models described earlier, or variations of them. In addition, perspectives or concepts of other models that have not been explicitly discussed here may include more recent approaches such as behavioral therapy, narrative, postmodern, couples therapy, or idiosyncratic therapeutic approaches.

All models using the systems approach have some features in common, including the ability to achieve a global perspective and a stated rationale for the treatment of families. If the major premise of these models is that the organization, structure, and transactional patterns play a leading role in determining the emotional health of family members, it follows from systems theory that a therapeutic change within these components can be used to bring about a healthy result. A change in the family system should lead to a change in the functioning of the system. Thus, in treating families the focus is on the disturbance in the system and how to effect a change that will improve the functioning of the system.

Despite the common theme of changing the system, *the focus of change* and *the mechanisms of change* are two areas that differentiate family systems models from each other. Focus on system variables such as power allocation, division of labor, patterns of intrafamilial affective expression and involvement, familial communication, and family subsystems are some areas that differ in the amount of prominence they receive in the therapy session. Mechanisms of change that vary between models include: defining boundaries, directing or restructuring family behavior, assigning tasks, solving problems, using negative sanctions and positive reinforcement, negotiating change, guiding and educating families, and facilitating communication. The McMaster approach differs from other therapeutic approaches in several key areas. In the following section we discuss six critical areas that differentiate the McMaster approach from other family therapies. We discuss these points in order to highlight the McMaster approach and not to review or critique other models or other perspectives.

- **Theoretical base.** The McMaster model is based on a *family systems approach* in which the family is viewed as systems within systems (individual, marital) that relate to other systems (extended family, school, church/synagogue, workplace). In the McMaster model, the dynamic family group cannot be simply reduced to the characteristics of the individual or interactions between pairs of members. Clarification of the family *as a system* helps to identify the locus of difficulty and stress in the system so that the therapist is able to identify the aims, the objectives, and the methods of therapy. This approach differs from therapies in which the individual is the focus within the family context. It also differs from family system models in which the emphasis is on subsystems, repeated transactional patterns, the family structure, or family processes that are far removed from the immediate family or the presenting problem.

- **Time frame.** The McMaster model is *time-limited* as the number of therapy sessions is limited (typically 6–12 sessions) rather than unlimited or possibly lasting for several years. If desired, families can work on one set of problems and return at a later period to work on other issues. Also, the McMaster model focuses on problems of the *here-and-now* as opposed to inter-generational patterns, past origins of problems, or systematic analysis of childhood issues.

  With the help of the therapist, family members learn how to label interactions (both affective and behavioral) and their effects (again, both affective and behavioral), particularly concerning everyday transactions. The therapist stresses the importance of what is happening *currently* rather than what has happened in the past. This is not to say that traumatic events or long-standing problems are ignored or have no place in the therapy session. If the problems that occurred in the past affect the present-day functioning of the family (as is often the case), then clearly they may be very important to understand current issues. The emphasis, however, is for family members to address present concerns, resistances, or blockages to problem solutions.

- **Therapist-family member relationship.** The *degree of openness* in the therapist-family relationship and the prominence of the *role of the therapist and family members* are linked. In the McMaster approach, the belief in clear and direct communication between therapist and family members, and between family members themselves, is a very important part of the model. Since the model draws on communication theory, this emphasis is not really surprising. Clearness and directness is often liberating for family members as well as for the therapist.

  The roles of the therapist and family members are also distinguishing features in many family therapy approaches. Often the therapist acts as a director, facilitator, manipulator, educator, and guide. When using the McMaster approach, however, the therapist functions as a catalyst, clarifier, and facilitator. Family members are responsible for doing most of the work during their course of treatment; the therapist facilitates openness, clarity of communication, and development of effective problem solving abilities. Of course, as a clinician, the therapist may be an educator at times; but the emphasis, by far, is on the active collaboration of family members and therapist throughout the treatment period.

  Family members are expected to fully participate in the family assessment sessions and to be open and direct in identifying, clarifying, and resolving family issues. One goal of the model is to help family members become adept at identifying and solving problems themselves. Family members learn how they are responsible to find answers to their problems. This approach is in contrast to directive models in which the therapist takes responsibility for delineating a problem and finding a solution. In the process of evaluating and working toward a solution to a problem, each family member becomes involved and helps in their own, and each other's, development.

- **Insight.** On a more abstract level, a clear philosophical issue in the approach to family treatment is on whether insight into the family's problems is necessary for change to occur or whether insight follows change and is not necessary to initiate the process. Psychodynamic and psychoanalytic models posit that insight is necessary for change. In contrast, models based on system theory (like behavioral models) do not consider insight a necessary ingredient for change.

  In the McMaster approach, *insight into a problem is not a necessary or sufficient ingredient for change to occur in the system.* Concern is not for what produces pathology in the individual but with *the process occurring within the family that produces the behavior.* Therapy is directed at changing the system and thereby changing the behavior of the individual.

  Many methods are available to effect a change in behavior and they are often directed at an individual. For example, behavior models often target specific behaviors in a patient and positively reinforce good behavior or negatively reinforce poor behavior. Other models use paradoxical approaches to effect change, manipulate space or boundaries, recreate communication patterns, or assign tasks and homework. The McMaster model incorporates assignments and tasks that have been agreed upon by family members, but it also uses bargaining, mediation, and conciliation to effect changes. The treatment sessions are used to teach families the techniques they need for negotiating on concrete issues. Once family members learn the techniques, they will be able to generalize to many areas of life. The aim of negotiation in the family therapy process is to allow the maximum satisfaction within each individual while taking account of the family system. Negative sanctions may on occasion be used to change behavior, but the therapist should emphasize choice as much as possible. During any course of treatment family members may or may not accept the proposed change. Whatever option is chosen, possible consequences are discussed and treatment sessions are used to address the effects of the change.

- **Clarity of concepts and treatment.** The degree of *clearness in the method of treatment* also differentiates family models. In contrast to other models, systems theory allows for relatively easy conceptualization of each person's behavior in the system and permits a clear understanding of the therapeutic process. The importance of clarity of concepts and methods should not be underplayed. As developers of the McMaster model, we feel that if the treatment concepts are consistently applied, then therapists will be reasonably effective in the majority of cases that they treat. The reliability and validity of constructs used in the McMaster approach ensures that the methods of evaluating and treating families will be readily teachable to nonexperts, transferable to different settings, and applicable to a variety of family problems. In addition, the clinical-research link is up front and can clearly be tested empirically. In fact, because of our interest in testing the model, early in our program we made a decision that if a concept could not be operationally defined it would be excluded from the model. Some concepts that held our clinical interest (particularly those from a psychodynamic background) were excluded because we were unable to operationalize them. Our care in defining the model ultimately made it easier to describe the treatment component of the McMaster approach. We were able to break down the therapeutic process of the McMaster model into a series of simple, discrete components that can be taught, analyzed, and measured.

- **Transportability.** Related to the degree of clarity is the *ease of transporting the ideas, concepts, and techniques* that make up any treatment approach. Because of the emphasis we had originally placed on having clearly defined constructs, the McMaster approach is easily transported from one setting to another. Our interest in teaching the model and conducting research was the driving force behind the insistence on concept definition. Another reason we set up clear definitions was a reaction to events that periodically occur in the field of family therapy. That is, while it is fascinating to watch a "master of therapy" in action, it is difficult, if not impossible, to transmit the therapeutic approach to someone else. Since therapeutic skills are tied to the therapist involved, there is no systematic description, and the concepts are impossible to teach. Further, some techniques (e.g., manipulation) can be destructive if novices try to imitate the master but do not have a clear understanding of the concepts—either because they have not been defined or because they have been defined so poorly that several interpretations are possible. Clarity of concepts and methods, therefore, minimizes dependence on a charismatic therapist and reduces idiosyncratic approaches to therapy. Finally, if it is unclear what a therapist is doing with the patient or family members, then he or she is not a good role model. Unclear or inconsistent approaches may promote dependence on, rather than independence from, the therapist.

Early Stages in Developing the McMaster Approach

Once the basic framework of the McMaster model was delineated, Epstein and colleagues worked on setting up the treatment structure and defining the therapeutic process. The clinical and research work focused on ongoing family therapy even as work continued with a sample of "normal" nonclinical research subjects.[12] The juxtaposition of working with clinical and nonclinical families in several pilot projects helped in understanding variations in healthy and unhealthy family functioning. On the basis of their original pilot studies, Epstein's group developed a Family Classification System that consisted of a series of family dimensions describing areas in family life. The group focused attention on dimensions they felt were of prime importance in understanding families and on developing more effective therapeutic methods. As the research and clinical work progressed, the conceptualization of these family dimensions was reworked until they made theoretical and clinical sense, and were carefully defined. The family dimensions evolved into a classification system called the Family Category Schema.

Despite making progress, limitations in the research methodology became apparent when work began with the schema. The original goals of the studies were to find predictors of outcome, to develop measures of affective interaction within therapy sessions, and to evaluate therapeutic outcome. Because Epstein and his colleagues strongly believed in the need to integrate clinical and research perspectives, they decided to test some of their ideas empirically sooner rather than later. Epstein's experience at Columbia had already demonstrated to him the importance of understanding and questioning research findings and incorporating them into the therapeutic approach. The early studies highlighted the iterative process that is so crucial when developing an evaluation and treatment model.

For example, because they had not developed precise operational definitions of the therapeutic transactions they were interested in studying, Epstein and his colleagues soon found that they were not able to collect precise or reliable data. The questions posed to the therapists in the early research protocols elicited only the overall impressions of the therapists as to what actually took place during each session. The researchers discovered that an objective rating of transcribed sessions revealed a totally different picture of the treatment reports completed by the therapists. Some of the difficulties revolved around coding affective interactions. Other difficulties arose when deciding who was speaking to whom during the session, or who was angry with whom. It became clear that trying to measure concepts, particularly affective concepts such as welfare, positive, and neutral emotions, was problematic.

Results from these preliminary studies helped the research team rethink the research process and its goals. Epstein and colleagues learned to appreciate a long-term, programmatic way of thinking. It led the group to develop a more defined model and a therapy manual so that any therapist involved in the study would be treating families in approximately the same manner. Creating a treatment manual is now seen as an elementary step when testing a therapy model. At the time, however, it was assumed that rigorous training in the model, combined with frequent discussions of therapy sessions, ensured that therapists practiced the same method of treatment. Epstein and his team learned firsthand the importance of standardization in research protocols and the inadequacy of relying on clinical impressions and imprecise conceptualizations.

Early research experience also taught the team that in order to make real progress, they would need to develop instruments that would effectively measure the key constructs of the McMaster model. After reassessing the line of research they had already completed, the team decided to build on their findings and to develop two major streams of work to take place concurrently. The two areas of focus were family treatment and instrument development. Because these areas were developed in tandem by both researchers and clinicians, it was possible to identify and correct problems or incorporate advances in therapeutic or methodological techniques with relative ease. We now believe that the continuous interweaving of clinical and research work—that occurred from the beginning of the model development—is one of the major strengths of the McMaster approach and one reason why this model has endured.

- **Family Treatment.** The work that had begun in Montreal continued when Epstein moved to McMaster University in Hamilton, Ontario. It was in Ontario that the Family Category Schema evolved into the McMaster Model of Family Functioning. Not only were the concepts of the model now fully defined and operationalized, they were reevaluated with a new audience. That is, Epstein and his colleagues enlisted a group of students to see if the theoretical model could be packaged and taught by others so that it was both "teachable" and "learnable." Epstein did not want the model to be dependent on charismatic teachers only to gain acceptance. The developers presented their ideas at each stage of progress to students and varied groups in the university community. These included psychiatrists, psychologists, social workers, researchers in the social and behavioral sciences, and family physicians. Feedback from these professionals was incorporated into the model.

All of the years of clinical and research work that Epstein and colleagues had undertaken were nicely coalescing into the completion of the McMaster Model of Family Functioning. Work on this model was finalized a few years later after Epstein moved to Brown University with two of his colleagues, Duane Bishop and Gabor Keitner. At Brown, the clinical/research group completed a treatment model and treatment manual that was a blueprint for conducting family therapy. They drew on their years of research and experience that had started in Montreal and continued in Ontario. The result, the *Problem Centered Systems Therapy of the Family*, was a detailed guide on how to evaluate and treat families following the theoretical framework of the McMaster Model of Family Functioning. The treatment manual was completed at the same time that a new teaching and training program was being instituted for clinicians in their treatment of families. The therapy model and the McMaster approach soon became one comprehensive package with a structure that combined clinical, research, and teaching components.

• **Instrument Development.** As they worked on the McMaster model and the treatment manual, the research group set about to develop much needed assessment instruments. The development of the model and the instruments were tied together very closely. Gaps in the research program were directly related to gaps in the clinical evaluation of the therapy sessions. Once again, the importance of the clinical-research link became apparent—in the absence of valid assessments, the research could not go forward. For example, many of the outcome measures were subjective ratings by either the therapists or the families. Not only were these subjective ratings open to bias, the correlation between these measures and more objective measures was unclear. Awareness of these drawbacks increased the desire to push ahead with a search for instruments that attained satisfactory psychometric properties yet were clinically meaningful.

The approach taken when developing the subjective and objective family assessment instruments was based on previous research work as well as on clinical experience of treating families. The first task was to devise a method to measure a family's functioning. Epstein's approach to instrument development paralleled his approach in the clinical and research areas. That is, the team needed to develop instruments that were reliable, valid, and applicable to a wide variety of settings. Also, the measures needed to have clinical utility and research applicability. The original model that the research group had worked on, the Goal Attainment Scale (GAS), was too individualized and too idiosyncratic. Epstein and his colleagues went back to the drawing board and consulted with clinicians, therapists, and researchers. The team wanted to know what questions therapists ask a family to learn how they solved problems, communicated, assigned roles in the family, and other aspects of a family's functioning. From a list of over 200 items, factor analytic methods were applied to derive several broad areas of family life.

The results were unsatisfactory, mostly because the data reduction yielded an assessment that seemed to be too far removed from clinical experience. Through an iterative process of testing and retesting the instruments, using clinical and research perspectives, the team finally became satisfied. A ruling dictum for the clinical/research group was that the model and the instruments had to have relevance and clinical sense in order for the team to retain the ideas in the research design. The Family Assessment Device (FAD) captured the elements of what was considered to be a good summary of a family's functioning. As work developed in refining the FAD, it became clear that the approach Epstein used stirred some controversy among those knowledgeable in the field of psychometrics. Several experts in psychometrics informed the team that they were going about their work in reverse. They were told that data for scale development should first be gathered by casting a broad net that had theoretical relevance for family functioning but was not necessarily connected with clinical work. Once the information was collected, the next step was to subject these scales to factor analysis in the creation of the final form of the instruments. It was only at that point that the scales should be put to actual use in measuring family functioning.

Because of the strong clinical background and commitment to their patients, Epstein, together with members of his research team, resisted the suggested approach to develop instruments since it did not make clinical sense. They looked for an alternative method that would be robust, meet criteria that would satisfy psychometricians, and still have clinical relevance. They consulted experts in psychometrics, one in the philosophy of psychometric work and the other in the clinical application of psychometric tests. The consultants spent a considerable amount of time in learning the orientation, background, and goals of what was becoming known as the McMaster approach to assessing and treating families. They advised the team that the original approach was acceptable provided rigorous psychometric procedures were followed to achieve acceptable reliability and validity for the instruments. These consultants stated that it was acceptable to do factor analytic studies of our instruments at later stages of development rather than at the beginning. Epstein and colleagues took their advice and realized, in hindsight, the correctness of adhering to their original position of keeping the focus on clinical relevance. We believe that the strength and the durability of the McMaster instruments are due, in part, to the fact that they are so strongly grounded in clinical experience.

Application of the Model and Assessments

The more successful the research team became in psychometric development of the assessments, the stronger was the understanding of treatment outcomes. This was indeed positive feedback for maintaining a strong link between clinicians and researchers and for adhering to clear and precise concepts. The development of the therapy model, completion of the treatment manual and the subjective and objective assessments led to the next phase of work. This involved the comprehensive application of the clinical approach combined with administration of the assessments to study families. In addition, it was now possible to initiate several research protocols involving varied patient and non-patient populations.

When the team moved to Brown, one of the first studies completed was a comparison of family functioning across several groups of psychiatric patients and their family members. Concurrent studies measured the functioning of families of patients with a variety of medical illnesses. The resulting database consisted of several hundred families with a wide range of family scores. These data allowed us to compare family functioning in medical, psychiatric, and nonclinical populations.

Once we established that family functioning differed between clinical and nonclinical families, the group designed several naturalistic studies that tracked changes in family functioning over the course of an illness. Findings from these studies led the group to begin work on treatment studies, using the McMaster approach as one of the treatment arms. Depending on the specific illness and research goals, we were able to adapt the McMaster model to fit a number of clinical and research needs. Currently, we are using the McMaster approach in several research projects that focus on determining the most effective combination of treatments (including pharmacotherapy, family, individual, and group therapies) for patients and their families.

Summary

Research in family therapy is a very complex undertaking and requires the input of colleagues with many different skills. Epstein began the family therapy work over 5 decades ago with an expressed interest in expanding his knowledge and abilities to further develop his profession and to provide the optimal treatment for his patients. He sought to learn as many approaches as possible to the problems he faced as a clinician, researcher, and teacher and then, with his colleagues, to develop a comprehensive and cohesive method to deal with them. Although obvious to many, it bears repeating that it takes a long time to develop the necessary expertise, know-how, and tools in order to ensure a successful clinical, teaching, and research program. Having some feeling and appreciation for the evolution of ideas—from early theoretical influences, schools of thought, and previous experiences—may generate a better understanding of the philosophy behind the McMaster approach as it is presented in the following chapters.

CHAPTER 2

The McMaster Model
of Family Functioning

This chapter focuses on describing the model, its assumptions, and the specific concepts, including family dimensions, that are key to understanding it. We begin with a brief discussion on our view of the "normal" family that has been helpful in setting expectations or anchor points of family functioning. Clinical uses, research studies, and methods for teaching the model are addressed in depth in other chapters in this book.

Health and Normality

To attempt to define a healthy or normal family may seem like, or actually be, a fool's errand. It is tempting to avoid this particular exercise, particularly for those of us who conceptualize the family as a system of interacting individuals as well as a system involving a number of other systems (cultural, social, political, economic, biological substrates). The variables to consider seem overwhelming. Nevertheless, the demands of a comprehensive, empirical research program of the family necessitate that a series of benchmarks of family functioning be developed. The markers of what is meant by normal or healthy are particularly important. Although the healthy family is not perfect, it manages problems productively.

Normality is an ill-defined concept, often meaning, "not displaying any particular problems." When defined in this exclusionary way, "normal" is not a very useful concept. While a normal family is described as not having a number of features, there is no positive statement about what a normal family is. Another way to define normal is to equate the concept with a statistical average. Measurements are taken on a sample and the average score is considered normal for the population. If the sample is representative of the total population, then something may be known of the characteristic being measured. However, too often this approach is flawed. For example, if the characteristic is the frequency with which spouses discuss financial problems, and the average is once per week, it does not tell us much about the families. It could be that the current life situation of the family influences the amount of discussion taken place (either more than usual or less than usual). Alternatively, it is not clear whether families with a once-a-week financial discussion are functioning better than families who discuss their finances more or less often.

We have taken the position that it is useful to equate the notion of "health" with "normality." Our reasoning is as follows. A healthy family is neither necessarily average nor merely lacking in negative characteristics. Rather, it has described positive features. In the sections below we use a composite family to describe a healthy functioning family according to the MMFF.

Functioning Continuum

It is important to remember that the McMaster model does not cover all aspects of family functioning.[13,14] Rather, the model focuses on the dimensions of family functioning that are seen as having the most impact on the emotional and physical health or problems of family members. We have defined functioning within each dimension as ranging from "most ineffective" to "most effective." We feel that "most ineffective" functioning in any of these dimensions can contribute to clinical presentation whereas "most effective" functioning in all dimensions supports optimal physical and emotional health. Any family can be evaluated to determine the effectiveness of its functioning with respect to each dimension. To provide a framework on how we view families, we describe a family's functioning on each dimension.

Systems Orientation

The MMFF is based on a systems approach:

> In this approach the family is seen as an open system consisting of systems within systems (individual, marital, or dyad) and relating to other systems (extended family, schools, industry, religions). The unique aspect of the dynamic family group cannot be simply reduced to the characteristics of the individuals or interactions between pairs of members. Rather, there are explicit and implicit rules, plus action by members, which govern and monitor each other's behavior.[8]

Table 2.1 Assumptions Underlying the MMFF[15]

- The parts of the family are interrelated.
- One part of the family cannot be understood in isolation from the rest of the system.
- Family functioning cannot be fully understood by simply understanding each of the parts.
- A family's structure and organization are important factors in determining the behavior of family members.
- Transactional patterns of the family system are among the most important variables that shape the behavior of family members.

The significance of these ideas for therapy is the fact that the therapist is not concerned with the intrapsychic pathology in the individual, but rather with the processes occurring within the family system which produce the dysfunctional behavior. Therapy is directed at changing the system and, thereby, the behavior of the individual. The concepts of communication theory, behavior theory, learning theory, and transactional approach are drawn on, although the infrastructure remains the systems model.

Value Orientation

Practicing clinicians must appreciate how cultural values play an important role in influencing human behavior. In depicting a normal family, we often use value judgments when describing behavior as, for example, the appropriateness of a family member's reaction of sadness or anger. However, the expression of many values varies by culture; therefore, the judgments of health or normality are relative to the culture of the family. Although we try not to impose our values in conducting therapy, we recognize that we do make value judgments. Throughout this chapter we will point out areas of family functioning in which cultural sensitivity may be particularly critical.

Family Task Orientation

A major function of the family unit is to provide a setting for the social, psychological, and biological development and maintenance of family members. During the process of fulfilling this function families deal with a variety of issues and problems or tasks which we group into three areas. If families are unable to deal effectively with these task areas, they are more likely to develop clinically significant problems or maladaptive behaviors.

- *Basic Task Area.* This is the most fundamental task area of the three. As the name implies, this area involves instrumental issues such as providing food, money, transportation, and shelter.
- *Developmental Task Area.* These tasks deal with family issues that arise over the course of developmental stages at both the individual level and family level. Individual level crises typically occur at infancy, childhood, adolescence, middle, and old age. Family level crises may occur at the beginning of a marriage, at the first pregnancy, or at the empty nest stage.
- *Hazardous Task Area.* This task area involves handling crises that may arise through illness, accident, loss of income, job change, etc.

Family Dimensions of the Model

In order to understand the structure, organization, and transactional patterns of the family, we focus on six dimensions of family functioning: Problem Solving, Communication, Roles, Affective Responsiveness, Affective Involvement, and Behavior Control. It is worth repeating that while these dimensions do not exhaust important areas of family life, we feel they have the greatest impact on the emotional and physical health of family members. Additionally, the McMaster model does not focus on any one dimension as the foundation for conceptualizing family behavior. Each dimension contributes to a fuller understanding of such a complex entity as the family. We have defined and delineated the dimensions and recognize that some areas of functioning may overlap or interact with each other. Each dimension is discussed and includes a definition, a range of functioning that we consider healthy or normal, and examples of effective functioning.

Problem Solving

Problem solving refers to a family's ability to resolve problems to a level that maintains effective family functioning. A family problem is an issue that threatens the integrity and functional capacity of the family and which the family has difficulty solving. Some families have ongoing unresolved difficulties that, nonetheless, do not threaten their integrity and functioning; these "problems" are not considered. In our early work, it had been surmised that ineffective families would have more problems than would more effectively functioning families. Research showed otherwise. Although families dealt with a similar range of difficulties, effective functioning families solved their problems whereas ineffectively functioning families were unable to do so.[7]

Family problems are divided into two types—*instrumental* and *affective.* Instrumental problems refer to problems of everyday life such as managing

Table 2.2 Stages of Effective Problem Solving

1. Identify the problem.
2. Communicate with appropriate person.
3. Develop alternatives.
4. Decide on alternative.
5. Act on decision.
6. Monitor the action.
7. Evaluate effectiveness.

money, obtaining food, clothing, and housing. Affective problems concern issues of emotion or feeling, such as anger or depression. Families whose functioning is disrupted by instrumental problems rarely deal effectively with affective problems; however, families who have problems with affective issues may be able to adequately address instrumental problems. Many problems present an overlap of both components of problem solving, but effective functioning families will solve most of their problems efficiently and relatively easily. Sometimes it can be difficult to elicit the steps they go through in solving a problem. In contrast, it is often easy to analyze problem-solving steps taken by families that present at clinics, for at a minimum, the presenting problem is an unresolved difficulty.

The McMaster model includes a sequential listing and operational definition of the stages in effective problem solving:

1. Identifying the problem. The problem identification stage includes: who identifies the problem(s); whether or not there is a pattern in the problematic behavior that occurs; and what type of problem (affective or instrumental) occurs. A pattern refers to the repetitive ways in which families do or do not accomplish their goals. At this point the clinician should make sure that the family correctly identifies the problem and does not distort or displace the issue to a less conflicted area.
2. Communicating with appropriate people about the problem. The communication stage considers whether the appropriate person(s) was contacted about the identified difficulty.
3. Developing viable alternative solutions. The alternative solutions stage includes the types of plans developed and considered in relation to the nature of the problem. In this stage it may be particularly problematic if the family sees only one option, or a limited range of options, when a problem does not have an easy or obvious solution.
4. Deciding on one of the alternatives. The fourth stage, the decision stage, concerns whether the family is able to come to a decision after considering alternative plans of action or whether they circumvent

this stage and act in a predetermined manner. In this stage one also looks to see if those involved in the action are actually informed of the decision.

5. Acting on the decision. The action stage addresses the degree to which the family carries out the alternative plan they have selected. Although the family may have decided on a course of action, they may not act on it, act in a limited way, or carry out the action completely.

6. Monitoring the action. The monitoring stage refers to whether the family has a mechanism by which they check to see if the decisions agreed upon are acted upon and carried out.

7. Evaluating the effectiveness of the action and the problem solving process. The evaluation stage addresses if the family is able to review what happened in the problem-solving process, if they are able to learn from the situation, if they are able to recognize successful mechanisms of action, and if they can discern inappropriate problem solving behavior.

Families exhibit a range of problem-solving abilities from the "most effective" families who have few, if any, unresolved problems to those "least effective" who may not even be able to identify the problem. As family functioning becomes less effective, family problem-solving behavior becomes less systematic. The result is that fewer problem-solving steps are accomplished.

Variations Within Normal

A normal family may have some minor unresolved problems; however, such problems should not be of a degree or duration that creates major disruption in the family. The family is able to resolve the majority of problems by: discussing the issues in an open and clear manner, identifying instrumental and affective components of the problem, communicating the problem issues in a timely manner, processing alternatives, making a decision, acting on the decision, and making sure their actions are carried out. Only the most effective families will actually be able to evaluate the problem-solving process. They will be able to manage all of the instrumental problems, though they may have some difficulty in handling affective issues.

Example:

The Simpsons cannot identify any major unresolved problems. A visit by the grandmother led to some difficulties with the children. They describe one son as cuddly, while the other son is more active and independent. The independent grandson, who did not receive as much attention from his grandmother, became jealous and acted up a bit when she visited. When his grandmother scolded him, his behavior became mildly problematic. Mrs. Simpson first identified the problem and then discussed it with her husband. At the earliest reasonable opportunity, Mr. and Mrs. Simpson discussed the problem with the grandmother. This was done so that the grandmother was able to support them in maintaining discipline. At the same time, Mrs. Simpson helped her mother-in-law relate more appropriately with each grandson.

As they dealt with the problem, Mr. and Mrs. Simpson were flexible and made reasonable allowances for the grandmother as she came from a great distance and was only with them briefly. They also respected her individuality.

Another problem involved the older son. He did not follow rules they had laid down about where he could and could not play. They tried a number of disciplinary measures. When the mother realized that they were not working, she reverted to a previous effective pattern of using rewards. Returning to a previously adaptive approach soon led to positive results.

The Simpsons are able to discuss problems in an open and clear manner and to identify both the instrumental and the affective components of each. They communicate about problems at the earliest possible time, process alternatives quickly, make a decision, and begin to act. They ensure that their decisions are carried out and they are able to describe reviewing previously effective and ineffective methods.

Communication

We define communication as the verbal exchange of information within a family. Non-verbal communication is, of course, tremendously important; however, we had originally excluded it from the model because of the methodological difficulties involved in measuring it. While we recognize that some progress has been made in the conceptualization and measurement of non-verbal communication, we feel that the focus should be on verbal expression. This is in keeping with our philosophy of assuring both the clinical and research utility of the model and our feeling that understanding non-verbal communication patterns may entail more complexity (e.g., cultural, social, and linguistic issues) than can be addressed with the model. Also, the MMFF focuses on the family's pattern of communication as opposed to an individual family member's style of communication. We have found that using this more global definition of communication is more useful for both the therapist and family members.

Like problem solving, communication is divided into *instrumental* and *affective* areas that encompass the same problems and issues as discussed in the Problem Solving dimension. Families can have marked difficulties with the affective component of communication but function very well in the instrumental area. Rarely, if ever, is the reverse true. Two other vectors characterize other aspects of communication and are also expressed in this dimension: the clear vs. masked continuum and the direct vs. indirect continuum. The *clear vs. masked continuum* focuses on whether the content of the message is clearly stated or camouflaged, muddied, or vague. The *direct vs. indirect continuum* focuses on whether messages go to the intended target or get deflected to someone else. For example, messages intended for one family member may be transmitted via a third person. In either case, both the sender and the receiver are involved in the family's communication patterns.

The clear versus masked continuum and the direct versus indirect continuum are independent. We can therefore identify four distinct styles of communication. The following stipulates the four styles and provides an example of each.[16]

Joan is late for a meeting with Bill. When she arrives, the following statements might be made:

1. Clear and direct. Both the message and the target are clear. Bill says to Joan: "I'm upset that you're late, but let's get on with the meeting."
2. Clear and indirect. In this instance, the message is clear but the intended target is not. Bill says to someone else who is present, "I'm upset with Joan because she's late."
3. Masked and direct. Here the context is unclear but it is directed at the intended person. Bill says to Joan, "Are you ok? You don't look well?"
4. Masked and indirect. The content of the message and for whom it is intended are both unclear. Bill says to someone else who is present, "People who are late are a pain."

At the healthy end of the dimension, the family communicates in a clear and direct manner in both instrumental and affective areas. At the less effective end the family communicates less clearly and less directly. Although we focus on verbal communication, we do note non-verbal communication, especially if it contradicts the verbal message. Contradictory non-verbal behavior contributes to masking and may reflect indirectness of communication. Also, the clinical situation may require that we look at other factors such as multiple messages, whether or not the message is received, and how it is interpreted by the receiver. These principles of communication are based on concepts delineated by Lederer and Jackson[17] and available in recent texts as well.

Variations Within Normal

Toward the lower end of the normal functioning range, communication around areas of conflict may not be clear and direct. There may be some brief occasions of beating around the bush (masking), not clearly stating one's point of view (indirect), or having trouble clearly hearing each other (masking or indirect).

> The Simpson family is clear and direct in their patterns of communication. There is no sense of hesitation or holding back, no talking around the issues. They direct their comments to the person for whom they are intended. Their talking is efficient and effective. Mr. and Mrs. Simpson discussed the problem clearly and spoke directly with the grandmother.

Roles

Roles are the repetitive patterns of behavior by which family members fulfill family functions. Families have to deal with some functions repeatedly in order to maintain a healthy and effective system. We identify five necessary family functions, each made up of a number of tasks and functions. Like the first two dimensions, these functions comprise instrumental, affective, and mixed components. In addition to necessary functions, other family functions may arise in the course of family life.

We begin with the five necessary family functions:

1. Provision of resources. Tasks in this area are largely instrumental for they are associated with providing food, clothing, money, and shelter for the family.
2. Nurturing and support. These functions are considered affective as they encompass the provision of comfort, warmth, reassurance, and support for family members.
3. Adult sexual gratification. Affective issues are prominent in this area for both partners must feel satisfaction with the sexual relationship and also feel that they can satisfy their partner sexually. The level of sexual activity required to bring sexual satisfaction between partners varies, with some partners being satisfied with little or no activity.
4. Personal development. Functions in this grouping embody both affective and instrumental components. The associated tasks operate around the development of life skills, such as helping a child start and progress through school, helping an adult pursue a career or vocation, and helping both child and adult develop socially.

5. Maintenance and management of the family system. This area includes several functions that involve techniques and actions required to maintain standards.
    a. Decision-making functions. Includes leadership, major decision-making, and final decisions where there is no consensus. In general, these functions should reside at the adult or parent level and within the nuclear family.
    b. Boundary and membership functions. Tasks are concerned with extended families, friends, neighbors, boarders, and dealings with any external institutions and agencies.
    c. Behavior control functions. This area involves implementation and adherence of behavior control functions including disciplining children and maintaining standards and rules for adult family members.
    d. Household finance functions. These instrumental tasks deal with monthly bills, banking, income tax, and managing household money.
    e. Health related functions. Caregiving, identifying health problems, making health care appointments (e.g., doctor or dental visits), maintaining compliance with health prescriptions—all are tasks related to this area of functioning.

Two additional and integral issues of role functioning include role allocation and role accountability. The concepts are defined as:

1. Role allocation. This concept incorporates the family's pattern in assigning roles: whether the assignment is appropriate, the allocation is done implicitly or explicitly, and whether the assignment involves discussion or is arranged by dictum. Questions may include: does the person assigned the function have the necessary skills and power to carry it out; is the assignment clear and explicit; are the tasks distributed fairly and to the satisfaction of family members?
2. Role accountability. This part of role functioning focuses on the ways the family ensures that functions are completed. Accountability ensures a sense of responsibility in family members and provides for monitoring and corrective measures.

In order to understand the roles in the family, it is important to identify both necessary and "other" functions, to determine if the roles are appropriately assigned, and to see if accountability measures are part of the family pattern. A healthy family is characterized by adequately fulfilled functions, clear allocation, and accountability in place. In an unhealthy family one or more family members are overburdened with family tasks, and account-ability and role functions are unclear.

Variations Within Normal

Normally functioning families will, for the most part, not have difficulties with provisions of resources, except when circumstances are out of their control (e.g., labor action, times of economic depression). Nurturing and support will be provided, although it may not always be immediately avail-able. At times there may be minor dissatisfaction with the sexual relation-ship. Periodic difficulties may occur in the areas of personal development and systems management. In normal families these deviations from effective role functioning do not lead to conflict. In some families, roles can be effec-tively handled by one individual. In the most effective families, however, there will be role sharing. Role sharing allows a family to deal with changes from the norm, such as illness in the family. Within the normal range of most families, members are able and willing to carry out most role functions and are not overburdened with their tasks. Normal functioning families do not always maintain complete accountability, nor are tasks regimented to such a degree that there is no give-and-take; some tasks are not carried out or there may be a delay in completing the task. The occasional lapses, how-ever, do not lead to family conflict.

Roles within a family may vary by ethnicity, religious practice, or lifestyle of adult members. The guidelines still provide a framework to gauge the effectiveness of a family's functioning.

The Simpsons are very clear about who carries out each of a variety of family tasks. They discuss the jobs each has, are comfortable with them, and do not feel overburdened. They share tasks in many areas, but are also clear about their separate areas of responsibility. For example, Mrs. Simpson takes care of the flower garden, while Mr. Simpson takes responsibility for the lawn and shrubbery.

The task of getting up on weekend mornings with the children is split, one doing so on Saturday, one on Sunday. Their mutual involve-ment in dealing with their children was repeatedly demonstrated dur-ing the course of the interview. The children clearly go to both parents for nurturing and support as appropriate, and the parents obtain their main support from each other. The couple is satisfied with their finan-cial resources and quite clear about their roles in handling and bud-geting their finances.

Both parents are satisfied with their sexual functioning. They can discuss this openly and are able to indicate their enjoyment in being personally satisfied as well as in satisfying each other. In the course of their marriage, Mrs. Simpson has become increasingly active in initiating sexual activity. They are able to handle issues such as one partner saying 'no' to sex with tact and sensitivity and without either one having a sense of being rebuffed.

This family is clear in their ability to discuss the allocation of roles. In doing so, they play to individual strengths and interests. They keep track of whether jobs allocated to each other are carried out; when one does not carry out the task, the other will fill in or point out the problem.

Affective Responsiveness

In this dimension, we examine the range of affective responses of family members by looking at the experience of family responses to affective stimuli. We are concerned with two aspects of affective responses, whether or not family members are able to respond with the full spectrum of feelings experienced in emotional life and whether or not the emotion experienced is consistent or appropriate with the stimulus or situational context.

We distinguish between two categories of affect:

1. Welfare emotions. These feelings consist of affection, warmth, tenderness, support, love, consolation, happiness, and joy.
2. Emergency emotions. These feelings encompass fear, anger, sadness, disappointment, and depression.

The quality, quantity, and appropriateness of the responses of family members are the foci of this dimension. The quantitative aspect of the degree of affective response ranges along a continuum from absence of response through reasonable (or expected response) to over-responsiveness. The pattern of overall responses of the family to affective stimuli is extremely important. However, in affective responsiveness, more than any other dimension, the emphasis is on determining *the capacity* of individual members to respond emotionally and *not* on their actual behaviors. A family responding with love and tenderness, but never with anger, sadness, or joy would be considered somewhat distorted. Furthermore, children raised in such a family may become affectively constricted which may hinder their own personal development. The more effective the family, the wider will be their range of emotions and the more appropriate will be their responses.

Two considerations should be kept in mind when assessing affective responsiveness. First, the *manner* in which family members convey their feelings is more appropriately conceptualized as an aspect of affective communication. Second, since affective responsiveness may be particularly marked by cultural variability, the clinician will need to be aware of and sensitive to cultural factors that may influence family responses. At the healthy end of the spectrum, a family will be capable of expressing a full range of emotions. In most situations, family members will experience the appropriate emotion with both a reasonable intensity and for a reasonable duration.

Variations Within Normal

Even at a fairly healthy level of affective responsiveness, one or more family members may have difficulty experiencing a particular emotion. One spouse may be more responsive over a range of emotions than his or her partner. Also, there may be times when members respond inappropriately or instances when there are episodes of over- or under-responding. Neither the differences in range of emotions, nor the periodic instances of inappropriate response are necessarily indicative of disruptive family functioning.

Members of the Simpson family display a wide range of affect that is appropriate and in keeping with the situation. They have suffered no major losses in their extended family, but can describe periods of sadness and loss in other circumstances. They respond with appropriate anger and disappointment to situations. They have a good sense of humor and are able to be affectionate and caring. They described how Mr. Simpson was more responsive across a range of emotions compared to his wife. He was able to help her get more in touch with her feelings and more openly express her feelings. It is important to understand that her *capacity* for feeling a certain way did not change, merely her expression of the feeling.

Affective Involvement

Affective involvement is the extent to which the family shows interest in and value for particular activities of individual family members. The focus is on the degree of interest in each other and the manner in which the interest is expressed. There is a range of styles of involvement, from a total lack of involvement at one end to an extreme amount of involvement at the other end.

We identify six types of involvement:

1. Lack of involvement. Family members show no interest or investment in each other. They share physical and instrumental surroundings and functions, much like a group of boarders.
2. Involvement devoid of feelings. There is some interest in this type of involvement but little investment of the self or feelings in the

relationship. The investment is demonstrated only when demanded and even then may be minimal; the interest is primarily intellectual.

3. Narcissistic involvement. The investment in others is primarily egocentric. There is no feeling of the importance a particular situation may hold for others.

4. Empathic involvement. Family members demonstrate a true affective concern for the interests of others in the family even though those concerns may be peripheral to their own interests.

5. Over-involvement. This style is characterized by over-intrusive and over-protective behaviors shown by family members toward each other.

6. Symbiotic involvement. Involvement is so intense that the boundaries between two or more members are blurred. Symbiotic involvement is seen only in seriously disturbed relationships in which there is difficulty in differentiating one person from another.

There is a large range of styles in the area of affective involvement, with empathic involvement being the most effective and healthy form. As families move in either direction away from the empathic style, they become less effective in their family functioning.

Variations Within Normal

Variations within this dimension can still be in the healthy range. For instance, there will be instances of narcissistic interests by some family members as well as occasional episodes of over-involvement. However, these incidents are not continual and usually are focused on an individual member rather than on the entire family. Family members take an active interest in what is important to one another without over-identifying or personalizing.

> In the Simpson family, members show an active interest in each other. The children respond appropriately for their age. The parents take an active interest in what is important to each other even though their interests vary in several areas. They are able to respond to what is going on with each other without over-identifying or personalizing.

Behavior Control

The behavior control dimension defines the pattern a family adopts for handling behavior in three specific areas: (1) physically dangerous situations, (2) situations involving meeting and expressing psychobiological needs and drives, (3) situations involving socializing behavior both between family members and with people outside the family system. In this dimension, the focus is on the standards or rules that the family sets in these three areas and the amount of latitude they tolerate. This dimension concerns both parental discipline toward their children as well as standards and expectations of behavior that adults set toward each other.

1. Physically dangerous situations. There are a number of physically dangerous situations that the family needs to monitor and to be able to control behaviors of family members. Examples that apply to children include playing with matches or running into the road; dangerous situations involving adult behavior may be reckless driving, drinking to excess, or suicidal gestures. It is important to consider behavior of all family members when assessing this dimension. This area is particularly important when dealing with aged family members whose cognitive abilities may be diminished.
2. Psychobiological needs. Families adopt patterns of controlling behavior when meeting their psychobiological needs such as eating, sleeping, eliminating, sex, and aggression.
3. Socialization behavior. Standards of behavior are established by family members when dealing with socialization both within and outside the family. The distinction of in- and outside the family is necessary because the rules of acceptable behavior often differ between the two.

Families develop standards of acceptable behavior for each of these three areas. They also establish a degree of flexibility or tolerance in adhering to these standards. Both the standard and the latitude determine the style of behavior control.

The four styles of behavior control based on variations of the standard and the latitude are:

1. Rigid behavior control. Rules involve a constricted and narrow standard that allows little room for negotiation or flexibility across situations.
2. Flexible behavior control. Standards and rules seem reasonable to family members and there is an opportunity for negotiation and change.
3. Laissez-faire behavior control. At the extreme, there are no standards or direction and total latitude is allowed regardless of context.
4. Chaotic behavior control. The family shifts in a random and unpredictable fashion between rigid, flexible, and laissez-faire. Family members do not know which standards apply at any one time and they do not know how much, if any, negotiation is possible.

Flexible behavior is the most effective form, and chaotic the least effective. In order to maintain their style of behavior control, a family will develop a number of functions to enforce what they consider acceptable behavior.

Variations Within Normal

There are variations of very effective functioning within the normal range. Further, normal functioning families may not always use the most effective techniques. A family may be clear about the rules of behavior in general, while being indecisive, unclear, or lacking in agreement in a few minor areas. For example, although parents may disagree about minor aspects of table manners, family members are aware of the general range of what is and is not allowed. Any inconsistency should not be a major source of conflict. It is also important to keep in mind that this dimension does not apply solely to children. Partners should be able to describe acceptable forms of behavior expected from each other and be able to address the problem if those expectations are not met. One example is an expectation between partners that there is no drinking while driving. Another might be the expectation from each other to be home by a certain time and to call if there is a delay or change in schedule.

> Mr. and Mrs. Simpson are very clear about rules of behavior. They take a basic stance of allowing considerable exploration and activity by the children, and they tolerate a higher level of activity and noise than many couples would. However, they are very clear about what behavior is unacceptable and they intervene consistently when such behavior occurs. They make allowances when the situation calls for it (e.g., the grandmother's visit), but they maintain consistency within the framework. They also demonstrate superior techniques for handling the children's behavior. For example, during the interview when one child went to leave the room, he was politely, but firmly told to stay and close the door. When he persisted, he was told again, in a clear and slightly more forceful way. He responded as he was asked and immediately told, "Thank you, that's very good."

Table 2.3 provides a summary of family dimensions, goals, and key concepts of each dimension.

The McMaster Model in a Changing Social Environment

Since the MMFF was developed, there have been extensive changes in our society, in values and morals of families and of individuals, in views on marriage and divorce, and in the composition and makeup of family systems.

Values shifts have resulted in changes in the position of women in society and especially their role in the family. Varieties of family structure and organization include blended families, step-families, single parent families, same-sex partner families. Some of these changes have radically affected family life, have an enormous impact on both spousal/ partner and parent-child relationships, and raise important questions about the fundamental makeup of a family. Changes in family life have been matched by changes in methods of examining and evaluating aspects of family life. Finally, and not unrelated to these points, the MMFF has been practiced in environments that are culturally different from, and with different family structures, than that in which it was developed. Despite all the changes that have taken place in families, we feel that the structure of the model as well as the basic findings from our studies, albeit with a few clarifications discussed below, are still applicable for assessing and treating families. We take this opportunity to clarify a few points, expand on others, and present our view of how this model works, even within a changing social environment.

Family Composition

We believe that the organizational, structural, and transactional pattern variables are more powerful in determining the behavior of family members than are the intrapsychic variables. We do not dismiss the contribution of intrapsychic factors to behavior, but merely comment on our belief in the relative power of the variables. We also believe that the emotional health of children is closely related to the emotional relationship between their parents. When parental relationships are warm and supportive, children tend to be happy and healthy.

We recognize that with the variety of family compositions found today, two heterosexual parent families are not necessarily the norm. The relationship between divorced or separated parents has a profound effect on children. The more antagonistic the relationship between the adults, the more likely the effect will be detrimental to the children's development. Research is only beginning to be published concerning the effects of divorce on children's functioning, and the findings have been inconsistent and controversial. We are not aware of research on the functioning of families in same-sex households, but we would expect the basic principles of the MMFF to apply. That is, if the relationship between the parental partners is warm and supportive, the children will feel nurtured and accepted.

Cultural Variations

The MMFF was developed in Canada and in the United States. When it was developed, we did not realize the amount of interest this model would

Table 2.3 Summary of Dimension Concepts

DIMENSION: Problem Solving

GOAL: Successful achievement of basic, developmental, and crisis tasks

KEY CONCEPTS:
- Two types of problems: Instrumental and Affective
- Seven Stages in Process:
  1. Identification of the problem
  2. Communication of the problem to the appropriate person(s)
  3. Development of action alternative
  4. Decision of one alternative
  5. Action
  6. Monitoring the action
  7. Evaluation of success

Most effective: When all seven stages are carried out.
Least effective: When cannot identify problem (stop before stage 1)

DIMENSION: Communication

GOAL: Mutual understanding

KEY CONCEPTS:
- Two types of communication: Instrumental & Affective
- Two independent dimensions:
  1. Clear versus Masked
  2. Direct versus Indirect
- Above 2 dimensions yield 4 patterns of communication:
  1. Clear and Direct
  2. Clear and Indirect
  3. Masked and Direct
  4. Masked and Indirect

Most effective: Clear and Direct
Least effective: Masked and Indirect

DIMENSION: Roles

GOAL: Successful role integration

KEY CONCEPTS
- Two family function types: Necessary and Other
- Two areas of family functions: Instrumental and Affective

Necessary family functioning groupings:
A. Instrumental- Provision of resources
B. Affective—Nurturing and support—Adult sexual gratification
C. Mixed—Life skills development—Systems maintenance and management

Other family functions:
Adaptive and Maladaptive
- Role functioning is assessed by considering how the family allocated responsibilities and handles accountability for them.

Most effective: When all necessary family function are achieved have clear allocation to reasonable individual(s), and accountability is built in.
Least effective: When necessary family functions are not addressed and/or allocation and accountability not maintained.

(*continued*)

Table 2.3 Continued

DIMENSION: Affective Responsiveness	DIMENSION: Behavior control
KEY CONCEPTS: • Two groups of emotions: Welfare and Emergency	GOAL: Maintenance and adaptation KEY CONCEPTS: • Applies to three situations:

Most effective: When full range of responses are appropriate in amount and quality to stimulus.
Least effective: When very narrow range of responses exists (1–2 only) and/or amount and quality is distorted, given the context.
	1. Dangerous situations
	  2. Meeting and expressing psycho-biological needs and drives (eating, drinking, sleeping, eliminating, sex, and aggression).
	  3. Interpersonal socializing behavior inside and outside the family.

DIMENSION: Affective Responsiveness

KEY CONCEPTS:
• Two groups of emotions: Welfare and Emergency

Most effective: When full range of responses are appropriate in amount and quality to stimulus.
Least effective: When very narrow range of responses exists (1–2 only) and/or amount and quality is distorted, given the context.

DIMENSION: Affective Involvement

GOAL: Security and autonomy

KEY CONCEPTS:
• A range of involvement with six styles identified:
1. Absence of involvement
2. Involvement devoid of feelings
3. Narcissistic involvement
4. Empathic involvement
5. Over-involvement
6. Symbiotic involvement

Most effective: Empathic involvement
Least effective: Symbiotic and Absence of involvement

DIMENSION: Behavior control

GOAL: Maintenance and adaptation

KEY CONCEPTS:
• Applies to three situations:
1. Dangerous situations
2. Meeting and expressing psycho-biological needs and drives (eating, drinking, sleeping, eliminating, sex, and aggression).
3. Interpersonal socializing behavior inside and outside the family.
• Standard and latitude of acceptable behavior has four styles:
1. Rigid
2. Flexible
3. Laissez-fair
4. Chaotic
• To maintain the style, various techniques are used and implemented under role functions (systems maintenance and management.)

Most effective: Flexible behavior control
Least effective: Chaotic behavior control

generate in the United States, Canada, and overseas. To date, the model has been applied in a variety of cultural settings, usually via one of two formats. First, one of the developers/senior therapists presents the model to other clinicians or health care professionals in a series of workshops lasting up to one week. Alternatively, professionals in the field of health care have come from several countries to work with the Family Research Program at Brown in order to learn the model. English-speaking countries in which the model has been taught, or from which students have originated include: England, Scotland, Ireland, Australia, Israel, South Africa, India, and the Netherlands. Other countries where the model is being practiced are Mexico, Italy, Hungary, France, Japan, Chile, Argentina, Peru, and Spain.

One reason the MMFF transcends different languages and cultures is that, whatever the specific makeup and culture of the family, families still need to meet their basic needs and function as a unit. Superior-functioning families can be readily identified despite the variation in composition that we see in our own, and other, societies. Cultures likely vary in the emphasis they place on family dimensions or in how the dimension goals are expressed or fulfilled. Nonetheless, the emotional health of individual family members is related to the overall structure and function of their families. Correctly applied, this model can discriminate among families of widely varying levels of functioning. The model can be used in different cultures because it does not prescribe a specific outcome for families. Rather, the focus is on how a desired outcome is carried out within the family structure and cultural beliefs. Thus, the crux of the model lies in the process and ways of dealing with problems as opposed to applying specific solutions. The model focuses on the way in which families negotiate and resolve their differences and overcome obstacles whereas other models impose a "correct" solution to a problem by some external standard.

Dissonance and Accordance

A family in agreement or, equally important, not in apparent conflict, does not equate to healthy functioning of the family or within a particular dimension. In fact, a clinician may need to shake the complacency of a family if there is pathology present that is either not acknowledged or is being avoided by family members. This stance is in contrast to postmodern models which posit that clinicians should not be so directive with families.

General Functioning Dimension

Those who are somewhat familiar with our model might wonder why the General Functioning scale is not represented in this chapter. The model captures family dimensions that are seen as being crucial to a family's effective functioning. The General Functioning dimension was an outgrowth from the development of the FAD. This dimension was not, and is not, seen as part of the clinical evaluation of the family. It has been used very effectively, mostly as a research tool, sometimes as a teaching tool, but not specifically in a clinical setting when treating families. Further discussion of this scale is presented in chapters 5 and 6.

Treatment and Evaluation

Family therapy is not for everyone. Patients and family members may not need family treatment, may not be ready for it, or may need to supplement it with other forms of therapy. Likewise, a therapist may not be comfortable using family therapy or working with several family members at once. There is no doubt that family therapy can be a daunting task. But the richness that is available to the therapist, family members, and students who make use of a comprehensive family evaluation and treatment model makes the task well worth the effort. The following chapter provides the blueprint for how to work with and apply the McMaster model when assessing and treating families.

CHAPTER 3

The Problem Centered Systems
Therapy of the Family

Despite the variety of theoretical models underlying clinical work in the area of family therapy, there is no generally accepted framework within which to perform family assessment and treatment. The diversity of models can sometimes lead to an undisciplined approach to treatment just when it is most important for those treating families to be clear and consistent about the conceptual frameworks they use. The origins of the PCSTF[18-20] were conceived when Epstein and a colleague had previously worked together at McGill but had not observed each other's work with families for some years. While reviewing videotapes of each other doing family therapy, clear differences were observed with respect to the minor moves and interventions they both made. This was not the case for the major steps they followed which were strikingly consistent. Both therapists followed the same sequence of major steps that Epstein and colleagues labeled as the macro stages of therapy.

The effect of this observation was the realization that Epstein and his colleagues may have focused on the wrong level when they taught therapy skills. Taking a step back and looking at a higher level of abstraction actually made it easier to see clear stages in the treatment process. For example, many psychotherapists value the subtle interventions, strategies, and interpretations that make up the "art" of therapy. Observations of these two advanced therapists demonstrated significant differences in these areas yet striking similarities at a more general level of conducting therapy. Epstein concluded that the subtle interventions and strategies are the tools therapists use to build the therapy structure but the major structural components or *stages of therapy* are the essential building blocks of treatment. Since macrostages can be operationalized, therapists with a wide range of abilities and different therapy styles are able to follow them. This realization led the team to further delineate and analyze differences between the major and minor therapy moves and the utility of these concepts in teaching and research.

Basic Principles

Before detailing the PCSTF, we discuss several principles that underlie the treatment model. Some issues were touched upon in chapter 2, but here we elaborate since understanding our approach to family therapy is essential for treating families successfully.

Emphasis on Macro Stages of Treatment

We use the term *macro stages* to define the major stages of treatment. They are the large sequential blocks of the treatment process (assessment, contracting, treatment, and closure) that incorporate a number of substages. Therapists make use of a variety of strategies and interventions in the course of leading a family through these macro stages. *Strategy* refers to the options and courses of action that may be taken to successfully complete a macro stage. We differentiate the macro stages and the strategies required to negotiate them from the micromoves, the specific interviewing and intervention skills, such as those outlined by Cleghorn and Levin[21] and Tomm and Wright.[22] Several texts are available that provide updated techniques for honing interviewing skills.[23–26] Micromoves constitute the numerous interventions made by a therapist while carrying out the macro stages. They may include techniques for labeling, focusing the family on a problem, and clarifying communication.

Neither the macro stages nor the micromoves should be confused with style that reflects the personality of the therapist and includes qualities such as the choice of wording, use of gestures, and method of confronting. This aspect of therapy is often noticeable when observing a gifted therapist and should not be confused with the general strategy or micromoves the therapist is using to complete a step in the macromove sequence. One advantage of the PCSTF is that it asks therapists to focus on the *stages and steps* in therapy. The therapist does not need to change personality to become a good therapist or to use the model. Because of an emphasis on macromoves, the McMaster approach accommodates therapists with a variety of clinical styles.

In addition to varying in their therapeutic style, therapists also vary in their repertoire and number of micro level skills. Generally, we can say that the wider the range of skills available to therapists, the more effectively and efficiently they will carry out treatment. We anticipate that expert therapists will use the full range of their skills and advanced techniques when applying the PCSTF approach. Less experienced therapists will use the PCSTF as a basis for a structured treatment approach on which they can continue to develop more focal skills. Overall, we believe that if the treatment concepts are consistently applied, if the steps and sequences defined in the therapy approach are adhered to, then most therapists (including beginning therapists) can be reasonably effective in the majority of their cases.

We emphasize that the macro stages of therapy are the most important level of focus. We are aware that specific strategies and micro-level intervention skills are important and will discuss them when we feel they are important for an adequate and efficient completion of a given stage. However, since a major premise of the PCSTF treatment approach is that completing the steps and sequences of the macro stages yields effective results, they remain the focus of this chapter.

Collaborative Set

The PCSTF stresses active collaboration with family members at each stage of the treatment process. This idea of collaboration between the therapist and family members is the forerunner of the concept of therapeutic alliance that is so popular today. The importance of the therapeutic alliance reinforces our early identification of this principle as a focal part of the therapy process. The family must agree to and be a part of this collaboration throughout the therapy process or else there is no therapy. The therapeutic contract is based upon this total mutual commitment to work at the therapy.

Open and Direct Communication with the Family

The therapist explains his or her actions in open, direct communication with the family at each step in the therapy process and makes sure that family members clearly understand and agree to what he or she is doing. The open approach ensures that the family accepts and is prepared for each step and fosters a collaborative response on the part of the family to the treatment. An important corollary of this principle is that indirect or paradoxical interventions are *not* used in the McMaster approach.

Focus on the Family's Responsibility to Effect Change

The PCSTF focuses on the family's responsibility to change by emphasizing that family members actually do most of the therapy work. Family members are directly involved in identifying, clarifying, and resolving the difficulties and problems of the family. The ideal role of the therapist is that of a catalyst, clarifier, and facilitator. The therapist facilitates the achievement of objectives such as family openness, clarity of communication, and development of active problem-solving abilities on the part of the family members. In the process, family members become aware of their strengths and their shortcomings and develop effective problem-solving methods that can be generalized to resolve future difficulties. They are trained to become their own family therapists and problem solvers, thereby diminishing the need for the therapist.

Emphasis on Assessment

When conducting an assessment, the therapist elicits information about the structure, organization, and transactional patterns of the family. Additional family problems are often revealed in the assessment stage. Before proceeding with any therapy, we believe it is necessary to understand the family system and its problems and strengths as fully as possible. The diagnostic work-up must be thorough and complete before the treatment is prescribed, much less embarked upon. A surgical analogy would be to make an incision in the general area of pain and then to poke around hoping to find the true source of the problem.

A surprising but welcome clinical finding resulting from our thorough approach to assessment has been the degree to which it facilitates the therapy process and leads to more satisfactory outcomes. We find that in many cases, after completing a thorough assessment stage, the healing process has begun and little remains to be done to achieve a satisfactory outcome. This may be due to several factors. When the assessment stage is properly executed, it brings about a fruitful engagement process that induces family members into an active collaborative functioning throughout treatment. The assessment procedure filters out the poorly motivated and strongly reinforces the positive motivation for treatment where it is present—even in highly latent form.

In uncomplicated cases family problems become so clearly defined by a good assessment that well-motivated families quickly become aware—often with minimal input by the therapist—of the steps that need to be taken to achieve satisfactory problem resolution. These families are often able to develop and achieve the necessary actions on their own initiative.

When confronted with a family emergency or acute crisis, a different and more active intervention may be necessary. Appropriately dealing with immediate issues may delay the full assessment, but should not cancel it. Family therapists often think they understand the family and its dynamics after resolving a crisis situation. Seeing a family in crisis, however, does not give a comprehensive view of family problems or strengths. The therapist may need to deal with the crisis before completing a full assessment and proceeding to other stages of the model and treatment.

Inclusion of the Entire Family

When seeing a family for the first time, we prefer that all family members living at home are present. We may subsequently include significant extended family and outsiders actively involved with the family. This allows us to obtain a full range of views, resulting in a comprehensive assessment of the situation, an indication of potential allies and supports, and direct observation of parent-child and sibling interactions. It is also an opportunity to clarify the general course of action for everyone. To assess the parents' sexual relationship we either set aside a separate session for the parents or have the children wait outside the therapy room. Although we would also prefer that all members participate in the total treatment process, in some situations it may be clinically advisable to exclude some family members. Basic therapeutic values and ethics and the therapist's judgment must be relied upon when a decision needs to be made regarding exclusion of some family members. It is our experience that, except when the parental sexual relationship is being discussed, the need to exclude members occurs very rarely. Finally, despite the concern of some postmodern therapy models, family members are not likely to be hurt by exposure to the family therapy process.

There are several reasons for including all family members in the therapy process. First, the PCSTF evaluates the total family system, not just one or two members. The therapist cannot know the family system if an important family member is missing; the assessment will remain incomplete. Also, there is often one family member who is carrying a disproportionate burden of the family's problems. If appropriately supported, this person can be very helpful in outlining the true nature of the family's issues. In each family this role may fall on a different person; by having all family members come in there is a greater chance of including him or her in the treatment process. Second, a full assessment may suggest that the total system needs changing or that only one or two components need changing. Because change in part of the system will, by definition, change the total system, all family members are involved. Third, even when a member is not directly involved in specific interactions, he or she may be helpful in an informal role of co-therapist or auxiliary therapist. In fact, a major strength of the PCSTF approach is training family members to positively intervene and be more effective problem-solvers within their own family. Finally, the presence and participation of all family members allows the therapist to better evaluate the change processes in the system.

There are exceptions. In emergency cases, we vigorously attempt to have everyone present but will not refuse a beginning initial assessment solely on the grounds of all members not being present. Reasonable medical illness and the inability of an acutely psychotic individual to participate without major disruption are other exceptions. When a significant member, such as a spouse or the identified patient, fails to show for an appointment, the situation obviates against open and collaborative assessment and must, therefore, be dealt with directly by confronting the difficulty before beginning treatment. We insist that members who are a focus of discussion attend, so that if issues involving them arise they will be present for discussion.

When no emergency exists and a significant member has not shown up, we will sometimes cancel the session, pointing out that it makes no sense to begin the process without the presence of such an important member. We let the family members know that if they want our help it is their job to bring the absent member. We encourage this by scheduling another appointment. Our experience is that the therapist's confidence, clarity, sensitive understanding, and intervention usually result in the desired members being present for the assessment.

Emphasis on Current Problems

The focus of therapy is on the specific problems of the family. These include the presenting problems as well as those identified during the assessment.

Focus on Family Strengths

Because of the focus on healthy families during development of the MMFF, our approach to treatment explicitly recognizes that all families have strengths that should be recognized and fostered during treatment. Since a major tenet of the PCSTF approach is to develop as much independence and responsibility as the family can handle, it is important that the therapist accurately assesses the strengths of family members as well as their limitations. A related issue is the therapist's acceptance of the family's methods for accomplishing tasks. If the family has worked out strategies for dealing with particular issues, and the strategies are effective, we do not attempt to change them, even if they appear unusual or unorthodox.

Focus on Behavioral Change

The emphasis of the PCSTF is on changing current behavior of the family. Family members' desires for change in attitudes, beliefs, or opinions are reformulated into requests for change in observable behavior. These changes in behavior are the defined goals of treatment. The behavioral focus does not deny the importance of cognitions or affect, but recognizes behavioral change as the most expedient since it is *public and measurable.* Cognitions and affect are addressed in the PCSTF, but the goal is to promote change in behavior.

Time Limitations

The PCSTF is time limited in that it is tailored to a set of 6 to 12 sessions spaced over a period of weeks, months, or a year. Session intervals and the length of the individual sessions will vary depending on the issues involved in each case. Early assessment sessions may be longer depending on the needs of the case, the setting, and the stamina of the family and the therapist. Later, task-setting treatment sessions may be as short as 15 to 20 minutes. For some families, a thorough assessment with all family members present is sufficient to clarify issues and address the presenting problem. In general, however, we expect the assessment stage to take one or two sessions, with the remaining four to ten sessions focused on treatment. In the assessment and early treatment sessions, the family may be seen weekly. If all goes well, the sessions may be spread out to every 2 weeks, then to once a month, and, if still needed, to once every 3 to 6 months. During these intervals, the family works on the identified problems and the actions that were agreed upon in the family sessions. Families are encouraged to contact the therapist if they need help during the session intervals.

We stress limiting the number of treatment sessions for several reasons. First, imposing limits on therapy sessions stimulates therapists and families to more active involvement in the therapeutic work, thereby facilitating change. The objectives of the therapy are more clearly in the forefront of their work together. When no limits are set, families and therapists often develop a mutually satisfying relationship that they are reluctant to relinquish. Therapy drags on for long periods to the mutual enjoyment of all concerned but with no demonstrable relationship between length of therapy and effectiveness of results. Second, holding family members to a limited number of sessions communicates to them that the therapist is confident in their ability to work at effecting change. This approach emphasizes strengths, rather than weaknesses, of the family and often leads to a reduction of doubt and anxious tension often experienced when the family first comes in for treatment. Third, concern for the cost-effectiveness of treatment is another reason for limiting the number of therapy sessions. Long-term multiple sessions are very expensive and may be an exorbitant use of limited skilled resources.

If a therapist feels that treatment should go beyond 12 sessions, a re-evaluation of the treatment situation should take place and, if possible, a

Table 3.1 Basic Principles of the PCSTF

• Emphasis on macro stages of treatment	• Entire family present
• Collaboration with family members	• Address current problems
• Open and direct communication	• Focus on family strengths
• Family responsible for change	• Behavioral change
• Thorough, complete assessment	• Time-limited

consultation sought. Certainly there are times when the therapy is going well yet requires more sessions due to the complexity of issues being dealt with or new problems that have arisen. These situations are less likely than cases in which the therapy has gotten off track and become bogged down. Although it may be the inexperience of the therapist, even experienced and skilled therapists get caught in a pathological family system. Putting a limit on the number of sessions, with consultation and discussion built into such limits, is a useful mechanism to have in place.

Two points related to the time-limited nature of the model may need clarification. While learning the model, therapists may need two full sessions to complete a satisfactory family assessment. They may feel daunted by this and pressured to begin treatment. Families usually respond positively to a thorough assessment, however, and feel reassured by a therapist's desire to understand the family before offering a prescription for treatment. Second, even after completion of the therapy, family members are encouraged to call upon the therapist in the future for any further family work that may be needed.

Stages of Treatment

The four macro stages of the PCSTF are: (1) Assessment, (2) Contracting, (3) Treatment, and (4) Closure. Each stage contains a sequence of substages, the first of which is always orientation.

A major problem in clinical work is that practitioners assume that patients know what the therapist is doing and in what direction the therapy will move. Too often, we have found that patients and family members do not know why they are meeting, what to expect, and what is expected of them. The effect is dehumanizing to patients and families, not because therapists are unsympathetic, but because we presume a knowledge and understanding on the part of the patients and families about the way we work. From the moment family members come in, we orient them to what we are doing and seek their permission and agreement before proceeding from one step to another. We try to make them as aware as possible of what we are doing by being both clear and explicit. This is done out of respect for the families

Table 3.2 Stages and Steps in the PCSTF

1. Assessment Stage	2. Contracting Stage
A. Orientation	A. Orientation
B. Data gathering	B. Outlining options
C. Problem description	C. Negotiating expectations
D. Problem clarification	D. Contract signing
3. Treatment Stage	4. Closure Stage
A. Orientation	A. Orientation
B. Clarifying priorities	B. Summary of treatment
C. Setting tasks	C. Long-term goals
D. Task evaluation	D. Follow-up

we work with and our belief in their right to know exactly what is going on at all times. Further, we believe that therapy is more effective when families are aware of and in agreement with what is being done.

The orientation to the assessment stage is quite detailed and sets the tone and direction of therapy. Orientations to later stages of treatment are briefer and used to indicate a change in the focus and task. We use the orientation to explicitly set rules and expectations. The family's agreement with the summary at the end of each stage allows us to confront possible resistance at later treatment stages by reiterating to the family the agreement that was previously obtained. After a general orientation, each substage is approached systematically, with the therapist guiding the process. At the conclusion of each step, the therapist and family members review and reach agreement on what has been accomplished before they move on to the next stage. As we review each stage, the goals and methods for assessing achievement will be discussed.

Assessment Stage

The first, and in many ways the most important, macrostage is the Assessment Stage. This stage has three main goals. First, the therapist orients the family to the treatment process and establishes an open, collaborative relationship with the family. Second, the therapist, with the family members, identifies all current problems in the family, including the presenting problem. Third, the therapist identifies family dynamic patterns that appear to be causally related to the family's problems. The specific family issues that the therapist has formulated are presented to the family and accepted as accurate or amended as needed.

Because of the importance that the PCSTF places on a thorough evaluation of the family system, the therapist should take as many sessions as necessary to complete a full assessment. The number of assessment sessions required will vary due to the therapist's expertise and the nature of the family's problems. Beginning therapists can be expected to take longer in the assessment stage; advanced therapists may take longer with more complex problems and families. Paradoxically, we find that extra time in the assessment stage often reduces the number of task-oriented treatment sessions required. Several reasons may account for this. A thorough assessment results in delineation of the issues involved in the family, provides each member of the family with a chance to offer his or her opinion on family matters, helps family members focus on the issues, and provides an opportunity to tease out problems that family members did not recognize. In addition, the inherent family strengths, as well as deficits, are made clear. Such exposure often points to obvious solutions the family may have missed, thereby cutting down the number of actual therapy sessions required.

If more time is needed to complete the assessment stage when a session comes to an end, we summarize our findings to that point and clarify that we require more information before a decision is made regarding diagnosis and treatment. At this stage we seldom space the sessions more than a week apart. Most families appreciate that relatively long-standing problems can wait for completion of a thorough assessment. Although we urge therapists to take as long as necessary to complete the family assessment, we realize that this may become a problem if the evaluation takes so long that the family loses interest. Earlier we discussed the strategy a therapist can take in an emergency situation. An unduly long assessment may be due to the therapist's inexperience, lack of focus, or numerous/complicated family issues. We believe that by following the model the therapist will obviate these problems in most cases.

The assessment is based on family member reports. The therapist confirms the impressions by observing the family's behavior in session. At any time, the therapist may confront and clarify contradictions between the stated information and observed behavior and between information offered by different family members. The therapist's impressions are condensed and fed back until the family agrees that an honest appreciation of the family's functioning has been obtained.

The therapist takes care to gather firm evidence to support his or her hypotheses about the family before putting them forth as opinions. If the therapist has a strong clinical hunch and no confirmatory evidence, it should be presented to the family as such, either as a hunch or an impression. Family members can be asked their opinion about the validity of the impression. This approach prevents the therapist from taking off into flights of fantasy without evidence, yet allows him or her to test clinical hunches and exercise clinical intuition. It engenders confidence and respect on the part of the family for the therapist's objectivity, impartiality, and respect for data. Further, it reinforces the role of family members as participants in the treatment process.

If there is substantial disagreement, but the therapist has sufficiently clear data to make an accurate judgment, the therapist can suggest: "Okay, you (we) disagree in this area, so let's agree that it is at least problematic in that respect and move on to another area I wish to explore."

The assessment stage consists of four steps: (1) orientation, (2) data gathering, (3) problem description, (4) clarification and agreement on a problem list.

Orientation

We orient the family by clarifying why they think they are there, what each member expects will happen during the session, how they think the session was arranged, and what they hope the outcome will be. This often provides useful information and helps avoid later resistance. The following suggests wording that the therapist (T) might use:

> I'd like to find out from each of you what you thought was going to take place here today? I'd also like to know why you think all the family is here? And I would like to know what you'd like to see come out of this session? What do you particularly want to see addressed or have an answer to?

We condense and feed back their ideas and then briefly outline our ideas, including why we understand the family is there, what we already know about them in general, what we plan to do, and what we hope to achieve. At this time we obtain their permission to proceed. We also explain our rationale for seeing them as a family.

> T: Fine. Now that I have your ideas, let me explain mine. I asked you to come in because I need to have a clear idea of how you function as a family. This gives me a clearer understanding of the entire picture and helps me to work out with you how things can be more helpful for John and all of you. I know you have concerns about John's getting upset and being hard to manage. That obviously affects all of you and not just John. Part of the reason it's important to meet with all of you and understand how you function is that I know that the way a family functions influences what happens to each family member. So, before deciding on a possible treatment, I need to have a clear picture of how you function as a family.

I'm going to jump around a bit to find out about your family and ask a number of questions in different areas. Some may seem unrelated to John's problem, but they're important for me to know about. I'll clarify as I go along to make sure that I have a correct impression of how you operate as a family. At the end of the session, I will summarize where we seem to be at that point. Do you have any questions? Is that okay, then? Can we go ahead with my finding more about your family?

Data Gathering

With this step, we gather data about the presenting problem, overall family functioning, additional investigations, and other problems. The therapist asks family members what *they* think are the problems in the family. Each family member is asked his or her opinion. This helps to focus them on the issues, gives them an outlet to express their feelings, and creates an atmosphere for listening and discussing. In the following sections we pose several questions that may be used to help focus the family and the therapist. By listing the questions emphasizing different areas of family functioning, we do not mean to suggest that the therapist needs to ask each and every one. The questions are provided as an aid to understand the family system.

Presenting Problem(s)

The therapist begins by asking the family to describe the problem(s) that brought them to treatment. Sufficient time is spent in gathering data so that the therapist develops an accurate picture of the nature and history of each problem. The therapist explores the factual details, the affective components of the problem, the historical perspective, the precipitating events, and who is mainly involved in the problem and how.

An example will help. A teacher's telephone call about John's problems, what the teacher said, and the mother's observation of John's withdrawal and increased disobedience are factual details. The mother's reaction of frustration and later helplessness, the father's fury at John and at the mother for not disciplining him, and John's feelings of guilt and sadness are affective components of factual details. Details that the problem began 6 months ago, got better for a short time, and then deteriorated are historical components. The father's recent change in jobs may be a precipitating event, and John's entry into adolescence is a developmental issue.

When describing the presenting problem, we use the MMFF dimensions to frame the issues. In this example, we explore how the family attempted to solve the problem, how they communicated about it, and what behavior control issues may be involved. In exploring the problem, other issues may arise and be defined as difficulties. The mother may feel that the father does not support her in dealing with any of the children, the father may feel that the mother does not understand his situation, and John recognizes the conflict between his parents, gets upset, and runs away. After discussing the problems, we feed back our understanding of each issue and make sure that everyone agrees that we have a clear understanding.

> T: At this point I'd like to make sure that I understand things correctly. We seem to agree that (1) John has been harder to manage, particularly for you (mother). John, you and your sister both notice your mom and dad disagreeing, but this upsets you more than your sister and you take off, which gets you into even more trouble. (2) Both of you (mother and father) are not able to get together and solve problems. This makes both of you unhappy and increases the tension between you. (3) You (mother) feel that your husband has not been supporting you—not just with John, but also with the other children. And (4) you (father) have been down because of changes at work and because you don't feel your wife is understanding of the work situation. The effect is you feel you're failing not just at work but also as a husband and father. (5) The family is having trouble adjusting to dad's job change. All of this has developed in the past six months and was not the case previously. Dad's job change seems to be the biggest stress associated with it all. Do I have it right to that point?

Overall Family Functioning
The next step moves from an assessment of the presenting problems to an exploration of overall family functioning. We first orient the family to this change in focus.

> T: Now I'd like to switch to get a general idea of how you operate as a family. Is that all right?

The therapist assesses the family on the six dimensions of the MMFF: problem solving, communication, roles, affective responsiveness, affective involvement, and behavior control. The assessment focuses on detailing strengths and difficulties in each area of family life and helps us determine aspects of overall family functioning that influence the emotional or physical health of family members. At this stage of the evaluation a critical point to keep in mind is that the assessment focuses on the family's overall functioning and avoids developing formulations based on data related to the presenting problem, data that by their nature are more likely to be negative. The assessment is approached tactfully, directly, and honestly. We explain what we are doing and discuss all issues openly. As we examine each dimension, we feed back to the family members our understanding of both their assets and their shortcomings in each particular area. We emphasize strengths since doing so is supportive and central to the therapeutic planning that will follow.

The following section suggests a line of questions to ask family members when assessing each dimension. A thorough clinical exploration of each area will lead the therapist to an accurate assessment of the family's functioning, and their strengths and weaknesses, while focusing on an important area of family life. For those who are less experienced in conducting family interviews or who prefer a more structured set of questions, the McMaster Structured Interview of Family Functioning (McSIFF), described in chapter 5 (and included in Part II) may be used to pinpoint areas of difficulty that the family is experiencing.

Clinical Exploration—Problem Solving

We ask family members to identify family problems that have come up within the past two to three weeks so that we can explore *the family's problem solving ability.* We indicate that all families have problems and that we are interested in problems they have solved and those they have had difficulty with. After identifying a problem, we ask them to describe it in some detail. If it was largely instrumental in nature, we ask about their responses and reactions to facing a similar problem so that we can explore the affective component of the problem. If all the problems they encountered in the past two to three weeks were instrumental, we ask them to identify the last problem they can remember where people had trouble with their feelings, were upset, or felt down. After identifying any given problem, we explore the family's attempts at resolving the problem, using the stages described in chapter 2. As we explore what the family did or did not do at each stage, we feed back our understanding to family members to make certain that we have correctly identified how they handled the stage in question. The following are examples of questions that might be used to examine each step of the process [27] (also see Table 4.1, p. 108).

Questions on identification might include: When that problem arose, what did you think was going on? Did you feel anything else was involved? Did you all see the problem the same way? (Here we would explore specific differences, as well as elaborating on the instrumental and affective components of a given problem.) Who first noticed the problem? Are you the one who usually notices such things? Who else notices problems like that?

Questions regarding of the problem to the appropriate resource would be: When you first noticed the problem, what happened? Whom did you tell about it? Is that who you would usually tell? When did you tell them?

Did any of the rest of you notice the problem but not tell anybody? What stopped you? Is that the way the rest of you see it?

To *assess the development of alternatives* step, we would ask: What did you think of doing about the problem at that point? Did you think of any other alternatives? Who thought of the plan? Did any other people have ideas? Did you share them?

Decisions and actions might be probed by: How did you decide what to do? Who decided? How did you decide on that alternative? What did you expect might happen if you used your other alternative?

We check on *monitoring the action with questions* such as: When you decided on your choice of action, did you follow through? Who did what? Do you usually check to see that things get done after you have decided? Who usually checks?

Questions on evaluating success of action might include: How do you think you did with that problem? As a family, do you ever discuss how you think you did in handling problems? Do you ever go over the problems and what happened?

Finally, we ask *summary and general questions* such as: Is that the way you would generally handle problems such as this? What is similar to your usual pattern? What is different? Do problems such as that make it hard for you as a family to function well? What other areas do you feel create problems? (With the last question, if other problems are identified, we might revert to questions about the steps the family took to explore the newly identified problems.)

In exploring problem solving, we make sure that we have a solid understanding of the family's handling of instrumental and affective difficulties. These questions are also useful in exploring the presenting problem. In addition to understanding the presenting problem, it is helpful to know about the identification and communication of the problem, development of alternatives, action taken, monitoring the action, and evaluating the effectiveness of the action.

Evaluation of Functioning. Generally, the fewer unresolved problems, the healthier the family. Also, the more problem-solving steps accomplished by a family in pursuing a solution to a problem, the healthier the family. If a family differs widely in its ability to solve problems, the therapist determines which problems are causing the most difficulties for the family's functioning. Difficulties with instrumental problems receive a more negative rating than difficulties with affective problems. At the healthy end of the dimension we conceptualize a family with few, if any, unresolved problems. When family members encounter a new problem situation, they approach the problem systematically and evaluate the outcome of their attempt to solve the problem. Moving towards the disturbed end of the spectrum, the family's problem-solving behavior becomes less systematic (they accomplish few problem-solving steps), and they are more likely to deny or mislabel the problem. At the very disturbed end of the dimension, families consistently deny or mislabel problems, have long-standing unresolved problems, and problems tend to generate much conflict within the family system.

Clinical Exploration—Communication

In assessing communication, we observe communication patterns that occur during the assessment process. We purposefully stimulate discussion and interaction among members to produce observable behavior. We observe how they handle information that we feed back to them. We ask a number of questions to explore *the extent and nature of communication in the family.* Examples would be: Do people in this family talk with one another? Who does most of the talking in the family? We ask individuals who they talk with and try to pin down the frequency, regularity and pattern: Do you feel you can tell things freely to others in the family or do you have to qualify or be guarded about what you say?

To *assess the clarity-masked or direct/indirect aspect of this dimension,* we ask: How did he let you know that? How do you get the message? What is she telling you? What did "Mary" say just now? What did you make of that? Can you tell how "Ellen" feels about that? Does she let you know things that way all the time or just around feelings? Do members in the family let you know they have understood what you are trying to say? How do they do that? Do you feel that you can get your ideas across to others in the family? Do you feel that others understand you? What happens if they don't? What happens when you try to tell others about things? What about when you try to tell others about your feelings?

Evaluation of Functioning. We are primarily interested in producing a rating of overall family communication. Other factors being equal, the following rules of thumb are useful:

1. The level of health/pathology in the parents' communication pattern should be weighted more heavily than the level of communication functioning in the children.
2. The lower the level of communication functioning in a single member of a dyad, triad, the lower the overall rating of the family.
3. The greater the number of family members at a low level of health in the communication area, the lower the overall rating of the family.

In evaluating communication, the therapist considers both the clarity and the directness of the communication within the family.

1. Clear versus masked communication: Optimal clarity is achieved when the information transmitted is relevant, concise, and consistent with other communications. Communication is masked when a sequence of messages contains contradictory information (e.g., a message is given and then immediately contradicted), when contradictory messages are given at different levels (e.g., nonverbal message contradicts verbal message), and when the communication simply does not make sense because it is out of context, vague, woolly, or clouded.

2. Direct versus indirect: For effective communication, the message should be clearly directed, both verbally and nonverbally, to the intended receiver. Communication is indirect when it is either directed to an inappropriate person or directed towards no one in particular.

At the healthy end of the dimension, we conceptualize a family that communicates in a clear, concise, and direct manner in both the instrumental and affective areas. As we move toward the disturbed end of the dimension, communication becomes less clear and direct and affective communication becomes particularly distorted. At the very disturbed end of the dimension, we conceptualize a family in which communication is consistently masked and indirect in both the instrumental and affective areas. Problems in distinguishing affect being experienced versus affect being communicated are discussed below, under affective responsiveness.

Clinical Exploration—Roles

Following are examples of questions that can be used to evaluate different areas of *role functions in the family*:

Questions of provision of resources include: Who brings in the money? Are there separate bank accounts? Is there a common checking account? Who gets the groceries and prepares/plans meals? Is it always the same person? Who buys the clothes for the family members? Do you have a car? How do you all get to work, school, other activities?

Questions on nurturing and support include the following types of questions directed to each family member: Who do you go to when you need someone to talk to? Who do you go to when things get to you or when you are upset? Is it helpful when you talk to them? If there are small children, we ask which parent usually comforts the children. How do they handle it when a child gets upset? What do they do? Do the mother and father do similar or different things? How do the mother and father divide their availability to the children? Do they talk about supporting each other and making themselves available for comforting the children?

Questions on adult sexual gratification are completed with the parents alone unless the children are very young. When children are asked to leave, it is done with a statement such as, "I would like you to leave long enough for me to ask your mom and dad specific questions that only involve them. We will not be talking about you while you are out of the room. Any plans that may affect you will be made only with you here. Is that okay?"

With single parents we explore how they meet their sexual needs. With spouses, we start with questions similar to the following: How do the two of you feel about the affectionate and sexual aspects of your relationship? Are you both satisfied about all aspects of you sexual life? Would you change any aspects of your sexual life if you could? How? (If initial findings indicate the need, more complete sexual functioning assessments might be indicated.) Who initiates sexual contacts? Has your sexual life always been as it is now? Was it better or worse before? How often do you have sexual relationships? Is it satisfactory to each of you? Do you feel that you satisfy your partner? Do you feel that you know what is most pleasurable and satisfying to your partner? Do you personally feel satisfied by your partner? How do you say "no" when you want to? Can you do that easily? How would either of you like to change sexually?

Examples of *life skills development questions* are: Who usually oversees what is happening with the children's education? Who usually helps the children with homework? Who usually deals with the school? How do you handle the stages the children go through? Who usually gets involved with problems that children face growing up? Who is responsible for teaching manners? Who gets involved in sex education of the children? Who is responsible for dealing with the children as they relate to others? Who discusses their vocational choices? Adults go through stages too: who helps and gets involved in those discussions? Who is involved in discussions about changes in jobs? How do you help each other develop?

Examples of *maintenance and management of the systems* are: Who is involved in major decisions? Who has the final say? Where does "the buck stop?" Have you decided on the size of your family? Who decided that? Who keeps track of the health of family members? Who decides when you see the doctor? Who handles the money or monthly bills? Who gets involved in large purchases? Who cleans the house? How are house repairs handled? How is the decision to paint or remodel the house taken? How efficiently and effectively are these things done? Who looks after the car? Do you share these tasks or is it the same person all the time? Who handles the discipline of the children?

Questions on allocation include: How do you decide who does the jobs? Do you talk about it? Would you like the decisions about who handles jobs to be done differently? Do you feel that some people have too many jobs? Do any of you feel overburdened by your jobs? Do you think it is reasonable to expect people to do the jobs or do you think some people are doing jobs they can't handle? What is it about the jobs or the people that makes you think that?

Questions on accountability include: How do you check that a job gets done? Who does that? What do you do if it is not done?

Evaluation of Functioning. When evaluating a family's role functioning, the therapist considers the following:

1. Are all the necessary functions being fulfilled?
2. Are family members satisfied or dissatisfied with the way responsibilities are shared?
3. Has the family reached a consensus regarding the allocation of roles? If consensus has not been reached, it is possible that one or more role functions will be poorly fulfilled.
4. Is the allocation of family members to roles appropriate? A family can err by expecting someone to fulfill a function that he is not capable of carrying out, or by overloading a particular individual with too many functions.
5. Has there been an appropriate allocation of authority (power) to go along with the allocation of a particular function? For example, a family cannot ask an older child to baby-sit and then not provide him or her with the power to maintain reasonable control.
6. Is there a procedure within the family for making sure that jobs are carried out?
7. Is there cooperation and collaboration within the family in fulfilling role functions?

At the healthy end of the dimension, we conceptualize a family that fulfills all necessary functions. Such a family reaches a consensus on the allocation of roles, collaborates and cooperates, allocates both authority and accountability to ensure that functions are completed, and has some room for flexibility and shifting of roles. As one moves toward the disturbed end of the dimension, we conceptualize families that accomplish the basic functions less and less effectively. At the most disturbed end of the dimension, one or more of the basic functions are not being fulfilled and there are major problems with allocation and accountability.

Clinical Exploration—Affective Responsiveness

This dimension considers the pattern of the *family's responses to affective stimuli,* but focuses more than any other dimension on the individual as the locus of response. It is important to understand how this dimension is distinct from affective communication. Affective responsiveness refers to feelings that the individual experiences while affective communication refers to how family members transmit to each other the emotions they are experiencing. If someone does not experience an emotional response, then he or she cannot communicate it. When evaluation of affective communication leads to the judgment that there are significant disturbances or deficits, affective responsiveness may or may not be problematic. If there is clear communication of a full range of appropriate emotion, affective responsiveness is considered healthy. The absence of affective communication, however, does not necessarily indicate that no affect was experienced. Also, the fact that affect was experienced does not mean that it was necessarily communicated.

The following *questions elicit information regarding emotional responses*: What was your response to that? How did you feel then? What did you feel besides that? Do the rest of you feel that way? What is similar about your response? What is different? Do you ever sense that you do not experience feelings that you should feel, or that you think others do? Are there any feelings that you experience more intensely than you think is reasonable given the situation? Are you a family that responds with a lot of feelings? All feelings? Or some more than others? Which feelings do you not respond to or express? Do any of you feel that you are a family that under-responds in terms of emotions? Which emotions do you feel that you under-respond with?

We then discuss with the family as a whole, and with each individual member, their experiences regarding the following emotions: love, kindness, affection, tenderness, anger, depression, sadness, hurt, fear and tension, and rage or hate. As we assess each individual, we check whether he or she or the family feels that they under- or over-respond in each area. While doing this assessment, we may gain further information about affective communication by asking the rest of the family how the person lets them know their feeling.

Evaluation of Functioning. Ratings are based on whether the affective response is appropriate in intensity and duration in a particular stimulus situation. Given the variety of stimuli and possible emotional responses, evaluation takes into account the total scope of emotional responsiveness. At the healthy end of the dimension, we expect family members to possess the capability of responding with a full range of emotions and with appropriate intensity and duration. We rate families at the very disturbed end of the dimension if they are extremely constricted in the range of emotions with which they respond or are consistently inappropriate in quality or quantity of the response. Families rated as functioning at a healthy level may have one or more members who may not be capable of responding emotionally with the full range of affect. The affective responses of other family members, however, fill the gaps in the emotional spectrum. Families can be rated in the healthy range even if they occasionally respond with inappropriate affect or experience occasional episodes of under or over affective responsiveness.

Clinical Exploration—Affective Involvement

The following questions can be used to clinically explore *affective involvement of the family:*

> *For Any Family Member.* Who cares about what is important to you? Why do you think they care about it? How do they let you know they are concerned for you? Do they ever show too much interest? When "Bill " talks about that, what effect does it have on you? What were you thinking (or feeling) while they were talking about their interests? What activities, interests, or areas are important to you individually or personally? How does the rest of your family respond to these? Are they interested? Are they *too* interested? Do you feel they are interested because it is important to you or for their own sake? Do you feel that other members of the family go their own way and do not care or notice what happens to you? Are others in the family really interested in what you do or do they just minimally respond?
>
> *For Parent–Child Dyads.* We ask children questions like: Who bugs you most in the family? Do you feel people in the family are overprotective or over involved in your life? How do they do that? How do you handle it? How do you get them to stop it? If a child responds in a way that indicates problems, we ask the parents how they see it and what they think is going on. We also explore this area with siblings. We ask the parents questions such as: How do you relate to each of the children? Do you listen? Does the child make it easy or difficult to relate to him or her? Do you feel your relationship with the child is close enough? If there are difficulties, we have the parents spell out the issues and what steps they have taken to improve them. We also ask the children concerned for their views of the situation.
>
> *Evaluation of Functioning.* In rating the family in this dimension, the therapist considers whether family members show an appropriate

amount of interest and concern with each other, whether they are overly engrossed in each other, or whether their involvement is restricted to sharing physical/instrumental surroundings and functions. We are interested in the nature of their involvement, how much they give of themselves and invest in understanding and being supportive of other family members. We evaluate whether they are interested primarily for their own sake or for the sake of others. Different styles of affective involvement are rated along a dimension. The least effective involvement is presented at either pole with lack of involvement and symbiotic involvement. Slightly more effective, but still problematic, is involvement devoid of feelings at one end and over involvement at the other. Healthy involvement is characterized with positive interest but without intruding extensively.

Clinical Exploration—Behavior Control

This dimension is explored with statements and questions such as the following: All families have rules. They also have ways of *handling behavior in certain situations.* In which areas are rules most important in your family? Are the rules clear? How do you handle dangerous situations? Can you give me an example of such a situation and the rules you have for it? Is that the same for everyone or does it vary from person to person? If so, how? Do you have rules for table manners, going to bed, dressing, bathing? Are they consistent in each area or do they vary? How fixed are the rules? Do you make allowance for special situations? Are the rules the same for everyone? Do you expect everyone in the family to eat together?

Are the rules clear about how you relate to each other? Can you give me an example? Do you allow hitting or yelling at each other? Do the rules vary from time to time? Is the rule the same for everyone? How much freedom are you allowed? Can you discuss the rules? Do you know what's expected of you in terms of behaving with people outside of the family? Is that the same as behaving with each other inside the family or different?

Are there any particular rules that anyone in the family feels are really unfair? Mom and dad, do you agree on all the rules? Which ones do you differ on and how? Do you kids know that mom and dad agree, or do you feel that they disagree? How do you know that they agree or disagree?

Tell me about how you enforce the rules? Does it vary depending on who is doing the enforcing? Do you know what to expect if you break a rule? Who's toughest in terms of punishment and consequences? Do they stick to being tough or do they give in later? Mom and dad, do you ever feel that the other one doesn't back you up?

Evaluation of Functioning. To determine an evaluation rating for behavior control, the therapist must decide if there is a sufficiently stable pattern of interaction among family members to identify family rules and the consequences for infraction of these rules. If there is not a sufficiently stable pattern, the two most likely styles are laissez-faire or chaotic. A number of other concepts are used in making the evaluation. Are the rules clear and understood by all family members? Has the family reached a consensus regarding these family rules and consequences for infractions? Are the standards of behavior appropriate for the age (maturity) of each family member within each of the areas described? The standards of behavior could be either too high or too low. The standards could be appropriate in one area (or situation) but not in others. Is there an appropriate amount of rigidity/flexibility in the enforcement of rules? Ideally, there should be sufficient flexibility within the family system to permit modification of the rules when special circumstances arise. A family can err by being either too rigid or too flexible (e.g., in physically dangerous situations for young children, relatively little flexibility would be expected). Are the consequences for infraction of the rules clear, understood, appropriate and flexible? Are the responses to infractions applied in a consistent manner?

At the healthy end of the dimension, we conceptualize a family that has clearly defined standards of behavior that are appropriate to each family member. While a family is consistent in its enforcement of its standards, there is sufficient flexibility in the system to permit exceptions to the standards. As we move toward the disturbed end of the dimension, standards become less clear or appropriate, or become increasingly rigid and authoritarian. At the very disturbed end of the dimension, family standards are completely absent, chaotic, or totally inappropriate.

Dysfunctional Transactional Patterns

Throughout the assessment stage, the therapist is aware of and recognizes the occurrence of potentially dysfunctional transaction patterns. In contrast to other family therapy models, we do not spend time detailing transactional patterns, particularly if it is distracting. We make note of the pattern and proceed with the rest of the assessment. When the pattern does present, it is usually in association with the presenting problems. We prefer to keep the problems in focus rather than be side-tracked by a specific transactional pattern early in treatment. If, during later stages of the assessment stage, the therapist recognizes a consistent dysfunctional transactional pattern that is associated with problems in several dimensions, he or she may label the process directly and see if the family agrees with the statement. Alternatively, the therapist may question the family regarding the transactional process so as to make the transactional pattern obvious. In this way, a specific transactional pattern may be included in the problem list for a given family.

For example, scapegoating is a problem that requires both exploration and observation. The therapist considers scapegoating as a transactional process when discussion around conflictual areas leads to a shift of focus from the topic area onto a given individual. We may label the process and see if the family agrees with statements such as:

> T: I hear what you're saying, but I would like to comment that each time we discuss ——, the topic shifts and it almost seems easier to deal with Joe as a problem than it is to deal with —Does this happen at home? Do you think it's a problem?

We may explore the responses going on in the potential scapegoat. We do so by asking questions when a possible scapegoat acts in a way that is guaranteed to draw attention onto him or herself. Questions could include, "What were we talking about just now? What's your reaction when that topic comes up? What do you feel like doing? Are you aware of jumping in at such times and changing the focus so that attention falls on you?"

We may openly challenge the scapegoated individual and enlist his or her agreement to change the pattern through the use of supportive or confronting statements such as, "I notice that you jump in each time we approach this area and begin to explore it. We've talked about that and you obviously find it uncomfortable. Is that right? I wonder if you could agree to hold back and let me explore the area. I know it's difficult, but I also think that if we can explore it and deal with it and then you won't have to feel so uncomfortable."

The next step of data gathering is to consider the need for additional investigations. Use of the systems approach in family therapy extends the factors that are usually considered in the assessment and diagnostic process. As the Group for Advancement of Psychiatry [28] pointed out three decades ago, the family's behavior can be influenced by factors at numerous levels such as the physical universe, biological systems, intrapsychic status of individuals, small groups (in this instance, the family), extended social systems, and value systems. In addition to what has previously been described, the diagnostic work-up comprises the necessary individual and family members' psychological and biological information as well as data about the family's broader social system such as the extended family, school, place of work, patterns of social recreation. Failure to make this point explicit has often led to the erroneous impression that a systems approach does not involve data obtained from such investigations. In fact, such investigations are basic to a comprehensive evaluation of the family.

The data gathered in the family work-up will determine whether further investigations are needed. In the case of children, additional work may include developmental history, pediatric examinations including all necessary laboratory and x-ray tests, biopsychosocial assessments of a child, intelligence, and other psychological investigations. For adults, the therapist might request a psychosocial history and formulation, a psychiatric examination, medical history and a physical examination, all the necessary laboratory and radiological tests, and psychological assessments as appropriate. Neurological investigations are becoming even more important as imaging technologies such as CAT, MRI, and PET scanners are increasingly sophisticated and available. Neuropsychological assessments have also become a helpful and useful part of the diagnostic work-up. New information gained in these investigations may add to an understanding of the family's functioning.

In concluding the data-gathering step, we ask if there are any other significant problems or difficulties that we have not touched upon. If there are, these are explored in appropriate detail.

Summary of Evaluation

The MMFF provides a conceptual framework for understanding the functioning of clinically presenting families and for assessing their effectiveness on each family dimension. We cannot overemphasize the need for as careful an exploration as we have described to be a regular part of the assessment process. Assessment of families on each of the family dimensions is clinically useful in two ways. First, the therapist is able to assess areas of strength instead of the more negative picture gained by only looking at the presenting problem. Identified strengths can be used in therapy. Second, exploration of the dimensions often turns up significant family problems other than the presenting problem. The fuller assessment allows the therapist to be aware of problems that will be operative during the course of treatment.

Problem Description

As noted throughout the data gathering stages, the therapist indicates problems as they are identified during the assessment process. Therefore, by the time this stage is reached, the identified problems should be reasonably clear to the family and to the therapist. The purpose of the problem description step is to summarize the identified difficulties and to develop a formal list of problems to be addressed. First, family members are asked to indicate the problems they are able to identify now that a detailed list has been completed. The therapist adds any additional difficulties he has noted. The list should highlight the major issues but still be comprehensive.

Often the presenting problem is broken down into two or three more specific problems or redefined as a more general problem. For example, a presenting problem mentioned in an earlier section was John's difficulties at school. This problem can be subdivided into: (1) John's grades have been slipping for the past three months, and (2) his mother and father don't agree on the seriousness of the problem. As a more general problem, the issue can be redefined as: (1) the mother and father don't agree on other issues, and (2) the children tend to test their parents even more when they disagree. To this list the therapist may add any other problems identified by the assessment of the McMaster dimensions—or any special evaluations collected from the additional investigations.

Problem Clarification

The final step in the assessment process is to obtain partial or complete agreement regarding problems listed by the family or therapist in the problem description step. The family usually agrees to the list if the therapist has been active in clarifying and obtaining agreement during the evaluation of the presenting problem and the dimensions of family functioning and in the feedback resulting from the other investigations. Two types of disagreements can arise. First, family members may disagree among themselves, in which case a therapist attempts to negotiate a resolution, reopens the area for further exploration and clarification, or obtains a temporary "agreement to disagree." If the problem differences are minor, the therapeutic process can go on and the differences will resolve in the course of the therapeutic work. An example of this type of situation might be where one parent may feel the child is lazy and performing very badly at school, whereas the other parent feels the child is showing behavior normally appropriate for his or her age. This usually resolves itself as family members become more collaborative and understanding of each other. If the differences regarding the child's behavior extend more deeply into basic disagreements about values related to child rearing and goals for the children, then there could be an impasse further along in the therapy process.

The second type of disagreement may occur between the family and the therapist regarding problems added to the list by the therapist. If the therapist considers the differences relatively minor in importance as far as the central therapeutic issues are concerned, he or she may decide to come to an "agree to disagree" solution for the moment and return to them later in the therapy process. If the therapy has gone well, these disagreements usually dissolve in the course of dealing with the more important issues and rarely have to be dealt with again. An example of this type of disagreement is that of a family where the father drinks moderately heavily and there is disagreement between the family and the therapist on the degree of the drinking and its effect on the family. If this is not the central issue and the problem drinking is not too severe, the therapy can go on if the therapist shelves the disagreement. When the therapy goes well, the question of the father's drinking invariably comes up and is usually resolved by the family without any disagreement and with the father's participation. Rarely do the initial differences of opinion of this type have to be formally brought forward.

In the case of a father's severe alcoholism that is a marked factor in family problems (e.g., violence, disruption, personal difficulties), disagreement between the family and the therapist about the presence and importance of this issue would be basic and would preclude the continuation of the therapy process. Were the therapist to "agree to disagree" in this case, he or she would be colluding with the existing pathological family system which would obviate any successful therapy. The disagreement would have to be resolved by the family's accepting the problem as is, or they would have to withdraw from the therapy process with the option of resuming the procedure should they change their minds. While some postmodern therapists view recognition of the problem as an issue to work on, our position is that fundamental problems should not be minimized or ignored, especially if they have a serious impact on the family.

In cases of basic disagreement, specific areas may be re-explored, or the family may be asked to think about them for a period of time (1 to 2 weeks) and return for more discussion. With continued disagreement, the family might be offered a consultation with another therapist rather than termination. The assessment stage ends when mutual agreement is reached on a problem list. We cannot emphasize strongly enough the importance of basing such a listing on a full, thorough, comprehensive history before embarking on therapeutic interventions. Treatment should not begin without a full knowledge of the problems and strengths of the family.

Contracting Stage

The second macrostage is contracting. Its goal is to prepare a written contract that delineates the mutual expectations, goals, and commitments regarding therapy. The steps in this stage are: (1) orientation, (2) outlining options, (3) negotiating expectations, and (4) contract signing.

Orientation

The first step is to orient the family to the tasks in this stage and obtain their agreement to proceed.

> T: If we agree on the problems, let's discuss what to do about them. Is that okay?

Outlining Options

We outline the treatment options to the family. The therapist presents each option and indicates the realistic consequences of each. Although specific options may vary according to each situation, in general, at least four are presented: (1) the family continues to function as before without attempting any change, (2) the family attempts to work on problems without therapy, (3) the family seeks another type of treatment or therapy, or (4) the family engages in the PCSTF in an attempt to solve their problems. It is important that the therapist articulates consequences of any option that is presented.

> T: You have a number of options. You may choose not to do anything about the problems we've listed and make no changes. I'm sure you will hope that things will improve somehow, but they may also stay the same or get worse as a consequence of that choice. The second option is to try and work on changing the difficulties on your own now that we've clarified them. Third, you may decide that you want a different kind of treatment not involving all of you. The difficulty there is that you've all agreed that family issues have a part to play so that option would be like trying to balance a checkbook with only half the figures. But it is an option that you have. A fourth option is that we agree to work together and deal with the problems as a family. Which option seems best to you?

For each option it is the therapist's responsibility to clarify what his or her function, if any, might be (some of the options would require no input from the therapist), and to explore the consequences of each. If somebody is significantly depressed or suicidal, the options and consequences are quite different than if the problem is minor in nature. After presentation and discussion of each option, the therapist asks for the family's decision regarding the choice of option. In reaching a decision, it is important that input from each family member be solicited. The goal is to obtain a consensus among all family members regarding their choice. Sometimes treatment can proceed without agreement from the children, but it is necessary that the marital partners agree before proceeding. If after discussion of the pros and cons of each option, the marital dyad cannot agree or disagree regarding the choice of option, the therapist can ask the family to think about their decision and schedule a return appointment to finalize the decision.

It is crucial to obtain a full commitment to participate in treatment. The commitment cannot be coerced. If family members are not willing to make such a commitment, the therapist *should not* attempt to persuade or entice the family into treatment. If the family chooses not to enter treatment at this time, we respect their decision. Families can always return for another trial of therapy in the future. We have had many positive experiences terminating some families on this basis and then having them return at a later time ready to begin work. There is no ill will with the choice and they are left with the assurance that they can contact us any time if they change their minds. This is further evidence that we respect their opinions, values, and goals while making it clear that we cannot proceed without full involvement from the family. If the family chooses treatment, we proceed to the next step.

Negotiating Expectations

The goal of the negotiating stage is to formulate a set of expectations that each family member wants to see occur if treatment is successful. Treatment goals are stated in concrete, behavioral terms to allow for clearly identifying and assessing progress. The therapist monitors the process so that unrealistic goals such as wishing "to never again fight" are moderated into more reasonable statements like "to be able to disagree and get angry but resolve the problem without a physical fight." The treatment goals address all of the problems on the problem list that was generated during the assessment stage. The therapist clearly states that not all expectations will be addressed or achieved immediately, but that this phase of treatment is devoted to clarifying long-term treatment goals.

The therapist may make suggestions about their negotiations and indicate his or her own expectations, including the commitment from family members to attend each session and to work on the issues conscientiously. The family is given an estimate of the number of therapy sessions, with the proviso that this can be changed should the situation call for it. Additional expectations of the therapist regarding specific problem behaviors should be made clear. For example, if the identified patient is taking medication, the therapist includes medication compliance as one expectation of the patient. The therapist also makes clear that there is no acting out behavior, physical or sexual abuse, suicidal behavior or threats during the course of treatment.

The main technique for establishing these treatment goals is to have each family member negotiate with every other family member what they will want from each other (i.e., how they want each to change) if they are to feel they have been successful in treatment. Thus, the family is given the major responsibility for defining their expectations of each other and of treatment.

The therapist's major function during this process is to facilitate maximal interaction between family members and to ensure clear, behaviorally defined expectations of change. It is particularly important that the therapist does not allow vague or abstract demands, but rather helps the family members become more specific and arrive at behaviorally defined goals. For example, in response to a statement of, "I want my spouse to be more loving," the therapist attempts to clarify and specify what changes are desired. "Does more loving mean a hug a day? Spending more time talking with you? What does it mean to you?" The goal is to reach a set of specific targets for change. "I want my spouse to show love by: (1) spending more time with me; (2) listening and stating what he or she hears me say when I talk; (3) going away with me without the kids at least once a year; (4) initiating sex more often."

Once the expectations have been clearly defined, each individual negotiates the specific issues directly with the appropriate family member. In the example above, the two partners negotiate with each other. In addition, the therapist is responsible for raising any problems on the problem list that were not addressed by the family during the negotiating process. If there are difficulties during the negotiation of expectations and the family refuses to address all problems on the problem list, the therapist returns to defining the problem list.

> T: I thought you agreed as a family that this issue is a problem. You seem to have changed your views. So maybe we need to back up and go over it again. How do each of you see this issue?

It may be that the problem has been resolved and no longer is an issue for the family. If the problem is still important, the therapist again outlines the family's options and if the family still chooses to engage in treatment, the therapist returns to negotiating the expectations with the new agreement to work on the problem as delineated. The same process occurs if new problems are identified as part of the negotiating process.

> T: That seems like a new problem that you didn't mention before so we need to take some time out from detailing your expectations and be clear about this issue.

Contract Signing

After completing a list of treatment expectations, the therapist prepares a written contract that lists the problems and specifies what has been agreed to as a satisfactory outcome of the problem. The therapist's negotiated conditions of treatment are also included as part of the contract. The therapist and the family members sign the contract. It is emphasized that the family will do most of the work, but it is made clear that the therapist will work also. We indicate this clearly by letting the family know that as part of the family sessions we will discuss the progress made on negotiated tasks. After signing the contract, the family and therapist agreed to work on 2 to 3 tasks until the next therapy session, scheduled for 1 to 2 weeks later.

Background: The family consists of Mr. and Mrs. Stewart and their three teen-age children, one of whom is developmentally disabled. They presented for treatment after Mr. Stewart was diagnosed with major depression following an incident at work for which he received a warning. Mrs. Stewart had recently returned to work after an absence of several years. Her change in schedule and availability, along with Mr. Stewart's depression, resulted in major disruptions in the household. Following a thorough family assessment, the therapist felt that the family's functioning was unhealthy in several family dimensions.

Family members had difficulty in naming family problems, usually avoiding any discussion of issues. If they did bring up a problem, they were unable to resolve it or follow through with any possible solutions. Family members also got into heated arguments. Although Mr. and Mrs. Stewart had a reasonably good rapport, their communication had deteriorated because of the recent stressors. Mr. Stewart tended to get caught up with others' problems at work; he became overinvolved, had trouble expressing himself, and would get angry. The roles in the Stewart family were skewed, with Mrs. Stewart taking on major responsibilities in the household as well as caregiving for the handicapped child. She felt pressure to contribute to the household income, yet felt that she was not getting enough help around the house. When her mother resumed work, the older daughter was left to watch her disabled brother. The youngest, a 16-year-old son who recently quit school, contributed little to the household chores. In addition, he called his parents' work places two or three times a day, disrupting them because he felt bored at home.

Family members displayed a lot of anger, and were unable to show signs of affection or caring for each other. The daughter, who was becoming more withdrawn from family members, resented the added burden of looking after her brother. She began eating excessively to the point where she became obese. Her brother exacerbated the situation by teasing her relentlessly. During the assessment, it became clear that so much attention was given to the disabled child that the older and younger siblings were acting out, each in their own way in order to gain attention themselves and to show their resentment. The parents were torn between care for the disabled child, making ends meet, and trying to deal with two teens acting out to gain parental attention and approval. This family was so dysfunctional that there were several areas that the therapist could target for intervention. After discussion with the family, they agreed to work on areas that warranted immediate attention, with the understanding that they would continue to work and revise the problem list as needed. After helping the family negotiate expectations, goals, and tasks, the therapist and family members chose specific issues and set up the following contract as shown in Table 3.3.

Treatment Stage

The third macrostage is the treatment stage. The goals of the treatment stage follow closely from the previous assessment and contracting stages. The goals are to develop and implement problem solving strategies in order to change the identified problems. Two major therapeutic techniques in the PCSTF are used to accomplish these goals. First, treatment interventions are focused on producing behavioral change in the family through task setting. The therapist helps the family set tasks to accomplish between meetings and then helps the family evaluate the success or failure of these tasks. Second, several techniques are used in the therapy session to promote cognitive and behavioral changes that will increase the family's abilities to successfully address their problems. Each of these interventions will be described in detail below.

The treatment stage consists of four steps: (1) orientation, (2) clarifying priorities, (c) setting tasks, and (4) task evaluation.

Orientation

The first step is to orient the family to the new stage and to obtain their permission to proceed. We do this with a statement such as, "Well, now that we have agreed to work together, how would you like to begin?"

Clarification of Priorities

This step involves ordering the problem list to establish which problems the family wishes to tackle first, second, and so on, in order. The therapist reiterates the identified problems and treatment goals and asks the family

Table 3.3 Family Treatment Contract

FAMILY NAME: Stewart

Problem list: *Mother & Father*
• Mother feels pressured, not getting help around the house, especially with handling
   children. Father not getting enough attention from spouse, has trouble expressing
   himself, gets too involved in work problems.
   Therapist noted that the father had a quick temper and was clinically depressed.

• *Parents & Children*
   Parents could not sit down and discuss issues with children.
   Parents bothered that son disrupts them at work. Also bothered that son quit school.
   Parents upset with daughter for not sticking to any weight program.
   Therapist noted parents were not consistent with children and did not follow through
   with disciplining children.

• *Children*
   Daughter was resentful of time she had to look after her younger brother. Felt
   neglected by parents and needed more attention. Her weight problem was a third
   issue.
   Younger son was not contributing to any household chores. Son lied to parents,
   teased his sister constantly, and, since quitting school, did nothing constructive.

Tasks: *Mother & Father*
Mother and father will set time aside each week to discuss children's behavior and
   how husband can help spouse regarding household duties (2 to 4 ways).
   Father will discuss work and family issues with spouse.
   They will say two positive things about each other during the week.

• *Parents & Children*
   Son will return to school and will not call parents at work. Son will contribute to
   household chores, including looking after his brother twice/week. (If son calls them
   at work or does not do chores, they will take away his privileges: no TV, no
   borrowing the car, or staying in the house, depending on the offense and discussion
   between parents).

(continued)

Table 3.3 Continued

Daughter will stick to one diet for at least 4 months. Mother can ask about diet only once every 3 weeks.

Parents will go out with daughter once/week to a movie or dinner.

Family will discuss how they are doing, ½ hour together per week discussing each other's interests and feelings, if each is following up on his/her tasks

Therapist's expectations:

All family members will attend therapy sessions and call in advance if they cannot attend.

Family members will complete tasks and be prepared to discuss the outcome in therapy.

Family will revise and adjust problem list as needed.

Father will take prescribed medications for depression as indicated.

Signatures:

* _____   _____
  Family Member   Date

* _____   _____
  Family Member   Date

* _____   _____
  Family Member   Date

* _____   _____
  Family Member   Date

* _____   _____
  Family Member   Date

* _____   _____
  Therapist   Date

to prioritize their problems. We prefer to follow the order established by the family because allowing the family to set the priority list reinforces the general emphasis of our approach, i.e., giving as much responsibility as possible for the therapeutic work to the family. If the family cannot establish priorities, or has ignored urgent problems that the therapist feels would impede therapeutic progress, then the therapist should intervene to change the priority list. Examples of urgent problems that demand immediate action are failure to identify suicidality, alcoholism, anorexia, and physical aggression or abuse.

In general, priority should be given to problems in communication and behavior control since problems in these areas can lead to difficulties in solving other problems (due to poor communication) or to chaotic behavior that disrupts treatment (due to behavior control). We make it clear that we do not consider the family to be passive partners in the therapeutic process.

Setting Tasks

Two types of principles guide the task setting, general principles and specific principles.

General Principles

Taking the family's first priority, the therapist asks the family to negotiate and set a task that, if carried out in the next week, would represent a move in the direction of meeting their expectations. The negotiation includes identifying individual responsibilities. If the family is unable to do this, the therapist suggests a task and checks to see if it is agreeable to the family.

In negotiating and assigning tasks, the following general principles are considered:

1. The therapist is open and direct with the family about the purpose of the assigned tasks. We do not use paradox or other indirect methods of producing change.
2. The tasks address changing the specific dimensions of family functioning (from the MMFF) that have been identified during the assessment and problem listing phase.
3. Tasks are directed at changing dysfunctional family transactional patterns.
4. Tasks have maximum potential for success, particularly in early stages of treatment.
5. The task is reasonable with regard to age, sex, and sociocultural factors.

6. Tasks are oriented toward increasing positive behaviors rather than decreasing negative ones. Families often ask someone to stop a behavior rather than asking him or her to do something. We prefer to request positive actions.

7. A task is behavioral and concrete enough so that it can be understood and evaluated.

8. A task is meaningful and important to everyone involved.

9. Family members feel that they can accomplish the task and they are individually able to commit themselves to carry out their part.

10. Emotionally oriented tasks emphasize positive, not negative feelings. Fighting, arguing, and open display of hostility are strongly discouraged.

11. Tasks fit reasonably into the family's schedule and activities.

12. Overloading is avoided. A maximum of two tasks per session is usually reasonable.

13. Assignments to family members are balanced so that the major responsibility for completing a task does not reside with just one or two members.

14. Vindictiveness and digging up the past are avoided, with the focus placed on constructive dealings with current situations.

These principles are made explicit to the family in the form of suggestions or instructions when necessary. For example, if one spouse indicates he or she wants the other to "stop being so negative" (violation of principle 6), we would respond with a statement such as "I'm sure you do, and while I can understand that, it's harder to ask someone to stop doing something than to start doing something. So what would you like him or her to do in the next week that would give you the sense that he or she is trying and that would begin to help in solving the problem?"

There are several suggested tasks that the Stewart family negotiated as part of their contract. Other examples of negotiated tasks that follow the above principles are:

- A 16-year-old son agrees to come home by an agreed upon time. The father agrees to take the son to a ball game later in the week if he does well, and to deal with the son if he is late. The mother agrees to back the father and send the son to him. She also agrees to spend more time with her daughter, who agrees to keep her room tidy.

- The father will take the mother out once a week/month (e.g., to dinner, a movie, a sports event); the mother agrees to go as an indication of her willingness to negotiate and compromise with the expectation that her partner/husband will agree to the needs or desires that she expresses. The older son agrees to baby-sit and the younger son agrees to behave.

• The couple agrees to set aside 15 minutes after supper to talk about "good things." The children agree to clear the table and do the dishes to support this activity.

Once tasks have been assigned, it is important to designate a family member to monitor and report on performance at the next therapy session. Designating a monitor increases the involvement of the family, increases all members' expectations regarding sense of responsibility and accountability, and raises individual self-esteem. The role of the monitor may be rotated among members or may vary with tasks (e.g., one member reports on one task, someone else on a different task). The role of the monitor should be given to a member who is objective, not actively involved in the area being dealt with, and most likely to keep the family at the task.

Specific Principles

In the following section, we outline common tasks we use with the PCSTF.

Task Setting—Problem Solving

Tasks to address difficulties in problem solving can be focused on any of the seven stages of problem solving. If the family has trouble *identifying problems,* one task is that individual family members bring information about potential problems to the next session without discussion (discussion involves the next step in problem solving). If the family has trouble *communicating the problem to an appropriate resource,* a family task is to identify an appropriate individual and discuss the problem with this person. This process can be practiced in the session using role-play between family members.

Another task at this stage is to ask the family to *develop a list of alternatives* to solve a particular problem. The assignment can be made to the family as a whole or each individual member can be asked to develop a list of possible solutions to a problem. At this point the family does not attempt to arrive at a decision regarding alternatives, so as not to preclude open exploration of options. Next, the family discusses the pros and cons of problem-solving options and *makes a decision.* The family *takes the agreed upon action* to solve a problem and *reports back* to the therapist on what has taken place, including whether or not all details have been completed. The family is asked to *discuss how they feel about their efforts* on a given problem and to *compare their effectiveness and methods* in relationship to other problem situations.

Task Setting—Communication
Tasks assigned to address communication problems can be roughly categorized according to the type of *communication problem in the family*. The most basic and commonly used task is to instruct the family to spend a set amount of time together talking about personal issues. The interaction can be a quid pro quo positive communication with each party talking for 3 to 5 minutes about positive, personal issues. These can be positive events in the past, events that occurred that day, or dreams about the future, whether related directly to the family or not. At the end of the period of talking, other family members feed back a synopsis of what was said to practice communicating positively, listening, and letting other family members know that they have been heard. A specific order of turns can be determined, or the family can draw lots or flip a coin. A specific time can be designated in advance for this communication session. When the major communication difficulties are between spouses or partners, another commonly used variant of this task is used. The task may involve the parents spending time talking together and the children agreeing to spend time elsewhere to provide the parents with an opportunity to talk privately with each other.

If the family has *difficulties with masked communication*, family members can be instructed to ask for clarification when anyone is unclear. Often this request for clarification can be put in humorous ways: "Was that another fuzz ball?" or "You really lost me on that one" or "Back up and play it again." If *indirect communication is problematic* for the family, individual family members can be instructed to respond to indirect communication about them with a statement like: "Rather than talk about me, could you please talk to me." Other family members noticing indirect communication can also be instructed to state: "You are (we are) talking *about* Dad; instead you (we) should talk *to* Dad." Other types of communication tasks are:

- When John speaks, tell him what you heard him say. Ask him if that is what he said.
- Before trying to give an answer, ask Sue whether or not she wants an answer.
- Begin by saying, "I need to talk to you just to let you know what I'm feeling and thinking. I really don't need an answer, but I want you to know what I think."

Task Setting—Roles
Problems in allocation of roles are addressed by instructing families to develop a list of regular household tasks and to discuss who should be

responsible for each task. Children and adolescents are asked to state the jobs they would like to take responsibility for as a way of meeting their family obligations. Attention is given to having the family discuss the appropriateness of the individuals assigned to different tasks, with particular emphasis on the individual's capacity and ability to complete the task. To address *problems in accountability of roles,* the therapist may assign a specific family member to keep track of whether or not jobs are completed and to check the adequacy of performance. If individuals within the family do not meet their responsibilities, the family is given the task of devising an intervention or given instructions to help the individual meet his or her responsibilities.

Task Setting—Affective Responsiveness
In developing tasks in this dimension, the focus is on two major areas that are often difficult to address. They are the handling of rage, anger, and aggression by both sexes and all ages and the capacity to feel and express the widest range of welfare emotions. In Western culture, males typically have more difficulty with this than females.

If possible, the first tasks assigned focus on the feeling and expression of welfare emotions. Possible *tasks in the welfare affect problem area* are:

1. For the spouses/partners to kiss and hug each other on leaving or returning home and at other times that may be appropriate for a given couple. Each should be instructed in how to be receptive to the other. This task could involve the children as well, setting up tasks for them to express and allow them to feel welfare affect at socially appropriate times.
2. Setting time aside during the week for the couple or other family members to say nice things to each other and to hold or stroke each other. Another task might be learning how and when to compliment each other and, after being complimented, responding positively ("thank you").

The *tasks for coping with emergency emotions* such as rage, anger, and aggression usually center around two major problem areas, helping individuals overcome their fear of feeling and expressing anger. Such people are usually over-controlled and over-inhibited in relation to the perception and expression of rage and anger. The therapist will need to desensitize them to the experience of feeling rage and help them learn that expressing rage will not result in an excessive outpouring of destructive hostility. The tasks consist of teaching members of the family who have problems in this area to:

1. Learn how to recognize and anticipate anger-provoking situations.
2. Learn how to think the situation out before expressing anger and express it when appropriate.
3. Teach individuals how to express their anger in a calm, constructive, assertive, and respectful manner.

When first setting these tasks, individuals are instructed to attempt the task at certain fixed times during the day, preferably at the time of structured talking to each other. Individuals will learn that they do not have to express their affect at the time it is felt. This allows them to have a feeling of safety and security that they will not be out of control at the time of perception, and they will be able to express their feelings in a structured manner with the controls in place as they learned. By going through these tasks, family members will understand that the perception and expression of such feelings can be handled in a constructive respectful manner without destroying the objects of their anger.

In contrast to the inability to express anger and rage, some individuals express excess amounts of rage and frequently are under-controlled. Tasks in these situations center around having family members signal the under-controlled individual at the time of excess or otherwise unacceptable expression of rage. The signal can be taken as a sign to immediately stop the expression of rage. He or she should stop and apologize. Later, he or she will review or role play to learn how to express his or her rage in a constructive, controlled, respectful manner.

Task Setting—Affective Involvement

Two major areas requiring task development are lack of involvement, and overinvolvement. Tasks addressing lack of involvement are structured between dyads, triads, or the group, as appropriate. Each week time is set aside when family members talk about current interests in their jobs, hobbies, friendships, sports, or other activity. Family members listen, ask appropriate questions, and compliment each other whenever possible. The goal of the task is to acquaint members of the family with each other's interests, their way of looking at things, how they get enjoyment and satisfaction, and their anxieties. These exchanges generate feelings in each member that the others are involved, interested, and concerned. The task setting in an overinvolved situation is to get the overinvolved individual to back off when one—or several members—are enmeshed with each other. Family members give each other a chance to speak, but do not push each other past a certain level of detail seen as intrusive. The family finds a balance between communicating the essentials of an issue or situation without intruding into the privacy of others. Members who have borne the brunt of over-involvement only speak to the level or degree with which they are comfortable. For those who have been subjected to overinvolvement, it is important for them to understand that, despite the enmeshment, some basic level of information is necessary to communicate. Rather than cut off communication entirely, it is best if they find a level of communication so family members relate to each other in a satisfactory manner. The issue is a matter of degree and intensity.

In cases involving children and adolescents, just the basic facts related to a specific situation may be given in response to questions. Adults can expect answers to their questions only to the degree necessary. For example, where the child was or is going, with whom, and what activities they are going to participate in are legitimate questions. If the child wants to report a greater amount of detail that is acceptable; however, a "play by play" reporting is usually discouraged. The underlying principle is that children be allowed age appropriate privacy; the older the child, the more privacy is needed. This task is structured in situations where the parents insert themselves too much with the children's homework, duties, and friends. Only basic levels of instruction are called for with children and adolescents, i.e., the parents should expect them to do their work effectively and efficiently. Parents can be available for help when called on, but do not need to insert themselves into the nitty-gritty of activities of children or adolescents. In situations where difficulties revolve around homework, the child can be asked to agree to complete homework without the parents urging. The parents agree not to ask for or bring up the issue of the child's homework at home.

Task Setting—Behavior Control

Tasks in behavior control are centered around over-control and under-control. In this dimension the therapist makes sure to get agreement by all concerned parties to fulfill their part of the task and to assign specific tasks to all concerned parties. Tasks that are unidirectional do not work well. When all members on all sides of the equations are involved, there is a greater likelihood of success. In parental over-control:

1. The over-controlling parent agrees to reduce his/her involvement.
2. The over-controlled child agrees to meet specific expectations such as household chores, homework, etc. (without being urged) on a time-table he sets up himself that is acceptable to both parties and the therapist.
3. Both sides agree on the rewards and punishments related to these expectations.

It is sometimes a good idea to have the members concerned agree to appoint a third member of the family to be a monitor of the family's handling of the task. The therapist's input is also warranted in order to monitor the appropriateness of the task and the family's expectations.

In parental *under-control* the therapist asks all members of the family what would be acceptable controls instituted for all sides—who should apply them, and who should follow them. All details are worked out by participating family members. Once this is done, the therapist and the family members are able to structure the treatment tasks accordingly. The therapist should be as active in these negotiations as he or she needs to be—no more than the minimum necessary to keep the negotiations on track so that the family can develop an effective system of control.

When one parent is grossly ineffective—either because of being too rigid, full of rage, or helplessly ineffectual, it is important to free this person from being involved in the controlling situation. Agreement can be obtained for that person to have their role taken over by the other parent. If this is not possible, an appropriate sibling might be able to fulfill the task, a choice that is not optimally desirable, but may be practically necessary. In situations of behavioral control, the therapist has all members put forth ideas and participate actively in the discussion. Frequently adolescents or children who are labeled as rebellious, defiant, and refusing to obey are very helpful when they are allowed to express their opinions of what 'should' be done. Asking the children what they would do and how they might structure the situation if they were the parents can be a helpful means of evoking the appropriate parameters of a task.

In setting tasks for behavioral control, the most important issues are: adherence to the family's expectations concerning rules and standards, the clear spelling out of rewards and sanctions, and the definitive follow through. When an agreement is reached regarding expectations for adherence to certain behavior patterns, rules, and standards, it has to be clear that family members who have contracted to accept these expectations are now held accountable for them. If expectations are not met, the individual will be responded to as if he or she has chosen not to meet them and will be treated accordingly. If expectations are carried out, he or she will be rewarded as spelled out in the task assignment contract. The most basic principle in all tasks in the dimension of behavioral control is that members of the family and the therapist must know—in advance if at all possible—that all of the involved tasks will be carried out as assigned. If not, therapy is less likely to be effective. The following examples may clarify.

- The family of a child who has been delinquent in carrying out what has been expected of him in the past has contracted to reward him for carrying out assignments. If he completes his assignments, the family follows through with the reward. If there is no follow through, the child will not trust the parents and receives the message that nothing he can do will gain positive response from his parents. The child may conclude that negative responses are better than no response. Hence, he will be reinforced in his previous pattern of failing to do what is expected.

- Parents must be prepared to "go to the brink" if necessary in response to failure to follow through on tasks assigned to children. This is particularly clear in cases of adolescent acting out. If the family is not willing to take a stand, there is no point in assigning a task or in agreeing on a contract. For serious acting out problems it may be necessary to consider removing a child from the family, at least on a temporary basis. Alternative treatments, outside placements, and staying with relatives are options that may need to be considered.

- This latter approach is also called for when parents/partners contract with each other. The spouse of an alcoholic or other type of addict must be prepared to leave the relationship if the addicted one fails to follow through with their contract to abstain from the addictive behavior.

Task Evaluation

Task evaluation is a critical process in the PCSTF. It is essential that the therapist review the success or failure of the family to accomplish the task at the following session. The monitor and other appropriate family members furnish the information. If the task was accomplished, we provide positive reinforcement and highlight the positive aspects of the family's performance, including what particular individuals may have done to make things go so well. If a task, or part of a task, did not get completed, the therapist begins with some aspect of the task that the family was able to accomplish. This not only encourages the family, but also helps them to view the task and family work as an ongoing process. If the task was a complete failure, the ability for the family to sit down and discuss it may be seen in a positive light.

> T: Well, how did the tasks go? Okay, so _____ got done but _____ didn't. Is that right? We'll come back to the difficult one in a minute, but first, what made the other go well? Can you tell me what each of you did to help them go well? What did others do that made it easier for you to do your part?
>
> . . . That's very good and I'm sure you're pleased. Let's return to the area you had difficulty with.

We then explore the difficulty with questions such as: What was the problem? Did nothing get done or did you do part of it? Were you aware of thinking about it? What could others do that would make it possible? Do you think it's possible to do it? Do you agree that if the task were carried out it would make things better?

If all goes well, the process of task setting and evaluation continues, at times negotiating new priorities, at times re-contracting, until all contract expectations have been fulfilled. If the family fails to complete a task, the therapist discusses and clarifies with the family what went wrong and why. Failure to accomplish a task may provide important information about difficulties within the family that was not previously available or not fully articulated. It is important to assess any negative consequences or reasons for not completing the task. First, the task may have been too difficult or general in a particular situation. The therapist could suggest a simpler task having to do with the same problem. A failed task may occur due to family difficulties which were not identified or whose severity was underestimated by the therapist. In this case, the therapist cycles back to the assessment stage and renegotiates the problem list and priorities for treatment. A failed task may indicate to the therapist that his or her formulation of the problem is incorrect and the identified problem is associated with other factors not previously considered or underplayed. The therapist then refines the formulation which may lead to a different treatment focus.

Repeated failed task assignments may indicate that—without being aware of it or without informing the therapist—the family changed their chosen option from the original one of participating in family therapy to opting for no treatment. If this is the case, we give them an opportunity to formalize the change. If family members insist that they still want family therapy, we point out that they do not seem to be working at their tasks and that perhaps there is something wrong with the treatment process or the therapist's handling of the case. At that point, a consultation may be indicated. If the family rejects the suggestion of a consultation, we recommend termination of therapy since we have adequate evidence of failure. We feel that there is no point in denying if the treatment is inadequate. We respect a family's decision not to enter or continue family therapy. It may be that the family is in a process or stage of change [29] in which the family recognizes the problem but is not yet ready to take action. If the family wouldn't, or couldn't, complete the tasks as agreed on, or even complete the assessment phase, we suggest that we stop the sessions. We leave open the option for the families to return. Often families do return and, when they do, are eager to begin work.

Other Techniques

Throughout this chapter, we referred to techniques that therapists use while assessing and treating families. During the treatment phase of the PCSTF, a major part of each session is devoted to reviewing previously assigned tasks, and developing and negotiating new tasks. We thought it worthwhile to review a few strategies and the way they are commonly used during the treatment phase. The model is not dependent on these techniques, but they may be particularly useful because they can be applied across all stages of the treatment model. The strategies include: clarification of problems, labeling and interpreting transactions, and psychoeducation. These interventions focus on producing changes in cognitions that interfere with problem solving. The overall goal of these interventions is the same as task setting— to increase the family's abilities to successfully negotiate task assignments and resolve their problems.

Clarification of Problems
One of the continuing interventions of the PCSTF therapist is to clarify the family's problems so that the description of the problem, as well as its antecedents and consequences, are understood and agreed upon by all family members. The therapist feeds back clear descriptions of the family's functioning. This is done using language appropriate to the specific family. The process helps the family become aware of functions, processes, and family organization that had been unclear to them. With this new information in hand—or rephrased so that it is understood— the family acts quickly and effectively to address the problem.

Labeling and Interpreting Transactions
Consistent with the aim of improving its problem solving abilities, the family learns to recognize transactional patterns that interfere with optimal problem solving. The therapist teaches recognition skills as he or she labels and interprets dysfunctional transactional patterns during therapy sessions. He also labels the unacknowledged affect that occurs during the course of such transactional patterns. The labeling and interpreting process is based on observable behavior occurring in the therapy session. This process depends on the collaborative relationship developed between the therapist and the family.

Psychoeducation
When working with families in which one or more members have an identified psychiatric or medical problem, families often have inaccurate

assumptions, expectations, and information about the disorder and its consequences. Providing the family with information about the disorder, its etiology, effects, treatment, and course often alleviates any blocks to successful problem resolution. These types of interventions and their effectiveness have been well described by others nd will not be discussed here.

Closure Stage

The final macrostage is closure, consisting of four steps: (1) orientation, (2) summary of treatment, (3) long-term goals, and (4) follow-up (optional).

Orientation

As an orientation to treatment termination, we point out that the family expectations, as set forth in the contract, have been met and that therapy may now stop. If the family wants more therapy, the therapist can explore the issues or problems they wish to deal with and consider continuing treatment. Although treatment may occasionally be extended, most of the time families should be encouraged to resolve any new issues they want to work on. The family will be in a position to apply—by themselves and on their own—what they have learned in family therapy. They can be encouraged to get in touch with the therapist any time who can decide whether to see them for another session or not, depending on the situation.

Summary of Treatment

Family members are asked to summarize what has happened during treatment and what they have learned. The therapist confirms or elaborates on their perceptions, adding any insight that may have been overlooked. He or she asks family members what they will do if the problems that they worked on recur. This gives the family an opportunity to reinforce their understanding of the issues while the therapist is present, lets them recognize that family functioning is an ongoing process, and encourages them to realize that, as a family, they have learned techniques with which to address a wide variety of problems.

Long-term Goals

The therapist asks family members to discuss and set some long-term goals. The therapist asks them to identify how they will recognize if the family is functioning well or poorly, and what they will do if it is poor. Finally, the therapist asks the family to identify issues that they anticipate might either come up or become problematic in the future. The family is again reminded of their ability to cope with such problems by using what they have learned in family therapy. At the same time, the therapist clarifies that the family has an option of returning to obtain additional help if and when it is needed.

Follow-up

Therapy ends at this point, although an optional follow-up appointment may be scheduled if appropriate. When a follow-up visit is arranged, it is set far enough into the future to allow the family a full opportunity to deal with issues as they arise. It is also stressed that the purpose of the follow-up visit is to help the family monitor its progress and that it is not a treatment session.

Concluding Remarks

In most cases, the success of the therapeutic outcome reflects the degree of thoroughness and rigor that the therapist maintains in systematically following the macrostages and treatment steps. This includes adhering to the principle of keeping the family actively involved in working with the therapist at each step of the PCSTF. The therapist learns to function as an assessor, evaluator, diagnostician, clarifier, investigator, catalyst, facilitator, and, at times, a confronter. The therapist must be prepared to give major responsibility for the treatment to the family while remaining intently involved in the treatment process. Therapists using the McMaster approach will need to feel comfortable delegating responsibility to the family as members learn to work on their own family problems. The therapist also needs to feel comfortable terminating therapy when there is ample evidence that the family is not working on resolving their problems.

The family should be aware that the therapist expects full commitment to change. We do not believe in "seducing" the family into a state of positive motivation or in trying to convince a family to address problem areas. Families can seek other options or return for another trial of therapy if their motivation to change increases. We have had many positive experiences terminating some families for lack of action and follow through and having them return ready to work hard and prepared or willing to handle change. In effect, the family is told, "It is your family and you are entitled to handle things as you see fit. If you change your mind at any time we can review your situation and see if there are ways that you might want to change things." Such an approach indicates respect for the family's opinions, values, goals, and objectives. At the same time, the therapist makes it clear that he or she is not interested in participating in "sham" therapy or going through the motions of a therapeutic process which continues interminably without evidence of successful change. By developing the skills and approach detailed in the PCSTF, therapists can look forward to quite successful outcomes.

CHAPTER 4

Training in the Problem Centered Systems Therapy of the Family

The detailed description of the MMFF and the PCSTF in chapters 2 and 3 provides the groundwork for successfully applying the McMaster approach to evaluate and treat families. In this chapter we outline the implementation of our family therapy training program, established so that we could disseminate the model beyond our own program. Any reference to therapist training usually is omitted when explaining a therapy model. Yet even the best treatment model has limited value if it cannot be taught to others and transferred to different clinicians in a variety of clinical settings. Mindful of this, when Epstein and colleagues developed the model, they were particularly keen on ensuring that the model was readily teachable. As adjustments were made to the therapy model, the revisions became incorporated into the teaching component.

Despite years of experience in teaching and using the model, it is difficult to describe a training program that is suitable for all levels (beginning and experienced family therapist) in all settings (private clinic, hospital, academic center). Factors that influence the establishment of a program include the discipline, knowledge base, and experience that trainees bring to the program and the context in which they work. The level of interviewing and therapeutic skills that trainees have determines whether basic skills training needs to be addressed before family therapy training begins. The institutional setting and support affects the size and scope of any training program. Training undertaken by an established academic program or by peer-supervised student trainees will be modified by the specific goals and objectives of each. Success will be influenced by accessibility of audio-video equipment, one-way mirrors, availability of training supervisors and family participants, and communication among staff members. Since this model has been disseminated throughout the world, our description of a training program mirrors the approach we took in describing the McMaster model and reflects the treatment model. That is, since we cannot identify the needs of every agency, institution, or academic training program, we provide what we feel is a sound basis for learning the application of the McMaster approach.

First, we list a set of basic principles that guide our training program and then explain training procedures that we find successful when teaching clinicians to assess and treat families. We include a section on methods of evaluating trainees, trainers and the training program. We conclude by addressing training issues sometimes encountered in academic training centers, institutions or community agencies, or research programs. If viewed as a road map, the training program provides a strategy that helps therapists build a consistent, systematic, investigation of the family unit and applies a specific family treatment method. We describe the training program that works best for our needs but understand that individuals or teams of clinicians and researchers may need to make adjustments to fit their own program. The time frame of training programs may vary, depending on the training objectives, trainee experience, and the contextual atmosphere of where the training takes place.

Background

A major goal of the McMaster approach is to enable a clinician to categorize his or her observations of a family's functioning and to encourage a sensitivity and understanding of family life and family transactions in the therapy process.[12] A major goal of our training program, then, is to impart this understanding to each of the trainees so that they can become comfortable with the material and more effective in their role as family therapists. The program incorporates training for research staff so that assessments and family therapy are standardized when we test the treatment in research protocols.

When efforts to create a training program for the McMaster approach began in the 1960s, training responsibilities were not the prerogative of one clinical department. Although training activities were based in and carried out through an academic department of psychiatry, faculty from other departments routinely came together to develop, implement, and evaluate training programs. These experts from the Departments of Pediatrics, Psychiatry, and Family Medicine became the trainers and spent considerable time, effort, and resources to create innovative teaching programs, including the development of our own family training approach. Interactions with these different departments allowed us to incorporate clinical and nonclinical families into our program. Because of the input and feedback we received from professionals in many disciplines, we were able to adjust the model and training methods to meet the needs of members from a wide range of health care teams and institutions that provided family services within a large geographical region.

Since then we found that mixing disciplines in training groups works well—as long as the skill level of trainees are compatible. In fact, the skill level is more important than an individual's professional background when forming training groups. Individuals vary in the degree of experience and knowledge that they bring to training and in the amount of training they wish to acquire. They may view a minimal amount of training as a necessary part of their major training program or they may seek intense and in-depth training in a family-oriented modality. Obstetric and gynecology residents may want a conceptual framework upon which to understand family structure and organization. Family practice residents may also want to be able to complete a family assessment that helps them decide on the appropriateness of family therapy or obtain an understanding of how a family's functioning affects medical issues. Family therapists, counselors, and social workers may want to evaluate families to better understand difficulties that clients have in dealing with the world around them. Because training is often given to support professional development, we spend time in clarifying how the family treatment training fits with the individual, clinical, and institutional needs of the person being trained.

Clinical needs vary as well as individual needs. It seems pointless to train people in family work if they will never be directly involved in dealing with families and if the skills they are taught will not be beneficial in a particular clinical setting. Not infrequently students have requested family training when it is not appropriate. They may not be involved in clinical work that is oriented towards families and there is little likelihood that the situation will change in the foreseeable future. Sometimes we come across individuals who assume they know how to treat families and expect to advance more rapidly in their training than is realistic. To avoid any of these problems, trainers usually conduct an intake session with potential trainees to get a sense of individual goals, learn about previous training experience, clarify preferred learning style, and orient the trainee to the program. Such precourse evaluations help trainers place students in groups and in levels that are commensurate with their competency, enable trainees to get feedback on their strengths and shortcomings as they enter the program, and familiarize students with the necessary skill development for a particular training level. As trainers, we take the time to go over the commitments and requirements of the program and explain the effort needed to navigate an institution or agency's bureaucracy.

Inability to obtain a commitment from an agency will hamper the trainee's ability to develop the skills necessary to implement the treatment whereas inability to obtain a commitment from an individual may indicate potential trainee problems in dealing with family systems. We find that a discussion between trainers and agency staff about the needs, goals, and expectations of placing trainees in a program enhances cooperation and prevents misunderstandings. In addition, when health care professionals do not yet have solid skills in standard interviewing techniques, family therapy training has to be halted while basic skills are taught. It is appropriate to ensure that trainees have a certain level of skills before they are encouraged to take on family therapy training. Other prerequisites that help to ensure satisfactory functioning and progress in a training program include:

- Experience with a range and variety of human behavior in different personalities and different life situations.
- Appreciation for, if not an understanding of, the interacting influence of biological, psychological, and social factors on human behavior, including temperament, physical disability, intelligence, defense mechanisms, behavioral patterns, and ethnic background.
- Understanding how behavior is an adaptation to the environment and ranges from healthy through dysfunctional and involves personality, coping styles, and psychotic processes.
- Ability to be comfortable with one's own style of patient interviewing, yet apply basic techniques of listening, establishing rapport by responding to feelings, asking open-ended questions, and exploring problems with patients.
- Beginning experience in the professional role, including the importance of the health professional-patient relationship.
- Learning something about one's self and thereby one's ability to grow as a person.

Although trainees will vary in the amount of experience they have in each of these areas, they should be at a stage in their development where there has been some formal training addressing most, if not all, of these points.[12]

Basic Principles

When we presented the MMFF and the PCSTF in previous chapters, we began by stating several basic principles that are the foundation for our approach to treating families. We use a similar strategy to introduce our training program in order to highlight key elements of our approach to training and provide a rationale of their importance.[30] Themes underlying the McMaster approach parallel themes in the training program. For example, responsibility for learning is put on the trainee, the supervisor acts as facilitator or moderator and promotes independence as much as possible, and the orientation and outlining of expectations, so critical in treating families, is also critical when training therapists. There are specific, discrete tasks in training, a feedback mechanism to deal with problems, and periodic reviews to evaluate progress. Training is clear, direct, and focused, there is an expectation that learning continues after the program has ended, and there is an understanding that trainees can withdraw from the program without recrimination.

Teach One Model of Family Therapy

Since the MMFF is the theoretical basis for conceptualizing family life and is applied in the PCSTF, we first ensure that trainees have substantial knowledge of the model before they assess and treat families. More important, our experience has been that those who are new to the family field or those who are trying to understand a new family model, require in-depth immersion in one family approach before they can begin to incorporate other family approaches. Exposing beginners to multiple models creates conceptual confusion. We believe that teaching family therapy should demonstrate rigor and the serious consideration of issues. Presentation of multiple models early in training leads trainees to the deleterious view that treatment is made up of "a bit of this and a bit of that." Not only does this confuse the therapist, but families become confused in the therapy sessions if they sense that the therapist is wandering and there is a lack of focus. Once trainees have a clear understanding of the model and are fluid in the use of its approaches, exposure to and consideration of other models is actively encouraged. This approach is common to those who have extensive experience with one model but are conversant with and incorporate ideas and interventions from other schools of thought.

Categorization of Skills as Concept/Percept/Executive

In our training program we use a classification of family therapy skills categorized as conceptual, perceptual, and executive.[21,22,31] The MMFF is the underlying framework trainees use to develop conceptual and perceptual skills and the PCSTF is the framework used to develop executive skills.[32]

Conceptual skills include learning the definitions, concepts, and theories related to family systems models as well as the theory, concepts, and definitions of how a family functions according to the McMaster approach. In order to apply the model, a therapist will need a thorough knowledge of its ideas and how it works. Perceptual skills include the ability to perceive the data, that is, to accurately identify family behaviors and interactions and then relate them to the conceptual model. As these skills are developed, trainees recognize the actions occurring before them (via taped sessions or live interviews), correctly label the actions according to the concepts defined in the MMFF, focus on several issues presented before them, and prioritize the family problems, according to the model. Understanding a clinical case and translating the data into a conceptual framework is a key part of training, for it leads to the next set of skills learned in training, how to apply the model in assessment and treatment.

Executive skills include those needed to apply treatment concepts when assessing and treating families. Trainees learn an overall approach to treatment as well as a repertoire of specific interventions. Executive skills in the PCSTF are analogous to executive control functions of the prefrontal cortex, that is, the cerebral framework used for planning, initiating, monitoring, and sequencing our thoughts and behaviors. This set of skills increases as a therapist gains clinical experience. Within the executive level, trainees continue to use the conceptual and perceptual skills they learned earlier by adhering to the model and becoming proficient in its use. They learn conceptual and perceptual skills associated with a particular therapy approach (in this case, the PCSTF). As trainees move toward the advanced level, they recognize and evaluate their own performance and the performance of other trainees in assessing and treating families.

The classification scheme we use for training and evaluation has important implications, for each of the three skill categories require different training methods. The systematic progression inherent in this paradigm fits well with our view of teaching the McMaster approach as the sequence of our training program is geared towards acquiring skills by working through a series of tasks in a step-by-step manner. We begin the training by teaching conceptual skills, for this ensures that trainees share consistent definitions when discussing family issues. Once trainees grasp basic definitions and concepts, we initiate perceptual skills training. During perceptual skills training, therapists continue to obtain conceptual knowledge, particularly as they become exposed to a variety of families and family functioning. As trainees continue to improve their conceptual and perceptual abilities, we turn to developing their executive skills.

An example of this training paradigm is grasping the idea of scapegoating. At some point in their training, trainees need to know the definition of scapegoating and its ramifications (conceptual). This can be understood through many learning devices, including written material, lectures, learning tapes. Once they understand the concept, trainees will need to identify scapegoating in its many forms (perceptual). One way to learn this is by viewing videotape examples. After trainees correctly label scapegoating as it occurs in front of them, they will be ready to learn how to intervene when it comes up in treatment sessions (executive). Trainees begin learning the executive skills needed for treating families by role playing. As a trainee gains experience and starts to treat families, they discuss appropriate clinical interventions in supervision.

An example specific to the McMaster approach might include (mis)communication within the family. According to the MMFF, communication is conceptualized as moving along two continua, clear vs. masked and direct vs. indirect. After studying the MMFF, the trainee is able to define what these concepts refer to, understand the rationale for their use, and can distinguish parameters of the communication dimension vis-à-vis other family dimensions (conceptual). In a videotaped session or an observed interview, a father and mother are talking in the presence of their teenage son. Building on the knowledge gained from conceptual skills training, the trainee identifies whether the communication is clear or masked and direct or indirect. He also states why he came to such a conclusion (perceptual). As a therapist, the trainee learns different ways of intervening with the family, including labeling the process of communication and, possibly, soliciting or suggesting alternative ways of communicating (executive).

By the end of the training, the trainee will have mastered the model by using the conceptual, perceptual, executive paradigm. The trainee will be able to view a family session, know at what stage of the model or treatment process the therapist is engaged in (e.g., assessment stage, contracting stage), and be able to suggest appropriate therapeutic interventions.

Training Occurs Best in Small Groups

Rather than the traditional didactic method of large, open lectures, small group teaching and learning was the cornerstone of training at McMaster University. At Brown University, we continue to work with small groups of 4 to 6 trainees, although at times we may conduct one large orientation meeting. Because of the amount of feedback given to trainees, the use of actual families, and in-depth review of their cases, we have found it best to limit the number of participants when having group discussions. Also, we have experienced that learning is facilitated when responsibility is placed on the student and the small training group. In larger groups, individual trainees may not receive sufficient feedback or are able to avoid working by letting others take the initiative. Trainees learn family therapy and peer group learning skills, with an emphasis on group problem-solving and task orientation. Once they have completed the training program, peer group supervision is often continued as a valued learning experience.

Family Therapy Training Takes Time

As noted in previous chapters 6 to 12 sessions are adequate for treating the majority of family problems that a therapist encounters. Because the assessment itself has therapeutic value, it is common that the total number of treatment sessions ranges between three and five. In order to accomplish this schedule, the therapist needs to understand the model and its application thoroughly. We find that an extended training program allows trainees to digest and integrate family work into their everyday practice. We are often asked to conduct one or two-day training sessions on the McMaster approach. These workshops attract large numbers and a varied audience, but there are pluses and minuses to offering them. Although therapists are exposed to a useful model of family therapy, these seminars do not usually have a lasting effect. We find it helpful to acknowledge up front that learning how to assess and treat families in a systematic and comprehensive manner takes time. Trainees need to understand the influences that psychosocial factors in the family environment have on growth, development, and a family's functioning. Even an experienced therapist will need some time to change his or her thinking, especially if he or she is not used to either systems theory or its practical application.

Training is made up of two complementary dimensions, theoretical sections and clinical practice, which are interwoven throughout the training process.[12] Briefly, the theoretical component assumes a working knowledge of individual and family dynamics, methods of small group and family interventions, and systems theory. Clinical practice entails working with both families and small groups and receiving clinical feedback in supervision. We use seminars to integrate theory and its practical applications. Trainees may take up to 12 to 14 months to learn and develop basic comfort with the model, become familiar with the concepts and their use, and work with at least two families with different presenting problems. In the first 6 to 7 months trainees develop their conceptual and perceptual skills and use the following 7 to 8 months to learn and implement intervention strategies using their executive skill training.[32] Training is broken down into discrete steps and trainees complete tasks before moving to the next stage. Experienced family therapists complete conceptual and perceptual training in 1 to 3 months and begin supervision of cases in the following two months. The more prepared the trainee is and the more experience the family therapist has, the sooner he or she is able to apply the model.

Training Should Be Evaluated

The MMFF and PCSTF lend themselves to effective teaching and evaluation of skill acquisition. It is also important to evaluate the effectiveness of the family therapy training. It was our early family therapy outcome studies that forced us to attend to training in a disciplined way. Results of these studies demonstrated a great deal of variability among therapists, making it difficult to interpret our findings. We realized that training had to be systematized in order to evaluate the clinical work of our new treatment approach. In the process of tightening the training program, we found that evaluation had the added benefit of clarifying our training methods. To help us evaluate trainees on a regular basis, we developed adherence and competency scales that assess specific skills the therapist is learning. By separating adherence to the model from competency of the therapist, we are able to test and evaluate therapist skills as well as outcome evaluation. At the conclusion of the training program, we ask for feedback on the program and on the trainers. If a community agency is involved in the training program, the evaluation may include the impact of the program on service delivery.

In any evaluation process, part of the assessment includes whether or not goals and objectives are met. The strengths and limitations of trainees, trainers, and the training program can be discussed in such a way that the overall review is seen in a positive light, as an opportunity for learning or instituting changes. Getting input from all participants (trainees, trainers, agency staff), focusing on strengths but including areas that need work, being clear and direct when offering comments and criticisms are reflections of the McMaster approach as well as the evaluation of training.

Systems Issues and Goals Should Be Addressed Explicitly

There may be several distinct and competing constituency goals and objectives that need consideration when establishing a training program in an agency. Goals include that of the training program, the trainee, and the institution or agency that employs the trainee. Many programs pay attention to the training program, trainee goals and objectives, but overlook the employer. The goals and objectives of each component may be synchronous or divergent. Some goals may dovetail with an agency's mission, whereas others may be at cross-purposes. If objectives are similar rather than identical, invalid assumptions are often made. For these reasons, we find it best to spend time clarifying goals and objectives for all relevant parties. Clear and direct communication about these issues often prevents future misunderstandings, provides a focus on training objectives, and deals with misgivings about how training directives may interfere with the day-to-day running of an agency.

We would rather be more inclusive than exclusive when dealing with staffing concerns in private clinics or agencies and involve higher-level staff members, including experienced therapists, who may or may not be interested in obtaining more training. The inclusion of senior administrators and clinicians will more likely ensure institutional support, minimize negative institutional reactions, and facilitate dissemination of new approaches via supervision and in-service training programs. Involvement of senior staff (at least in the planning stages) may enhance the attraction of learning a new treatment approach.[30]

Training Is a Lifelong Process

It is important to be open-minded to new treatment approaches and to feedback from families and colleagues. Inherent in this training program is a belief in the importance of peer supervision and exposing one's style in order to keep improving one's therapeutic knowledge and skills and not drift into bad habits when treating families.

Program Content and Format

Orientation

We find it helpful to begin with a session that provides an overview of the McMaster training program, highlights that trainees will learn an approach to increase their understanding of patients and family members, and provides them with a specific method for treating families. If the training takes place within an agency or involves a subgroup within a department, we open the initial session to a larger, more inclusive audience, as a "kickoff" orientation. This serves several purposes. First, those not taking part in the training learn about possible program changes, in effect demystifying the training process and decreasing scapegoating and negative agency or department reactions. A more inclusive meeting also engenders enthusiasm and a positive boost for trainees who have been selected for the program.

To provide a reference point, we note that the teaching model is based on a transactional approach integrated within general systems theory and that the foundation for the training is the MMFF and the PCSTF. We explain that the paradigm for learning the McMaster approach emphasizes developing skills in three areas: conceptual (understanding concepts of the MMFF), perceptual (seeing and identifying the concept in the family before you), and executive (treating the family according to the PCSTF). When orienting trainees, we spend time on the training objectives so that there is a clear understanding about the goals of the program.

There are four objectives of the training program that may be adapted according to the needs of a specific program. First, trainees learn a conceptual framework so that they are able to formulate psychosocial problems irrespective of treatment recommendation. Second, trainees learn how to complete a consistent, systematic investigation of the family unit. Third, trainees learn how to provide family treatment to their patients and family members. Fourth, trainees learn to apply family systems concepts and family therapy techniques to a broad range of family types, problems, and services.[12,32] All participants should be clear about the training goals so that the training is focused and the evaluation of both trainees and the training program is clearly set.

Trainees briefly indicate their backgrounds, disciplines, previous clinical training and experience, special interests, past learning experiences, and reasons for joining the program. Trainers/supervisors provide background information as well. The detailed orientation is consistent with our model and is a good way to initiate small group learning. Since interdependence and co-operation are valued above independence and competition in training, this session helps create a sense of mutual responsibility to meet common objectives and provides information about individual trainee characteristics and group differences.[12,30,33] Small group learning has the added benefit of helping trainees develop peer group skills, group problem-solving, and self-directed learning—techniques they will use later in the program when treating families and when teaching individual family members ways to modify behavior. At this point the trainer provides an outline of the entire training program (see Figure 4.1), and highlights the small-group training format, the evaluation methods for trainees, trainers, and the program, the expectations regarding time and family case load commitments, and specific requirements of the institution, agency, or academic center in which the training occurs.

Training Sessions (Months One to Three)

The overview session for the first part of the training includes didactic material and family videotapes of the McMaster approach.[30] The objectives for the first session are to provide a background to the history and development of the model and an introduction to the six dimensions of the MMFF and the macro stages of the PCSTF.

Conceptual Skills Training

Seminars with assigned readings are best for developing and integrating the initial conceptual clinical and theoretical materials. Small group discussions center on the concepts associated with the MMFF, family systems thinking and its application to the model, and delineation of levels of family functioning (e.g., severely disturbed to superior). The amount of time and material that is covered varies with the knowledge and experience level of

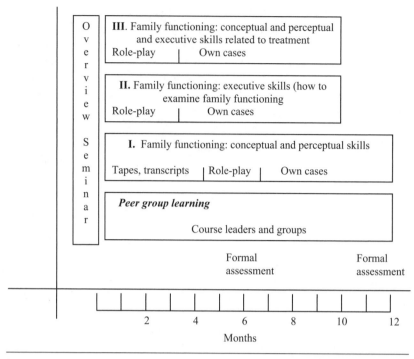

Figure 4.1 Outline of Training Program.[30]

trainees. Although trainees need to develop their conceptual skills training to ensure a common vocabulary, we keep a fairly quick pace in this part of training as the material is repeatedly considered during the subsequent perceptual skills training. Furthermore, although we want trainees to understand the concepts so that we can discuss practical applications, we do not want these seminars to become dry, theoretical, or nonclinically based discussions that have little practice utility. Trainees learn the basics of the McMaster approach by viewing tapes and reading materials. During months 1–3, topics covered include basic concepts and a thorough understanding of the MMFF dimensions: family problem solving, communication, roles, affective responsiveness, affective involvement, behavior control, as well as systems theory, family development, and family crises. In their readings, trainees become acquainted with the macro stages of the family treatment process: assessment, contracting, treatment, and closure.

Some trainers review one topic per week in-depth, using group sessions to cover areas in which trainees would like to clarify or expand their understanding of particular concepts. Sessions may cover discussion of one family dimension per week followed by presenting problems and transactional patterns of the family. Family transcripts and videotapes of family interviews are useful teaching materials to exemplify key concepts.

Perceptual Skills Training

Once trainees have a basic understanding of the conceptual framework of the MMFF dimensions, they begin to develop their perceptual skills. That is, after they understand a concept intellectually, trainees need to identify and label it when it is set before them. This stage of the training makes use of videotapes, DVDs, and direct observations of family sessions. If a videotape or DVD library has not yet been accumulated (or videotape equipment is not available), trainees need to find alternative sources so they can practice identifying the concepts they have learned in the training seminars. These may include transcripts of family sessions, audiotapes of family interviews, direct observation of their own family cases, or observation through facilities with one-way mirrors. Since the McMaster approach is used throughout the world, trainers may need to improvise according to the technical support available to them. Role playing may be used with students playing family members. They are given the task of playing a family with specific strengths or weaknesses on specific dimensions. This exercise allows them to experience (perceive) the effects that a family's functioning may have on particular family dimensions. One innovative trainer used the public library to borrow videotapes of movies with family scenes. Trainees then applied their knowledge of communication patterns, affective responsiveness, behavior control, etc., from the MMFF to identify family interactions.

All of the family material (including intake information and any individual or family assessment) provides the perceptual data that the trainee needs to assess the family according to the MMFF. Early in the perceptual skills training the focus is on assessment, with family interactions discussed and key family issues identified. Topics covered in the conceptual training sessions are revisited to help the trainee integrate the concepts into a cohesive framework. The focus is on identifying the elements of the MMFF, as well as transactional patterns and issues relating to family development stages and systems theory. A thorough assessment of the McMaster dimensions will lead to an understanding of the transactional pattern. Although as clinicians and health care providers we often focus on dysfunctional family interactions, the concept of transactional patterns is neutral—they can be functional or dysfunctional.

Training Sessions (Months Four to Six)

Once the trainee perceives and identifies concepts of the McMaster approach in a clinical interview, the training turns to developing the skills necessary

to complete a comprehensive family assessment. During this part of training the conceptual and perceptual skills are refined and reinforced and the
executive skills are introduced. There are several ways to approach this part
of the training depending on the experience and background of the trainees.

Role Playing

Initially the focus is on perceptual skill development, not therapist skills.
Trainees act as family members and are given explicit instructions, depending
on particular concepts the trainer wants to address. Generally when trainees
role-play, they use their own names, stop if they become uncomfortable, do
not escalate the pathology, and respond as they feel a family member would.
Some suggestions for role playing are:

- A family that has functioned well but is in crisis.
- Choose one dimension from the MMFF as disturbed and show its in-
  fluence on family life.
- A family the trainee has seen and a role-play of an individual from the
  family.
- Read parts from a transcript of a family interview.

At first, trainers play the role of the therapist. Observers identify the dimension of family functioning that is most disturbed. Trainees point out
which stages were handled well. The trainer stops the role playing at several
points and asks help from the trainees—whether or not he or she has collected enough data from the family and what steps should be taken next.
Trainers begin by having the trainees present a simple, one problem family,
instruct the role-playing trainees to be cooperative with the therapist, and
help the trainee get an insider's view of the family that is dysfunctional.
Trainers should be careful not to let the observer trainees flounder if they
have difficulty in identifying problems. Also, the trainer encourages comments and questions from the role-players as well as the observer trainees.

Conducting and Reviewing Family Interviews

Role playing *as family members* helps trainees perceive and identify concepts
of the McMaster approach in the clinical interview. Role playing *as the therapist* helps trainees develop skills needed to complete a comprehensive family
assessment. The training of assessment and treatment skills is based on the
PCSTF, the treatment arm of the McMaster approach. The first stage of the
treatment is assessment and derives from the MMFF that the trainees learned
in the first part of the program. The executive skill training begins with a
review of the PCSTF, followed by role playing as the therapist. An important
part of role playing is that the trainee feels comfortable asking questions of

all family members, balancing the interview among family members, and developing his own style of interviewing. The more a trainee practices, the more likely he will ask questions in his own words, and the less likely he will read questions or recite them by rote. This is important aspect of interviewing for, in addition to obtaining adequate information on a family's functioning, the trainee also needs to establish rapport with family members. Before remembering all the interview questions, trainees sometimes use a prompt sheet during the assessment. Table 4.1 lists prompts for each dimension to help a trainee cover the essentials of a family assessment.

Executive Skills Training

While honing their conceptual and perceptual skills, trainees begin their executive skills training when they assume the role of therapist. After one or two role-plays as a therapist, trainees become actively involved in seeing families for assessment. Depending on trainees' work situations, level of experience, and ability, there are several options for conducting the training. Trainees may do partial assessments (i.e., the orientation and one or two dimensions) with a family before attempting a full assessment. Having trainees deal with one task at a time reduces the trainee's anxiety and makes expectations clear. Alternatively, one trainee might be responsible for orienting a family and identifying the presenting problem, another trainee might be responsible for assessing one or two dimensions.

Another strategy is for trainees to complete full assessments, including orientation, presenting problems, and all dimensions. In each of these examples it is preferable that a trainee has her own family to work with but, on occasion, she may participate with an experienced therapist by assessing one or two family dimensions during an initial evaluation. In any case, sessions should be videotaped to provide feedback to the trainees. Audiotaped sessions are alternatives if videotape equipment is unavailable. For trainees who are practicing therapists, we suggest they assess one or two family dimensions in a regularly scheduled therapy session. The therapist orients the family by asking them to focus (20 minutes will suffice for an experienced therapist) on a specific aspect of their family's functioning. Therapists often report that they learn important information about the family that they were not aware of or that they would not capture using their normal interview process.

When trainees make judgments and evaluate a family's functioning, they use two skills. The first is a decision skill about whether or not there are sufficient data to make a judgment of the family's functioning. Once it is established that sufficient data are available, the trainee makes judgments about the relative effectiveness of the family's functioning in a particular area. This approach helps keep the training manageable and pinpoints any

Table 4.1 Family Assessment: McMaster Model Prompt Sheet*

INTRODUCTION
Problems as a family?
Discussed
Action
Resolved?

ROLES
Who does what?
Overburdened?
Fair?
Discuss?
Argue/Complain
Jobs Change
Jobs done/Who checks?
Does one person fail consistently?
Personal Development
How do you deal with rearing children?
Who does most?
How are kids doing in school?
How are kids doing with friends?
How are kids doing with interests?
How are kids doing with responsibility?
How are kids getting along in society?
Discuss adult sexual satisfaction
Discuss major changes
Help re: Career
Management
Final Word
In-law problems?
Nurture
Bad day, who do you go to?

PROBLEM SOLVING
Instrumental
Who identifies?
Who is told?
What approach is considered?
How did you decide what to do?
Did you come to a decision?
Follow through
Do you usually problem solve quickly?
Do you check?
Repetitive problems?

The order of dimensions follows that used in the McSiff.

BEHAVIOR CONTROL
Rules? (to kids)
Dangerous
Curfew
Hitting
Drugs
Drinking
Consequences
– known
– reasonable
Who punishes harder, Mother or Father?
Do the rules change?
Does anyone . . .
Drink too much?
Eat too much?
Take too many risks?
Have trouble with the law?
Embarrass in public?

COMMUNICATION
Hr/day spent as a family talking to and
with each other
Do people understand when you're talk-
ing about . . .
Everyday issues?
Feelings?
Do others answer for you or interrupt?
Do they talk about you in your presence
as if you're not there?
Forbidden subjects

AFFECTIVE RESPONSIVENESS
Pleasure, tenderness, concern, affection,
anger, sadness, fear
Can you tell me about a time you felt/
experienced
(*ask about pleasure, anger, fear...*) ____?
What was it like?
Other situations
Overreact ever?
Lose your temper?
Cry too easily?
Fear, terrified?

AFFECTIVE INVOLVEMENT
What is important to you?
Who pays attention to you?
Are others interested; how do you know?
Do they nag you?

difficulty the trainee encounters. Since a major tenet of the MMFF is that families have strengths and weaknesses, it is likely that families differ in their functioning across dimensions. Yet some trainees jump to conclusions without sufficient data or assume that functioning in one area of family life is identical to functioning in all family dimensions. If the trainee needs more information or clarification in a subsequent family session, families are usually amenable to follow-up questions. Other trainees go into too much detail and make an interview unnecessarily long or go off a tangent and lose their focus. Over time trainees learn to balance an interview, to keep it flowing, and to obtain the necessary information.

Whatever their experience or background, trainees find small group peer supervision extremely useful when learning how to apply the model. After the trainee conducts an assessment (whether partial or full), she provides a tape of the session for the trainer and other trainees to review. The trainee first comments on what she did well and what difficulties she experienced during the interview. Next, she summarizes the family data that she gathered and discusses her view of the family's functioning in whatever dimension(s) she assessed. Fellow trainees and the trainer comment on the therapist's interview, and include suggestions for improvement. As tapes are reviewed, trainees become comfortable in eliciting suggestions and feedback in peer group supervision and see their own progress, strengths, and difficulties. Because of the cooperative tone set from the beginning of training, trainees view these critiques as helpful. They also see differences in interview styles that remain within the context of the McMaster assessment. If a trainee has difficulty in specific areas of the family interview, seeing how other therapists ask questions is often very helpful. The following suggestions may be useful for trainees/trainers when reviewing family interviews.

Orientation

- Did the therapist elicit the family's expectations as to why they came to the meeting and what they thought was going to happen?
- Did the therapist make sure that the family understood the explanation?

Presenting Problem

- Did the therapist explore the problems with all appropriate family members?
- Was sufficient data gathered to allow for identification of the problem? If not, was the therapist able to identify why not (e.g., the family was highly chaotic, unable to identify problems themselves, contradicted themselves)?
- Did the therapist elicit the family's attempts to solve the presenting problem and their affective responses to the problem?

- Did the therapist identify other assessments if appropriate (e.g., psychological testing, neurological consult, school contact)?

When Focusing on the McMaster Approach

- Did the therapist ask appropriate questions to understand each family dimension?
- Did the therapist provide appropriate summaries, clarification, feedback, and explanation during the interview?
- Did the therapist focus (or refocus) the family, clarify data gathering, elicit specific examples, go over the problem list with family members?
- Did the therapist provide post-assessment options to the family?

Training Sessions (Months Six to Twelve)

Once a trainee has a reasonable grasp of the assessment process, he or she is able to work on completing a full, comprehensive family interview. The more families a trainee interviews, the more exposure he or she will receive to a variety of family situations and problems. In order to establish competency, we ask for a minimum of two full assessments with reviews completed by the trainer. When trainees have a sound conceptual understanding of the McMaster model and have demonstrated the knowledge and skills to conduct a full assessment, they are ready to continue with the family's treatment according to the PCSTF. Some training programs may stop at this point for two of the basic objectives have been met. That is, trainees have learned how to obtain a systematic investigation of the family unit and they have learned a conceptual framework with which they can formulate a family's psychosocial problems and level of functioning. If clinical intervention is recommended, trainees provide referral sources. However, if the trainee continues with the family in treatment (as is usual in our training program), she proceeds to the next stage of the PCSTF process, the contract stage.

Supervision at this advanced stage of training is concentrated on executive skill development. Conceptual and perceptual skills are still relevant, for the trainee needs to understand the concepts of the MMFF and PCSTF, identify them in the families being seen, and develop therapeutic skills as related to family treatment and management of family therapy sessions. The trainer reinforces the complementary relationship among the three skill levels when providing feedback. The format of the seminars continues to be small peer group supervision that is supplemented by individual case supervision. At this point in training we recommend that trainees videotape family sessions as direct observation of cases presents logistic difficulties for trainees, trainers, and family members. Videotapes, reviewed in small-group supervision, are unobtrusive and acceptable to most families, provide visual cues that are lost when sessions are audiotaped, help a trainee review her progress over time, and are useful for building a library for future training. As trainees gain experience, they prepare tapes in advance in order to go directly to difficulties encountered in sessions or segments where they would like feedback. All family members provide signed permission before any taping occurs. Tapes need to be stored properly to protect the families' confidentiality and it should be stipulated that the use of tapes is for training purposes only. Some programs specify a time frame when tapes of a family's sessions will be erased.

Since we provided detailed steps of the PCSTF in chapter 3, we do not repeat these when describing the training process. We do include an outline of the macro stages of the treatment model in Figure 4.2 and a summary guide in Table 4.2.[15,33] Readers may refer to chapter 3 if they need more information on specific stages of the therapy. As shown in the flow chart, therapists may seek consultation at any point during the therapy process. When conducting family therapy, key points to keep in mind are:

- Apply the stages as defined in the PCSTF
- Delineate presenting problems and negotiate tasks as they relate to the MMFF dimensions
- Recognize and utilize family transactions and interactions in family treatment interventions
- Intervene appropriately if the family does not follow through with tasks, has difficulty with them, or breaks the contract
- Discuss and manage issues related to engaging, assessing, treating, terminating, and providing referrals for follow-up care

Reviewing and Supervising Family Cases
The format in this stage of training parallels the format used when critiquing trainees' assessments of families. Trainees provide a brief background on the family session that will be viewed, comment on how they felt the session went, and draw attention to particular areas where they request feedback. This method of self-appraisal fosters a realistic assessment of their executive skills without being over-critical.

The following questions may be useful *before* the tape is played.

- Ask the trainee to summarize presenting problems, assessment of dimensions, and treatment contract.
- Ask the trainee to describe aspects of the family session, i.e., the experience of being with the family, the flow of the session, and any patient issues raised during the session.

- Ask the trainee to note what part of the session went well and where they might improve.

The following questions may be asked *after* the tape is played.

- Ask the trainee what part of the session went well.
- Ask the trainee where there could be improvements and what alternatives she might suggest.
- Ask the trainee what is the next step in the treatment process.

After the trainee has given her own critique, ask for input from all the trainees. Use the same set of questions to focus the discussion. Trainees become comfortable with this approach since it is the same format that is used when reviewing family interviews. As an experienced therapist, the trainer/supervisor may need to bring up additional therapeutic issues. These may include:

- Suggestions of other tasks as alternative options suitable for addressing the problems presented
- Review of transactional and interaction patterns
- Consideration of the need for consultation
- Discussion of personal reactions to family members as well as any transference issues raised in the treatment sessions
- Rationale for the spacing, duration, and content of the sessions

Training is completed when trainees have shown competence in assessing and treating at least three families. Trainees demonstrate their competency in treating families by engaging the family and keeping them in treatment, identifying transactional patterns within the family, successfully contracting with families for change, dealing with resistance appropriately, and maintaining clarity of treatment goals.

Evaluation

By separating training program into discrete tasks, several methods are available to assess a trainee's progress and determine areas of strengths and weaknesses on an ongoing basis. This approach is useful to correct misconceptions quickly, offer constructive criticism and positive reinforcement, keep trainer and trainee on track in the systematic use of the model, and draw attention to issues for subsequent training sessions. In addition, trainees value the feedback, learn to make adjustments, and become adept at evaluating their

Table 4.2 The McMaster Family Therapy Model

ASSESSMENT:	Determination of the family's problems.
Orientation:	Establish the basis for and approach to family therapy; e.g., (a) that a problem may be a dysfunction in the family system, (b) problems affect how the family functions. Explain what you are going to do and what you expect them to do.
Data Gathering:	Collect information concerning family functioning with regard to (a) presenting problem, and (b) how the family functions, more generally
Problem Description:	Discuss with family (a) how they now view their problems, and (b) how you view the problem.
Problem Clarification:	Clarify family's understanding of their problems, and obtain their agreement regarding problem clarification.
CONTRACT:	Establishment of goals and conditions of therapy
Orientation:	Establish agreement with family that assessment is done. Begin discussion of how problems are to be handled.
Outline Options:	Indicate options open to the family at this point; e.g., continue as they are, seek other help, work with doctor. If family chooses last option, the conditions of treatment are specified; e.g., number of sessions.
Negotiate Expectations:	Determine through discussion what the family expects from therapy and convey to the family what is expected of them.
Establish Contract:	Establish a written contract specifying negotiated expectations.
TREATMENT:	Treatment of the family's problems.
Orientation:	State to the family that treatment has begun
Clarify priorities:	Establish priorities concerning expectations
Task setting:	Negotiate, define, and assign tasks Designate a family member to report on tasks
Task Evaluation:	Have family member report on task completion Decide whether task was completed
CLOSURE:	Summary of treatment
Orientation:	State to the family that this is the end of treatment
Summary:	Summarize to the family, treatment received
Long-term Goals:	How they will handle new problems, or a recurrence of the original problem(s)
Follow-up:	Ask if they want follow-up meeting. Suggest one if you feel it would be helpful.

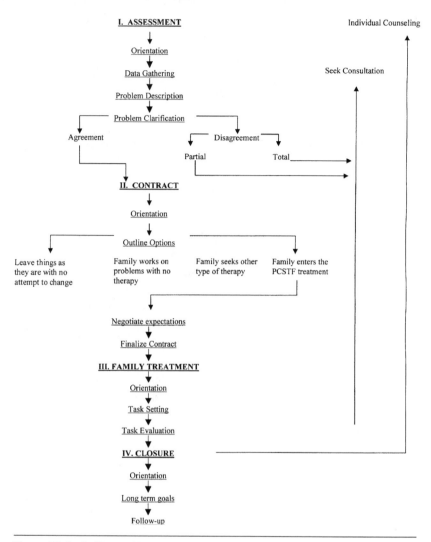

Figure 4.2 Family Therapy Macro Model

own therapy skills. This model parallels our overall teaching and research philosophy, i.e., seeking continuous improvement by learning how to view our work critically and accept criticism constructively. Our viewpoint fits well with the concept of quality assurance review that is in such widespread use today.

Trainee Evaluation

Self-assessment is used whenever appropriate. As noted throughout this chapter, the trainee is asked to outline his or her goals, rate his success in meeting them, and identify his or her strengths and areas that need more attention. Other group members comment, followed by a summary and evaluation by the trainer. Initially, trainees may be reluctant to expose their performance in a group context. At times, peer group members will be overly critical or positive. The trainer requires considerable skill in attending to the small-group processes inherent in peer group supervision. Because this method of evaluation is such an important part of our training program, the trainer must be clear, direct, and willing to confront any training issues in a respectful but firm manner. We use a variety of methods to evaluate conceptual, perceptual, and executive skill categories.

Essays, multiple choice, and true/false statements are appropriate for evaluating a trainee's understanding of *conceptual skills*. The McMaster Family Functioning Concept Test [34] is a paper-and-pencil test used to evaluate trainees or to gauge one's own knowledge and understanding of the McMaster concepts. Sample questions include:

- If a family can resolve affective problems, difficulties with instrumental problem solving are rare. True_____ False_____
- A young man comes home after having been given a ticket for speeding and says: "Cops are so annoying." This is an example of _____ and _____ communication.
- Three necessary role functions are: _____, _____, and _____.

- Give a one-sentence definition of Affective Responsiveness.

We use another pencil-and-paper test, the McMaster Family Functioning Percept Test,[35] to evaluate *perceptual skills*. The trainee determines which family dimension of the MMFF is best linked with a number of statements describing a particular family. Examples of items included in the Percept Test are:

- We know what to do in an emergency.
  PS_____ CM_____ RL_____ AR_____ AI_____ BC_____
- We avoid telling other family members about problems we see.
  PS_____ CM_____ RL_____ AR_____ AI_____ BC_____
- Some family members are unhappy about where they are going in life.
  PS_____ CM_____ RL_____ AR_____ AI_____ BC_____

The McMaster Concept and Percept Tests provide information to trainers if used as pre-tests or post-tests. As pre-tests they indicate the level of ability trainees have on entering the training program and help identify areas that may require the most work. As post-tests they are used to assign grades and place trainees in subsequent training groups. Difference scores may be one indication of the amount of skill development that has resulted from the training. If several groups use the same materials and tests, the gains made in training may also indicate trainer performance. Another effective method for evaluating perceptual skills is through the use of videotapes. Trainees view videotapes and rate families of preselected family sessions that have been conducted by a senior therapist using the McMaster approach. Trainees then compare their ratings with that of an expert. A third approach is to distribute short written descriptions of families, each illustrating several dimensions of the MMFF and key family developmental or transactional patterns. Questions related to family scenarios can be designed to elicit the trainee's comprehension of the dimensions of family functioning as well as appropriate treatment strategies related to the dimension problems.

Fourth, trainees may watch a brief segment of a family videotape and then indicate the main theme, transactional patterns, data and conceptualizations relevant to the McMaster dimensions, developmental issues, and other key issues. Trainees discuss their observations in one group session, or submit brief written responses for review at subsequent sessions. Finally, trainees may write up a family report. Depending on the experience and training levels, the families can be real or fictional, presenting clinically or not. (Trainers can also suggest a presentation of families taken from novels, movies, plays, or TV shows.) Trainees describe the families and patterns within the context of the McMaster dimensions and integrate an understanding of the family based on the McMaster approach to assessment and treatment of families.

Evaluation of *executive skills* involves family therapy outcome. Ultimately, the effectiveness of the therapist depends on her ability to bring about change in families that she is treating. We have described the self-assessment approach within the context of the small, peer group supervision. In addition, trainees' conceptual knowledge of the PCSTF is addressed using a true/false, multiple choice format. We designed two scales intended for use in a research project to ensure that therapists adhered to, and were competent in, the McMaster approach. We find these scales useful in focusing trainers and trainees when assessing executive skill development.

Examples of questions on the PCSTF Therapist Adherence Scale are:

- Did the therapist explain to the family her reasons for pursuing a particular topic?

1	2	3	4	5	6	7
Not at all		Some		Considerably		Extensively

- Did the therapist focus on problems defined in the assessment stage?

1	2	3	4	5	6	7
Not at all		Some focus		Considerable focus		Extensive focus

Examples of questions on the PCSTF Therapist Competency Scale are:

Collaboration:
- 0 – therapist did not attempt to set up collaboration with family.
- 2 – therapist attempted to collaborate with family, but had difficulty.
- 4 – therapist was able to collaborate with family.
- 6 – collaboration was excellent: therapist encouraged family as much as possible to take an active role in the session so they could function as a team.

Establishing and maintaining a focus in the session:
- 0 – therapist was unable to maintain a focus during the session.
- 2 – therapist was able to focus somewhat, but significant portions of the session were devoted to peripheral or unproductive discussion.
- 4 – therapist was able to maintain focus and to refocus discussion when distractions occurred.
- 6 – therapist maintained focus throughout session and, when appropriate, labeled any defocus that occurred and then successfully refocused.

Finally, trainees are required to write up family assessments, to outline a cogent treatment strategy, and to document ongoing therapy. This material is used to assess student progress in executive skill development and documentation as a skill itself. At the end of the training program, the trainer/supervisor completes a summary evaluation as shown in Table 4.3.

Trainer/Training Evaluation

Although our emphasis in evaluation centers on trainees' progress throughout the program, we purposely schedule evaluations of trainers and the training program on a regular basis. We do so (1) to adjust our training to

Table 4.3 Evaluation of Family Therapist

GENERAL COMPETENCIES

Attendance: _____   Participation: _____   Ability to use Supervision: _____

SPECIFIC COMPETENCIES (Rate 1 through 5)

Rating Scale: Excellent   5   4   3   2   1   Poor
(*3 = expected level of performance*)

A. **CONCEPTUAL/COGNITIVE:**
1. Knowledge of family concepts and systems theory: _____
2. Understanding of dimensions of family functioning
   according to McMaster model: _____
3. Recognizing when a family assessment is indicated: _____

B. **PERCEPTUAL/CLINICAL:**
1. Ability to engage in the family assessment process: _____
2. Ability to identify transactional patterns: _____
3. Recognition of affect in family members and in therapist: _____

C. **EXECUTIVE:**
1. Ability to do assessment and present problem list to family
   (at least three family assessments generally completed in year 1): _____
2. Ability to construct a treatment contract: _____
3. Ability to work with family on the contract: _____
4. Ability to pace work to family's level of functioning: _____
5. Ability to know when and how to successfully terminate: _____
6. Ability to identify other treatment needs in the family: _____
7. Overall clinical judgment: _____

OVERALL EVALUATION (check one) RECOMMENDATIONS

This trainee's performance is:

_____ Among the best   _____ Pass—Satisfactory performance
_____ Above expected level of   _____ Pass—Would recommend further
       performance   study in the following
_____ Meets expected level of   area: _____
       performance
_____ Below expected level of   _____ Fail—Needs to repeat this
       performance   assignment or makeup
_____ Unsatisfactory   experience otherwise

---

changes, new ideas, and research findings in the field of family studies, and (2) to adjust to new mandates from the health care system. A consistent belief of ours throughout the years has been that the McMaster approach must remain practical, teachable, and clinically useful for it to flourish. Our trainers have a minimum of three years experience in treating families and are supervised by senior level clinicians and teachers. Evaluation forms include ratings on course content and on individual trainers. Generic forms address items that may apply to any part of the training, such as course content, format, trainer abilities, use of audiovisual equipment, and reading materials. Specific evaluation forms include ratings on the effectiveness of the content, methods, goals, and objectives of a particular seminar series (e.g., advanced seminar on executive skill training).

Trainer staff meetings are held at mid-course and at course completion. These sessions are used to review the positive and negative aspects of specific seminars as well as trainees' performance and progress. During these meetings trainers and senior staff identify problems with particular training approaches either across or within trainee groups. They focus attention on format design, specific trainee group issues, or trainee problems. If a trainer receives lower evaluations than her peers, further investigation, supervision, direct observation, or pairing with an experienced instructor are options considered to assist the trainer. In addition to trainer evaluation, the program itself is reviewed periodically. We revisit the goals of the program and objectives of specific seminars to ensure that they are clear, achievable, and still desired. If one course/seminar compares poorly to others, we examine it in more detail and consider redesigning all or part of it.

Besides keeping a focus on program goals, a few key issues to bear in mind when developing a training program may be useful in its evaluation as well. For example, although trainers and trainees are aware of and must deal with small peer group supervision, group processes are a means to an end and not the end itself. The task of the group is to learn family therapy skills. Trainees may become preoccupied with the group process or a family's dynamics rather than concentrating on learning therapist or intervention skills. The organization of the training program and the format of small group seminars are designed to keep the training of the therapist as the primary objective. The orientation, outline for group meetings, routine structure, sequential development of conceptual, perceptual, and executive skills, followed by ongoing evaluations, are important for guiding and supporting both trainers and peer group supervision.

Finally, keeping the groups of trainers and trainees on task, progressing through the levels of development, assuring clarity of communication, and supportive feedback are reflections of the leadership of the training program. Similar to the evaluations completed on trainees and trainers, program evaluations are viewed by senior staff as addressing deficiencies in the training, so that we can correct, adjust, and improve our program. Generic ratings address the format of the program and small-group supervision, training objectives, and organization of seminars and supervision. Specific evaluations rate the effectiveness of the teaching format at different skill levels, the mechanisms for learning family therapy techniques, and suggestions for improvement in any aspect of the program.

Special Issues in Training

After presenting our research or the MMFF and PCSTF, a question we often encounter in professional gatherings is how to set up a training program to teach the McMaster approach. Given the variety of settings in which family treatment is conducted, we do not offer a fixed method that is guaranteed to work as is. Rather, we provide guidelines of our training program in such a way that those interested in setting up their own program will be successful in learning the McMaster approach. Some training issues are likely to arise regardless of whether the program is set in an academic department, hospital, community agency, public school, or private office. Other issues may arise that are specific to a setting or a program. We comment on a few of these issues.

Recognize Constituent Needs

Most institutions have their own goals and objectives. So too do the trainees and trainers. Before embarking on a new training program, it is important to clearly recognize and acknowledge different perspectives, needs, and competing demands so that common objectives can be agreed upon. An institution may be amenable to provide support for a program if it is clear that the training will have benefit beyond the training period. Trainees may be concerned with the utility of the McMaster approach to family treatment and may need assurance concerning its applicability to all family types. Trainers may need to be confident of the transportability of the model by knowing that trainees are able to sustain their learning without the continued presence of the trainer. Trainers need to be sensitive to senior clinicians who may feel threatened by junior staff learning a new treatment method. Some of these issues can be addressed by:

- Including the appropriate staff in discussions before establishing a training program

- Communicating the purposes of the program in a clear and direct manner
- Orienting trainers and trainees to what is expected of them and what they will accomplish
- Discussing how specific components of the program may impact on the system
- Negotiating with appropriate personnel to ensure a successful program particularly the senior personnel in the agency or program

Specify Goals for the Training Program

Program developers need to be as specific as possible when setting up their training goals. Not only will this strategy help in designing the format of the program and adjusting it where necessary, it will be easier to evaluate the success of the program and determine its relevance to the supporting agency. The following are examples of training goals along with the associated programs.

Academic
- Train residents in a medical training program to develop a psychosocial perspective from which they will gain a better understanding of the families they treat.
- Provide a model which would enable a physician to classify his or her observations of the family unit in areas of family living and transactional patterns.

Community Agency
- Train staff members so that they are able to assess and provide adjunctive family therapy as a treatment modality for appropriate client families.
- Extend family systems concepts and family therapy techniques to a broader range of clinicians/ therapists within the agency through staff development programs and supervision by those trained in the McMaster approach.

Research Program
- Train research interviewers so they can make accurate assessments of family functioning.
- Ensure reliability among therapists in order to test all, or part of, the therapy program.

Training Timing and Format

The timing and format of a training program is determined by the commitment of trainees, availability of families, institutional support, and participation in small-group meetings. We give three brief examples of diverse training programs.

Academic

In training that is currently based in the Department of Psychiatry and Human Behavior within the Brown Medical School, residents learn the MMFF and the PCSTF over the course of a two-year program. In the first six-month period, trainees meet weekly for 1 to 1½ hour seminars to learn and discuss the concepts and principles of the MMFF. They view (by direct observation and by videotape) demonstrations of complete family assessments conducted by senior level psychiatrists and experienced family therapists. The second half of the year is devoted to supervision of trainees as they learn how to conduct a family assessment and use the PCSTF. During the next year, residents follow their own family cases with an elective in family therapy supervision. Because this program is concentrated on learning the McMaster approach, trainees are expected to have reached a certain level of competency in their clinical knowledge and interviewing skills before they are permitted to participate in this series.

Community Agency

Training conducted within a community agency some distance from the medical school was done with minimal contact from trainers and with considerable reliance on peer group learning. The program took place over a 14-month period. Six months were used to develop conceptual and perceptual skill training, followed by eight months of executive skill training. Trainers met with the trainees once a month, while trainee groups met weekly. During the first phase of this program there were two groups, each made up of 12 trainees. In the second phase, which focused on executive skill training, the groups were divided into four groups of six trainees. Throughout the month trainers reviewed audiotaped sessions of the group meetings so that when the full group met, the trainers could identify problems, discuss specific goals for the ensuing month, and develop strategies to achieve the goals. In all of the groups, audiotapes were used to review family sessions during the peer group supervision.

One concern of agency administrators was that the program have a lasting benefit for the client-families that used the agency's services. Not only did the trained therapists implement the McMaster approach to assess and treat families, graduates of the program set up a series of in-house training seminars, 12 weeks in length, to help other agency staff understand psychosocial problems of the family. These seminars had the added benefit of providing continued support and training for the McMaster-trained family therapists. Also, since the treatment model could not address all of the problems that these families encountered, the graduates of the training program set up ad hoc committees to initiate spin-off programs, using the assessment and therapeutic skills learned from the McMaster approach.

Continuing Education Services

One education program was designed to provide interdisciplinary learning as well as more effective professional collaboration within a community. Classes were held one evening per week. Participants included community members who held senior positions in the ministry, medicine, education, nursing, social work, and related mental health care fields. As noted previously, a comparable level of development, more than an individual's background, was a key factor for ensuring success. Teaching methods in this program series were similar to what we have outlined in earlier sections. That is, the curriculum focused on theoretical and clinical practice with lectures, visual aids, small group seminars, role playing, and evaluation. Training for this program was adapted from the guidelines set forth in this chapter. An advanced aspect to this course was a consultation program set up for supervisors of family therapy. Under the lead of senior faculty, the supervisors presented video- or audiotapes of their supervisory sessions. While the focus of discussion became the process and techniques of supervision of McMaster trainees, supervisors soon brought tapes of their own therapy sessions so they could review and maintain their therapeutic skills.[33]

Research Issues in Training

Special considerations need to be incorporated into training related to research. We have developed a number of instruments for use as both clinical and research assessments. We alluded to a few in this chapter and provide more detail and discussion in the following chapter.

Training for Rating Tapes

If the research training includes ratings of family dimensions *by viewing* tapes, then training must impart the conceptual and perceptual skills necessary to achieve high inter-rater reliability. Over the years we have collected a library of tapes of family sessions conducted by experienced therapists. Trainees are assigned tapes to review and rate. Trainee ratings are then compared to known standards, discussed, and problem areas resolved.

Training for Interviewing Families

If the research training involves ratings of family dimensions *after* interviewing families, trainees are required to learn conceptual, perceptual, *and* executive skills in order to complete a reliable and valid McMaster interview. Training is the same as outlined in the formal training program with two important caveats. First, research interviewers do not need to explore a range of presenting problems—an aspect of training that often takes extended time and special attention. They need only assess problem areas to the degree necessary to complete a valid and reliable rating. Second, research interviewers need enough detail to provide family ratings in each dimension, but do not need to explore a dimension, nor its background, in detail. It should be clear to the interviewer and the family that he or she does not have the same role as the treating therapist. In our experience, research assistants, research interviewers, and paraprofessionals often find it difficult to stop exploring during an interview even though they have enough information to make an accurate rating. They become caught up in interesting clinical material. Regular meetings with the research interviewers, reviewing the task ahead of them, and staying focused on the issue usually corrects the problem.

Training for Conducting Therapy

Research protocols may include training in the McMaster treatment approach in order to test all, or part, of the therapy model. This type of training is best done with those who have already been trained in the model and have clinical experience with it. Training can then focus on consistency and adherence to basic principles to ensure that the research project therapy is carried out in a reliable and valid fashion.

Conclusion

This chapter provided a detailed outline of how to set up a training program, including the basic principles that we have followed in setting up our own programs in an academic center and in a community agency. In addition to program format and content, our training also involves guidelines of the methods by which we evaluate trainee, trainers, and the program. Finally, we discuss special issues that need to be considered, whatever the setting in which the training takes place. We recognize that individual training programs may need to make adjustments in order to be successful within their own organizations. However, if the family therapy training is grounded on the MMFF and the PCSTF, as outlined in this chapter, trainees should come away with an understanding of how to assess and treat families according to the McMaster approach.

CHAPTER 5

Assessments Developed
for the McMaster Model

A basic theme of the McMaster approach is linking the clinical utility of the model with its research and teaching applicability. Following this principle, we developed assessments that empirically measure key constructs of the McMaster model. The Family Assessment Device (FAD),[13,36] the McMaster Clinical Rating Scale (MCRS),[37] and the McMaster Structured Interview of Family Functioning (McSiff)[38] were developed by our research team to be used by clinicians, researchers, students, and paraprofessionals. In this chapter we present descriptions and scoring for each of these instruments, discuss the rationale behind their development and give examples of how they may be used as clinical, research, or teaching tools.

In developing our assessments, we assumed that a family is not likely to be perceived the same way by all individuals within the family. Family members likely view the family differently than participant observers (therapists) or non-participant observers (researchers/raters). It is our view that no one perspective is correct. These differences in perspective are interesting and worthy of study themselves. A good clinician will use his or her clinical sense as well as the family's insight to clarify or pinpoint problems and to correct, confirm or adjust perceptions. A researcher will use responses by clinicians and family members to test hypotheses, generate new hypotheses, check research assumptions, and suggest new lines of research. A student will learn to appreciate differences in assessment tools, objective and subjective measures, and what can and cannot be gleaned from clinical and research instruments.

We began our work on assessments by developing a self-report questionnaire, the FAD. This gave us measurable feedback from family members and allowed us to refine our constructs and test for reliability and validity. We then developed the MCRS, designed for use by a therapist or a trained rater after conducting an assessment interview of the entire family. Based on our experience with the MCRS and our observations regarding the clinical skills needed to make valid family ratings, we developed the McSiff—a semi-structured family interview schedule used to help a beginning family therapist or a paraprofessional rater collect sufficient information in the family interview to enable ratings on all dimensions of the MMFF.

FAD

Description

The Family Assessment Device[13,36] assesses family functioning on each dimension of the MMFF according to individual family members' perceptions of their family's functioning. In addition to the six subscales of the MMFF (i.e., Problem Solving, Communication, Roles, Affective Responsiveness, Affective Involvement, Behavior Control) the FAD includes a General Functioning scale that measures the overall level of the family's functioning. Sixty statements, geared to an eighth-grade reading level, describe various aspects of family functioning. Each family member over the age of 12 completes the pen-and-paper questionnaire by rating how well the statement describes his or her family. There are four choices (strongly agree, agree, disagree, strongly disagree) per item and 6 to 12 items for each dimension. Dimension items are purposely not listed in consecutive order. Each item matches only one dimension and may describe healthy or unhealthy functioning. The FAD takes approximately 20 minutes to complete.

Examples of questions about healthy functioning:
We talk to people directly rather than through go-betweens.
____ strongly agree ____ agree ____ disagree ____ strongly disagree

We try to think of different ways to solve problems.
____ strongly agree ____ agree ____ disagree ____ strongly disagree

Examples of questions about unhealthy functioning:
You can easily get away with breaking the rules.
____ strongly agree ____ agree ____ disagree ____ strongly disagree

We sometimes run out of things that we need.
____ strongly agree ____ agree ____ disagree ____ strongly disagree

The underpinning of the FAD is the MMFF that, as we noted earlier, is based on Judeo-Christian philosophy. Nonetheless, clinicians and researchers have found our model and instrument useful in a variety of settings and cultures throughout the world. We receive numerous requests to translate the FAD. We review the process of translation, back-translation, credentials of the translator, and their willingness to accept feedback. Once the FAD is back-translated into English, the original developers of the FAD and senior therapists provide feedback to ensure that the concepts have been understood and used correctly. The translators then send a final version of the translated FAD so that, through our clearinghouse, it will be accessible to others.

The FAD has been translated into 20 different languages and is currently being translated into 3 others. Translations of the FAD include: Afrikaans, Chinese, Croatian, Danish, Finnish, French, Greek, Hebrew, Hungarian, Farsi, Italian, Japanese, Malay, Norwegian, Polish, Portuguese, Russian, Slovenian, Spanish, and Swedish. German, Thai, and Turkish FADs are in the process of being translated. Several of the translations (i.e., the Croatian, Finnish, French, Greek, Hebrew, Hungarian, Italian, Malay, Portuguese, Russian, Spanish FADs) have been back-translated and reviewed by seniors members of the team. Many of our colleagues are in the process of validating the translated instruments in their own countries. Although we provide feedback and serve as a clearinghouse for FAD translations, we caution researchers to be aware of and to consult the wide literature that addresses important methodological issues when conducting cross-cultural studies, including translating and validating instruments, and making comparisons both within and across cultures.

Scoring

Endorsed responses are coded 1–4 for positively worded items and transformed for negatively worded items. Responses for each subscale are summed and divided by the number of items answered in that scale. If more than 40% of the items for a scale are missing, a scale score is not calculated and the dimension is designated missing. For example, the dimension that assesses Communication consists of nine items. As long as five of the items are answered, the score can be used. We have found that family members rarely have difficulty in answering questions.

Scores for individual items as well as individual dimensions range from 1–4 with a higher score indicating poorer functioning. The FAD scores are a family member's perception of his or her family functioning. Each family dimension has statistical validity and individual items making up the dimensions have face validity. This last point is more relevant to applied research and less of an issue when using the instrument for clinical care. The FAD may be hand-scored or a computer scoring program may be purchased for a nominal fee.

Development of the Scale

We originally designed the FAD as a screening instrument. The measure was needed to identify areas of strength as well as problem areas in the easiest and most efficient manner possible. We constructed the FAD to collect information on various dimensions of the family system as a whole, and to collect this information directly from family members. We designed the form so it would be useful to family clinicians and researchers. Details of the research studies that led to the development of the FAD are provided in a series of articles published in the last two decades. These articles include psychometric properties of the FAD, scale reliabilities, intercorrelations, and distribution of scores on family dimensions.[13,39,40] Briefly, our strategy in designing the FAD was to use the MMFF to define areas of family functioning that we wanted to assess. The first version of the FAD used a set of 240 items, each dimension consisting of a subset of 40 items. For each dimension we chose items that covered all aspects of that dimension. Within each set we selected the fewest number of items which, taken together, produced a scale with the highest reliability (Chronbach's *alpha*).

Because the resulting scales were intercorrelated, we returned to the item pool and selected the most highly correlated subset of items and created a General Functioning scale that would assess the overall health or pathology of the family. We returned once again to the original set of 240 items and selected items for the six dimensions using three criteria. First, the items had to be written for the relevant dimension. Second, the set of items making up a scale had to be as highly intercorrelated as possible so that the scale had maximum internal consistency. Third, items in a scale had to correlate more highly with that scale than with either the General Functioning scale or the remaining five dimension scales. The scale construction process was recursive. That is, each time the set of items making up a scale was modified correlations within the scale and between scales changed. The item selection stopped when the scale reliability was over a minimum (alpha = .70) and no item increased the scale reliability or increased the correlation of the scale with one of the other scales. We strove for a balanced instrument that would be clinically meaningful and meet rigorous standards when applied to research.

Not every concept defined in the MMFF is incorporated in the FAD; however, each dimension addresses all concepts necessary to assess the family's functioning in a particular area. For example, there is no question

Table 5.1 FAD Healthy/Unhealthy Cut-Off Scores, Means, and Standard Deviations

Dimension	Cut-off Score*	Nonclinical (N = 627)		Psychiatric (N = 1138)		Medical (N = 298)	
		$\bar{x}$	sd	$\bar{x}$	sd	$\bar{x}$	sd
Problem Solving	2.20	1.91	.40	2.32	.53	1.95	.45
Communication	2.20	2.09	.40	2.37	.44	2.13	.43
Roles	2.30	2.16	.34	2.37	.40	2.22	.39
Affective Responsiveness	2.20	2.08	.53	2.36	.57	2.08	.53
Affective Involvement	2.10	2.00	.50	2.32	.55	2.02	.47
Behavior Control	1.90	1.94	.44	2.14	.49	1.84	.42
General Functioning	2.00	1.84	.43	2.27	.51	1.89	.45

*Greater than or equal to cut-off score = unhealthy functioning in that dimension; less than cut-off score = healthy functioning in that dimension.

on the FAD concerning adult sexual gratification (Roles), but allocation of roles in the family and accountability are addressed. A clinician can ask adults about their sexual gratification in a family meeting. Also, in a clinical interview, the therapist detects visual cues and verbal intonation that is not captured in a pen-and-paper questionnaire. Of particular interest to clinicians and researchers are the healthy/unhealthy cut-off scores first published in 1985[39] and the mean scores of family dimensions for a variety of sample populations published in 1990[40] (Table 5.1). The cut-off scores were derived after experienced, senior level family therapists conducted comprehensive family assessments based on the MMFF, rated each dimension as healthy or unhealthy, and matched the clinician ratings with that of the family's FAD score. The means and standard deviations were calculated after pooling FAD scores from several hundred families. Details are provided in the referenced articles. A recent suggestion that the FAD be collapsed to two factors[41] is reminiscent of discussions that occurred when the FAD was originally being developed. We responded[42] in a similar fashion, i.e., the FAD must have clinical utility and not simply be a statistical construct with no relationship to the families seen in our clinics.

Strengths and Limitations

The FAD has a number of attractive features. It is an economical paper-and-pencil test that can be completed and scored relatively easily and in a short amount of time. It has acceptable data regarding reliability and validity, has been tested and found not to be influenced by social desirability, and has been used successfully in a variety of clinical and research settings, in different languages and cultural settings. Like most family assessments, it measures peoples' perceptions of their families. It provides ratings of a well-described, specific model that has proven useful in clinical work. The FAD gives a detailed picture of a family's functioning in several areas of family life and in the family's overall functioning. The FAD includes perspectives from all family members and has been tested in children as young as 12 years old. Each FAD dimension has documented acceptable reliability. The FAD provides a good orientation for family members to think about their strengths and weaknesses and is a useful introduction for a clinician to use in targeting problem areas in the family. Established cut-off scores indicate healthy and unhealthy functioning.

While we view the subjective perspective as a strength, there are limitations to self-report instruments. The FAD does not substitute for a thorough clinical evaluation of the family's presenting problems. As noted earlier, the FAD (like the MMFF on which it is based) does not address every aspect of family functioning. It addresses dimensions that we feel are critical to a family's functioning. Finally, the FAD score is a relative score that has no intrinsic meaning. For example, depending on the dimension, a score of 2.12 may or may not be considered unhealthy.

The FAD has been used as a screening tool to target at risk families, as a snapshot to measure change in a family's functioning over time, and as a way to indicate the strengths and weaknesses of a family. The following example shows how FAD scores on Problem Solving and Behavior Control can be used from a clinical and research perspective.

Case Study—FAD

The family consists of Mr. and Mrs. N, ages 45 and 42 respectively, a 13-year-old son (P) hospitalized with suicidal threats, anger outbursts, and school truancy, and a 12-year-old brother (M). The couple has been married for 14 years. Mr. N is a high school graduate and Navy veteran employed as a manager in a hardware store. Mrs. N completed two years of college and is a part-time secretary.

FAD scores:	Problem Solving	Behavior Control
Mother	1.66	1.66
Father	2.00	1.77
Patient	2.00	2.44
Sibling	2.16	2.11

The cut-off score for Problem Solving is 2.20. Although individual family members fall within the healthy range of this dimension, their perception of the family's ability to solve problems varies. On further discussion with family members, the therapist elicited the following information:

> Instrumental problems are reportedly handled competently. Family members report difficulty dealing with affective problems. They report reluctance in identifying emotional concerns and avoid discussing issues involving feelings. For example, family members report that there is a tendency to perceive and interpret open discussion of affective problems (e.g., the patient's angry feelings, the sibling rivalry between the patient and his brother) as being 'critical' and 'incriminating.' As a result, it is difficult for family members to sit down and solve problems.

Mrs. N is afraid that discussing strong affect will elicit Mr. N's "potential for getting really angry" and then he will "snap emotionally." Mr. N states that it's Mrs. N's "anxiety" about what will happen that's the problem, so he tries to avoid such conversations. Mrs. N takes it upon herself to deal with affective problems in the family ("I feel that I have to hold the family together"), especially when problems relate to the identified patient, P. Often, she internalizes these problems ("I feel them for P"). Her over-accommodation serves to distance her husband which then justifies her perception that Mr. N is emotionally cut off from her and her sons. Rather than overtax his already "overburdened" and "over-accommodating" mother, son M prefers to keep things to himself.

The cut-off score for Behavior Control is 1.90. In this family there clearly is a discrepancy between the parents' perception of their family's functioning and the children's perception. Although teenagers often rate their family's functioning worse than their parents do, our research has not shown that teen and parents scores differ significantly in a consistent pattern. The therapist used these scores to generate a discussion. His findings suggest the following:

> Rules for meeting the psychobiological needs of children and adults are generally appropriate. Parental disagreement over the rules for children becomes apparent when Mr. N perceives his wife as being over-indulgent and Mrs. N sees her husband as being harsh and rigid. When this occurs Mr. and Mrs. N are unable to discuss their differences (i.e., agree to disagree) for fear that such disagreement will result

in a conflict between them. The couple engages in their characteristic transactional pattern. Rather than challenge his wife, Mr. N retreats and reacts to such situations by making sarcastic remarks about his wife's need to monitor behavior. As a result, Mr. and Mrs. N are unable to sit down and discuss alternative ways to manage their sons' behavior. They were able to establish an unwritten rule that "aggressive acts are not tolerated." However, family members report that verbal aggression frequently occurs between the siblings. When this happens, especially when the patient is verbally aggressive toward his younger brother, the parents ask their younger son to "be nice to his brother." Mr. and Mrs. N admitted that when their older son displayed physical aggression, their solution was to enroll him in individual therapy which resulted in hospitalization after the aggressive behavior kept escalating.

The sons agree that their parents let them misbehave and ignore rules. They admitted that even when their parents try to enforce a rule or punish them, they resist by acting up. On the other hand, the children did not feel that they could talk openly in the therapy session about their parents' anger because they did not want to be the cause of a "blow-up." They felt comfortable, however, in answering the FAD. When the therapist asked if he could share their ratings, they were eager to do so in the "safety" of the therapy room and with the help of the therapist.

A transactional pattern that the therapist noted in other dimensions recurs in behavior control. The therapist suggested that Mrs. N fears her husband will respond with anger while Mr. N believes that intimacy leads to disappointment and hurt feelings. In behavior control, the pattern appears when the parents report great difficulty in cooperatively establishing and enforcing rules, ultimately resulting in ineffective behavior control of their two sons. The parents avoid and circumvent behavior control issues because they fear that any attempt to enforce rules will elicit emotional outbursts. When questioned, Mr. and Mrs. N agreed with the therapist's assessment.

Clinical Use

The therapist used the family FAD scores as a screen to get a sense of how family members perceived their functioning in two different dimensions. Scores on the Problem Solving dimension suggested some discrepancies between family members while the Behavior Control scores showed clearer discrepancy between the parents and children, with two of the scores suggesting moderate dysfunction. The therapist first sought permission from all family members to share and discuss individual FAD items. Then he used some of the family members' responses to problem solving and behavioral control items to elicit information, generate discussion, and point out where members agreed and disagreed. Family members are often fascinated with how others in the family have responded to the FAD items.

Since the item ratings list perspectives held by each family member, the therapist took the opportunity to orient each member to see differences in perspectives, and to compare and listen to each other's point of view. This exercise is useful for the family's upcoming treatment sessions as it sets the stage for discussions in which members try to resolve differences and conflicts within the family. The therapist used the FAD ratings as a starting point. From there, he conducted a thorough family assessment following the interview outlined in chapter 3.

Lack of discrepancy in members' scores does not necessarily mean good functioning. Family members often agree that major problems exist in some areas of their family's functioning. Families may even pinpoint the problems accurately but be unable to address the problem or come up with a satisfactory solution. In the case of the N family, the therapist explored the problem solving and behavior control scores in more detail. He was able to suggest some positive features about the dimensions (e.g., solving instrumental problems and establishing some basic rules), but also elicited difficulties (e.g., anger, lack of communication about problems), particularly between the parents. Once the therapist and family members discussed specific issues and examples of difficulties, the therapist recognized a common theme and was able to get family members to see how their behaviors affected each other as well as how those behaviors had unintended consequences. In this particular example, the parents' pattern of communication made it difficult for the children to express their feelings openly. Since the children felt comfortable answering the questionnaire, however, the therapist was able to note the discrepancy, bring it out in the open, and discuss the issues with all family members in a treatment session.

It is not necessary to use the FAD when treating families. This therapist routinely does so throughout the course of family treatment in order to assess change (or lack of change) in a family's perception of their functioning. He often shares the results with family members who are appreciative of being included in the process and who find each other's ratings instructive. In accordance with the model, the therapist first asks the family for permission to share the scores and then discusses the results with all family members present.

Research Use

From a research perspective, the family is the unit of analysis for most of our studies. Analytic strategies, however, clearly depend on the research question or area of interest. Descriptive statistics may focus on individuals making up a particular family or group of families with a characteristic of interest (e.g., a psychiatric disorder, specific development stage, family member at risk for school problems). Inferential statistics address more formal research questions such as hypothesis testing or model building. The focus might be on pre- and post- testing of a therapeutic intervention, within and between group comparisons, changes in functioning over the course of an illness/episode, predictors of response—or lack of response—to treatment, noncompliance, and risk behaviors, or clinical correlates of family dysfunction.

In the example given, the family's mean Problem Solving score was 1.955 (sd = .21) while the mean rating for the family's Behavior Control was 1.995 (sd = .35). Based on the cut-off scores, Problem Solving fell within the healthy range of family functioning while Behavior Control was considered unhealthy. Within-family analysis might focus on the discrepant scores of the patient versus other family members. In this example, the unhealthy rating of the Behavior Control dimension was driven by the patient's view of his family's functioning. Another approach might be to examine the differences or similarities between the parents' versus the children's perspective of their family's functioning. Using the above example, there was less apparent variation in the area of problem solving between parents and children than in the area of behavior control.

A researcher may be interested in comparing FAD ratings for different patient groups, including different illness categories (psychiatric, medical illness, chronic or acute illness). The mean family score may be considered one case of a family's perception of its family's functioning. The functioning of families in which one member is ill can be compared to the functioning of "normal" families in which there is no designated patient. Other comparisons of interest may be between family dyads (children versus parents), families at different stages of development, families with different household compositions, or families at different stages of their treatment or course of illness. Finally, FAD ratings can be used for making comparisons over time, including pre- and post-testing, particularly if an intervention is provided. FAD scores are used to measure change over time during the course of an illness episode or study, during a follow-up time period, or if there is an interim phase between two or more events. More complex studies might focus on a comparison of treatment interventions.

Two cautionary points that we have made in previous chapters are worth repeating. First, it is not surprising that family dimensions show different levels of health/pathology in the same family. There is no reason to believe that families perceive every area of their family life in the same way. While it is true that some families (or family members) rate their family's functioning uniformly poorly or well, our clinical and research experience suggests greater variability in the way families rate their functioning. Possibly because of this variability, we have not found a ceiling or a threshold effect when using the FAD. That is, there is no minimum or maximum number of family dimensions which, if rated good or poor on the FAD, automatically and uniformly establishes a family's functioning as healthy or unhealthy.

Second, the dimensions of the FAD have undergone rigorous statistical testing to establish validity and reliability. Because the series of studies on reliability and validity focused on the FAD dimensions (not items), we recommend that researchers use the family dimension scores for statistical comparisons, and reserve use of the FAD items for content analysis and interpretation.

MCRS

Description

The McMaster Clinical Rating Scale[37] is an assessment used to evaluate families according to the MMFF. A therapist conducts a clinical interview and uses the guidelines set up in the MCRS manual to rate families on their functioning. In order to obtain the information necessary to provide ratings, a rater must be thoroughly familiar with the MMFF. Ratings may be done by the clinician conducting the interview or by an observer-rater watching a tape or viewing the actual assessment. The rater should have the meaning of a dimension clearly in mind before rating a family so that ratings are made carefully, but not obsessively. The MCRS manual contains brief descriptions of the dimensions, anchor points, and rating guidelines for using the scale. Descriptions of the ratings are couched in operational and behavioral terms. They describe the type of functioning that should be present to qualify for a score (severely disturbed, nonclinical, and superior). Ratings focus on the *family system as a unit* and not on individuals, a mean score, or a summary of individual characteristics. Thus, one or two family members may have difficulty with some aspect of a dimension; nonetheless, the family *as a whole* functions effectively. Although each dimension begins with highlights of the dimension (in order to focus the rater), the manual by itself does not provide an adequate introduction to the MMFF.

Scoring

Each dimension is rated on a seven-point scale with 1 indicating severely disturbed functioning and 7 indicating superior functioning. A rating between 1 and 4 on any scale indicates that an individual in the family, or the family as a whole, is likely to need clinical help. A rating between 5 and 7 on

Table 5.2 Rating Key for MCRS – Communication Dimension[37]

	Very Disturbed			Non-Clinical		Superior	Insufficient Information
Communication	1	2	3	4	5	6	7	II

any scale indicates that disturbances in that area are minor and unlikely to lead to a need for clinical help. Anchor points describe each level of family functioning within each dimension and family characteristics at three levels of functioning: severely disturbed, non-clinical, and superior. A rating of 1 on the scale is the worst case scenario for that aspect of a family's functioning. A 5, denoting nonclinical, suggests that the family's functioning is not excellent but is at a level that is unlikely to require any intervention. We reason that most families have some difficulty in the more subtle aspects of family functioning, but these are not sufficient to evoke problems that lead families to seek help. We designate 5 on the scale to represent a level of functioning that, while not completely effective, does not lead to clinical presentation and represents a "normative" healthy level. Although some families obtain a 7 on some dimensions, it is rare for a family to receive a 7 on all family dimensions. The rating scale for communication is shown below followed by anchor points to rate the family's functioning.

Example of anchor points for family functioning in communication:

Severely Disturbed
1. The family does not communicate. Rather, there is silence/chaotic talking/irrelevant talking.
2. Instrumental messages are masked such that the content of the messages cannot be understood by other family members.
3. Instrumental messages are indirect so that even clear content goes to inappropriate family members.
4. A family's affective communication is masked.
5. A family's affective communication is indirect.
6. Messages are communicated clearly and directly by ordinary standards, but some members of the family still do not hear or perceive what is being said.

Nonclinical/Healthy
1. All information necessary for instrumental functions is communicated clearly and directly.
2. In most situations (70–80%) where communication of affect is required, it is clear and direct and received appropriately.

3. Only in the remaining 20–30% of situations are messages either inadequately clarified or inappropriately directed.
4. If a message is unclear, an attempt is made to clarify it.
5. Communication may sometimes be inefficient or inadequate, but not to the extent that it is disruptive.

Superior
1. A family transmits messages when they are called for.
2. All messages (instrumental and affective) are clear and direct with no misunderstandings.
3. If the recipient of the message does not completely understand it, he/she immediately asks for, and receives, clarification.
4. Messages are transmitted concisely and efficiently.

If it is unclear how the family should be rated, all three anchor descriptions (i.e., severely disturbed, nonclinical/healthy, or superior) should be reviewed. In cases where there is insufficient data to make a rating, this can be noted in the appropriate place on the rating form. The anchor point descriptions act as markers that the rater interpolates from to arrive at a rating. Each dimension lists a set of principles to guide the decision. A complete MCRS will have 6 dimension scores and 1 general functioning score. Using our clinical experience, we chose a 7-point scale because it has sufficient range to encompass a variety of family functioning, yet is sufficiently compact to be manageable by raters. For research purposes, we also felt that a 7-point scale would adequately differentiate within as well as across families.

Development of the Scale

There are several reasons why self-report inventories can create difficulties when assessing theoretical constructs. First, a significant body of literature provides evidence that beliefs and self-reports are not isomorphic with behavior.[43] Second, the decision about how to combine individual family scores into an overall rating entails a variety of methodological issues. Third, due to language differences or reading-level requirements, self-report questionnaires may not be useful for important segments of the population. There are several positive reasons for using interview ratings of family functioning. One of the most obvious is the interaction data and nonverbal cues available in interview settings with family members that are unavailable when using paper-and-pencil reports. The interview setting may provide greater flexibility in gathering information or more spontaneous responses. The clinician/rater may have an objective perspective of the family's functioning. Finally, the clinical interview is the most commonly used assessment in clinical practice. Thus, even while we were developing the FAD, we realized the need for a clinician-rated instrument that was based on our theoretical model.

Despite the importance of the clinical interview, few interview ratings are standardized. Not only did we immediately see the need for a standardized clinical rating scale, we felt the development of one would fit particularly well into our program by increasing the utility of the MMFF in both clinical and research settings. We conducted a series of four studies addressing the reliability and validity of the MCRS.[44] The first study sought to determine whether or not the dimensions of the MCRS could be reliably rated. We videotaped assessments of five families by senior therapists who had extensive experience in using and teaching the MMFF. Raters with different levels of clinical training (naïve, beginning, intermediate, and advanced family therapists) viewed and rated the tapes independently. Results indicated that the MCRS could be rated reliably on all seven scales. In the second study naïve raters received didactic training in the MMFF and the MCRS, completed trial ratings, and were given feedback on their ratings. Then they rated 31 families with a wide range of family functioning. Raters with minimal training demonstrated good interrater reliability.

The third study focused on the relationship between the FAD and the MCRS. The lack of correspondence between observational and self-report scales is generally thought to be due to differences in perspective (internal vs. external,[45] context (e.g., situational, home versus lab, clinic versus school,[46] or orientation (clinical based versus theory based).[47] The small to moderate correlations (average r ranges between .40–.60) that we found between the family dimensions measured by the FAD and those measured by the MCRS may reflect differences in perspective and context, similarities in a model based upon clinical observations, or, more likely, a combination of these factors.

The final study addressed the ability of the MCRS to discriminate between families that were expected to differ in family functioning. We chose families in which one member was acutely depressed. Experienced family therapists interviewed and rated the family at the acute stage of the patient's illness and when the depressive episode remitted. As expected, ratings of family functioning at the acute stage were, with the exception of one dimension, significantly poorer than family ratings at follow-up. The improvement in ratings of Affective Involvement did not reach significance. Since this was the healthiest family dimension at the acute stage, it was more difficult to show a significant change in functioning. Nonetheless, ratings for Affective Involvement improved, in the expected direction, to a level of healthy functioning.[44] This series of studies on the MCRS allowed us to demonstrate good interrater reliability and rater stability. Also, we found that the MCRS could be used effectively by relatively naïve raters and by experienced family therapists. Correlations among rated dimensions were shown to be moderate and consistent with theory, that is, during a depressive episode, familes of depressed patients exhibited greater dysfunction in more areas of family life than when their depressed member was not in a depressive episode.

Strengths and Limitations

The MCRS provides a clinician with a summary of each family dimension that is considered fundamental to a family's functioning. Because the instrument is based on a model of family functioning that is highly defined and behaviorally based, rating the dimensions requires fewer levels of inference than do other, more complex, and less behaviorally grounded models. The MCRS provides the clinician with a guide to enable him or her to do a comprehensive evaluation of the patient and family members, yet allows for an evaluation of only 1 or 2 dimensions if needed. This flexibility is useful when there are time constraints or patient/family limitations. Also, when a trainee is first using the model, it is often advantageous to practice on 1 or 2 dimensions before tackling all six areas of family functioning plus the overall functioning of the family.

The MCRS is based on a clinical interview in which the interviewer or an external rater evaluates a family system by addressing all components as laid out in the MMFF. Thus, areas of family strengths are taken into account as are areas of family weaknesses. Unlike other measures that may stress pathology, families can, and often do, receive ratings as high (very effective) functioning families. The MCRS provides clear guidelines for rating each family dimension. Ratings can be used as a continuous measure or as a healthy/unhealthy dichotomy. Finally, the MCRS correlates moderately with the FAD.

Because the MCRS is based on a clinical interview and taken from a well-defined model, training is necessary in order to conduct a valid assessment and provide reliable ratings. Thus, the ratings can be limited by the interviewer's lack of experience or familiarity with the model. The quality of the interview can also be affected by the style of interviewing. That is, if the interviewer focuses solely on the questions and the content of the interview, and neglects family interactions and non-verbal cues, then a faulty or inaccurate rating is possible. These limitations are more likely to occur with a novice interviewer or trainee and are not peculiar to this model or approach to therapy. As an interviewer gains more experience and confidence with the assessment and the model, the interview becomes smoother and there is a balance between questions addressed to family members, interactions with the family, and notice of non-verbal messages and cues.

Finally, the MCRS provides a summary score. A rating of 2 can suggest significant functional problems in the family but the rating does not specify which aspect of the dimension (e.g., allocation, affect, communication) is causing the problem. The following example describes one family's functioning on the dimensions of Communication, Roles, and Affective Responsiveness and the rating that was assigned to each dimension based on the MCRS. The ratings were used as an objective measure of family functioning at baseline and compared to the family's functioning after six months or end-of-treatment in a research study.

Case Study—MCRS

The family is Mr. and Mrs. S, age 37 and 33 respectively, a 14-year-old son and an 11-year-old daughter. The S family was referred for family assessment as one component of Mr. S's treatment plan following a 10-day psychiatric inpatient admission. Reluctant to seek treatment, it was only after nearly losing his job of 16 years (due to uncharacteristic and increasing disorganization, poor concentration, and irritability) that Mr. S sought psychiatric evaluation. He was experiencing significant psychomotor retardation, slowness of speech, constricted affect, and a profoundly depressed mood. His look was downcast with very little eye contact; thought content revealed low self-esteem. Mr. S believed he was a failure and had let down everyone who was important to him. Shame was predominant. He considered life was a hopeless bounce from one tragedy to the next and often wished he would die. Thoughts of suicide were present and disturbing to him; however, his devout religious beliefs deterred him from killing himself. Past psychiatric history revealed no previous treatment although there was evidence of at least one prior episode of major depression seven years earlier when Mr. S took a medical leave of absence and stayed in bed for nearly three months.

> *Communication:* The family acknowledged that they do not spend adequate time talking together as a family, nor do Mr. and Mrs. S spend time talking with each other. When they do talk, instrumental communication is generally clear and direct. Affective communication is considerably masked and indirect for they do not openly discuss their feelings. *MCRS rating – Communication = 3*

> *Roles:* The S family has established well-defined traditional roles that lend themselves to effectively accomplishing most necessary, instrumental family functions. Mr. S is the bread winning husband and father who has final say on all aspects of family life. Mrs. S is the primary homemaker and is quite ambivalent about her role. Her frequent disagreement with her husband's approaches and decisions places her in considerable conflict with her own religious beliefs and values of being

submissive to her husband. This appears to have strained their expression of nurturing and support as well as their sexual relationship. The children feel strongly connected to their mother and quite distant from their father.

Mr. S's depression and resultant withdrawal from his family intensified the family's feelings of isolation. There is significant discord between Mr. and Mrs. S with regard to Mr. S's acknowledged excessive involvement with a host of people outside of their family. Mr. S feels compelled to provide financial and personal support to his mother, siblings, and anyone in his church who asks him for assistance. Because he responds to these requests, he has amassed considerable credit card debt, much to the sacrifice of his immediate family. *MCRS rating – Roles = 4*

Affective Responsiveness: While highly constricted and uncomfortable in expression, the S family, in general, is able to experience the full range of welfare and emergency emotions. Mr. S has significant difficulty with the high degree of intensity of his emergency emotions (guilt, shame, sadness, and anger) while Mrs. S is "numbed" at this time to both her welfare (affection, support, happiness) and emergency emotions (fear, anger, disappointment). *MCRS rating – Affective Responsiveness = 3*

The therapist summarized the transactional pattern: As Mr. S became increasingly overwhelmed by the impact of his depression he withdrew. Worried and concerned, Mrs. S went to her husband only to be frustrated by his rejecting behavior. In her hurt and frustration, Mrs. S sought comfort in her children and in her excessive, unhealthy eating. She gained weight and lost self-esteem. Additionally, she experienced frequent headaches and generally "did not feel good." Mr. S then felt he was to blame for his wife's unhappiness and added guilt and shame to his burrow of hopelessness and further withdrew. The children, for the most part, remained on the sidelines. They were aware that "something was wrong with dad" and worried about him but kept their worry to themselves. This reinforced Mr. S's belief that he was protecting his family from his own problems. As this pattern progressed, Mr. S became significantly impaired and the family's functioning, particularly in the areas of affect and communication, deteriorated.

Clinical Use

Using the McMaster model as a guide, the therapist systematically explored the family's presenting problems in 2–3 assessment sessions and rated the family's functioning on each dimension. Initially the S family had a limited understanding of why they were meeting with the family therapist. The family was polite, attentive, and cooperative. When an individual was asked questions, each responded briefly but cautiously. Questions directed to the family as a group were met with long silences; eventually Mr. or Mrs. S responded awkwardly and with reluctance. Mrs. S finally said that her husband was not comfortable talking about problems and had intentionally kept them in the dark about his condition.

The family's tendency to respectfully wait and follow Mr. S's lead and to gain his approval before responding suggested important role definitions. Additionally, the discussion on Mr. S's thoughts about wishing he would die and his conviction that his family didn't need him evoked responses of disbelief from his family as well as powerful emotional expressions of nurturing and support. Noting the strong definition of roles within the family, the therapist showed respect in accepting the family's traditional hierarchy. This acceptance helped to establish and maintain trust between the therapist and family members that, in turn, further engaged the family in the assessment and treatment process. The assessment provided the therapist with significant information relevant to the McMaster dimensions of family functioning, particularly with respect to roles, affective involvement, affective responsiveness, and affective aspects of communication. MCRS ratings provided baseline measures that were used to compare family strengths and weaknesses on different dimensions and to gauge progress with the family's treatment over time.

The therapist used information gathered from the assessment to help the family negotiate expectations of one another around the identified problems. Predictable from the assessment sessions, negotiations around the affective problem areas were difficult at best. The S family was neither practiced nor skilled at addressing affective issues that they had studiously avoided in the past. Coupled with Mr. S's depression, the family initially began to panic at their lack of progress and Mr. S believed that all was hopeless. In this case, the family therapist thought that Mr. S would benefit from individual treatment. Gradually, through hard work, learning and practicing new skills, and with support and encouragement from the therapist and family members, the S family was able to negotiate their expectations, begin work on addressing their problem list, and progress to the treatment stage. Improvement was helped by individual and pharmacotherapy for Mr. S in addition to the family therapy discussed here.

Many therapists who use the McMaster approach observe that, when the assessment is conducted systematically and thoroughly, a significant portion of family treatment occurs during the assessment stage. The assessment process offers the family the opportunity to observe and discover their own family's functioning and, through new insight, determine a strategy to address family issues and improve their family's functioning. This proved true with the S family. The assessment phase lasted 3 sessions, the contracting stage another 3 sessions, while the treatment for the family included 8 family meetings. The time frame for assessment, contracting, treatment, and closure was 11 months. Mr. S's medication management and individual psychotherapy continued beyond the close of family treatment. As usual when practicing the McMaster approach, the therapist used one session for review and closure, offering the family additional sessions if they felt the need to review old problems or address new issues.

The therapist in this case was very experienced in the use of the MMFF and the PCSTF. He values the MCRS as a mechanism that keeps both the therapist and family focused on assessing issues and problems within the family, particularly in difficult to treat cases. Anchor points and rating guidelines help to ensure a systematic assessment of each dimension and provide a method of tracking progress (or lack of progress) in the family's treatment plan.

Research Use

The MCRS results in seven *family* scores, one for each of the six McMaster dimensions and an overall, general functioning score. The scoring method differs from the FAD scoring in which a mean score is derived from ratings made by each family member. The differences are important when considering research methods and use.

The case of the S family was part of a study that examined four arms of treatment: medication alone, medication with individual therapy, medication with family therapy, and medication with individual and family therapy. In this study we used the FAD and the MCRS to obtain subjective and objective assessments of family functioning in families of patients who had been hospitalized with major depression. One set of hypotheses focused on matching treatments to patient/family deficits. For example, if the patient and family exhibited poor family functioning at intake, a "matched" treatment would include family therapy. If the same family was randomized to receive "mismatched" treatment, family therapy would not be a part of their treatment. The S family was randomized to the "matched" treatment arm and therefore received family therapy in addition to the pharmacotherapy. In this example, an objective family assessment provided additional information about the problems encountered by Mr. S and his family. As a result of the family assessment and several family treatment sessions, the clinician recommended that Mr. S. obtain adjunctive individual therapy. Following the research protocol, Mr. S was dropped from the randomized part of the study so that he and his family could benefit from a combination of all treatments offered.

We are in the process of addressing several other research questions with the data we have collected for this study. They include: (1) the relationship between good/poor family functioning at the initial stage of the illness and over the course of the episode; (2) the family's functioning at index as a predictor of short- versus long-term outcome; (3) the association between subjective and objective measures and how they can be most effectively used to understand the patient's depression; (4) the clinical and psychosocial correlates of a family's functioning and the changes in functioning over time; and (5) the relationship between retention in the study, compliance with treatment, and dimensions of family functioning. The MCRS will provide an objective rating of family functioning for the above analyses. Depending on the specific question, we will dichotomize the MCRS score into healthy/unhealthy ratings or use the seven point scale as a continuous measure. As a more recently developed instrument, our use of the MCRS in research is less extensive than our use of the FAD. However, data that we have collected and analyzed with respect to the psychometric properties of the MCRS[44] have provided encouragement for our continued use of this instrument in research.

(McSiff)

Description

The McMaster Structured Interview of Family Functioning[38,48] is a structured instrument in which questions are asked of the family that address specific components of each family dimension of the MMFF. Throughout the assessment, information is elicited in order to determine whether or not a particular aspect of the dimension is problematic. The McSiff is an alternative means to arrive at an MCRS score when the interviewer is naïve, not clinically trained, or in the early stages of training. In fact, at the end of the 1 to 2 hour interview, the rater uses the MCRS scoring sheet to provide ratings on the family's functioning. In order to make it easier for the families and the interviewer, the sequence of dimensions examined in the McSiff interview differs from the sequence given in the MCRS.

The interviewer or rater who conducts the McSiff interview does not need to be a clinician or experienced family therapist, but should be familiar with the MMFF and have clinical interviewing skills. As the name implies, the McSiff is a structured interview that provides a road map through all the dimensions of the McMaster Model. The introduction to the McSiff discusses the importance of exploring each area fully and making judgments based on data gathering rather than on conjecture or intuition. The format of the instrument is explained and includes: (1) major headings of each dimension and what the interviewer should focus on; (2) instructions for the interviewer; (3) statements made by the interviewer; (4) questions that the interviewer should ask; (5) probes and follow-up questions; (6) interviewer rating prompt boxes; and (7) coding matrices.

Scoring

Prompt boxes appear throughout the interview to ensure that the rater has enough information to rate a particular aspect of a dimension. The following are examples of two prompt boxes used to rate two subcomponents of family dimensions: (1) role accountability (in Roles dimension) and (2) communication of affective problems to the appropriate person (in Problem Solving dimension). Detailed questions on these dimensions precede each prompt box. If all questions are answered, the interviewer will have enough information to provide a rating.

Example of Role Accountability:
Do you feel that jobs in the house are generally handled well by your family?
    If No: What is the problem?

Does anyone in the house consistently not do his or her job(s)?
    If Yes: Who?

What is the problem?
    Probe: Do they have the skills or ability to do the job?
                Do they have time to do the job?
                Do they take responsibility for household jobs seriously or not
                care? (i.e., is the problem lack of skills, time, or attitude?)

Do you check that jobs get done?
    Probe if Yes: Who checks?

If a task is not carried out what happens?

Interviewer Rating:
*The family maintains **good role accountability**?*   Yes   No
Comments: _____

_____

Example of communication of affective problems
to the appropriate person:
When you noticed the problem did you tell anyone?
Who did you let know about the problem?
    Probe: Did you let anyone outside the family know about the problem?
             If Yes: Who?
             Did you let the others know soon after noticing the problem?

Is this usually the way the family is told about a problem?
    If No: How is this different?

Interviewer Rating:

Affective problems are communicated to appropriate person? Yes   No

Comments: _____

_____

Individual questions within each of the prompt boxes are numbered. The interviewer uses a separate coding sheet to mark yes/no to indicate whether or not there is a problem in that area of family life. A total of 40 questions focus on components of each dimension, preceded by a grid that lists family roles and responsibilities. Once the interview is complete, the rater reviews the family responses and the answers from the prompt boxes to derive an MCRS rating on each of the family dimensions. The McSiff is used to help the interviewer determine a family's rating by flagging a specific problem area; at this time it is not used to generate a numeric score.

Development of the Scale

The development of the McSiff was stimulated by our clinical, teaching, and research activities. The lack of standardization of a clinical interview needed to assess a family's functioning became evident in a number of ways. First, it became apparent that the clinical interview of the family was a critical element in conducting a reliable and valid MCRS. However, even highly experienced clinicians varied in the quantity or quality of information they elicited in order to rate a family's functioning. Furthermore, experienced clinicians often used shortcuts in the interviewing process or drew conclusions that were not obvious to less clinically experienced raters. A beginning clinician or a naïve rater less familiar with the MMFF may feel that there is a lack of sufficient data to make a rating and prolong the clinical interview when more than enough data have already been collected. Novice clinicians often lose their focus and go off on a tangent during a clinical interview while novice researchers often get stuck on unnecessary detailed probes. The McSiff became a useful tool for: (1) training clinicians in conducting family assessments, (2) helping researchers maintain a good interview flow, (3) ensuring a comprehensive interview approach for either clinical or research purposes, and (4) keeping the focus of the interview on the family's functioning.

Responses to the questions on the McSiff provide enough information to enable the interviewer to rate the scale dimensions and to know whether a problem exists. A therapist might want to explore the problem in more detail and can do so by revisiting the issue during a therapy session. Once a research interviewer establishes whether or not there is a problem, he or she moves on with the interview as there is no need for further questions. The McSiff is useful in advancing a wider and more consistent application of the McMaster approach, both for those who do not have full clinical or research training and for those interested in applying the model but are not able to receive direct training from an experienced McMaster therapist. In addition to providing structure for conducting a clinical interview, the McSiff offers a level of specificity that the FAD and the MCRS does not. For example, the boxes that are interspersed throughout the McSiff pinpoint a specific problem in a specific dimension. The first example listed above focused on role accountability while the second example focused on communicating about affective problems. After a series of questions addressed to the family, the interviewer gives a rating and writes down comments as needed before continuing the interview.

Originally, use of the McSiff began as a teaching tool in the family therapy training program at McMaster University. Senior instructors in the program provided a list of questions they typically asked for each family dimension of the MMFF. Trainers organized these questions into a guide for students that would be suitable for any family. The sequence of questions followed what was practiced in clinical sessions and what is presented in the MMFF: problem solving, communication, roles, affective responsiveness, affective involvement, behavior control.[49] The first version of the McSiff did not address presenting problems of the family. After testing this instrument, we realized that families needed an opportunity to present their current problems and state why they were coming to the session. We also found it necessary to change the order of assessing dimensions. Based on trial and error responses to questions, we determined that the roles dimension was concrete and easily grasped by the family. We moved questions on role functioning to the beginning of the interview for they were highly specific, nonthreatening, and instrumental. We have since found that these types of questions reduce the anxiety of family members, help families become accustomed to the interview process, and help the interviewer develop a rapport with family members.

The dimensions dealing with affect (Affective Responsiveness and Affective Involvement) are the last dimensions addressed in the McSiff. Our reasoning for this placement is to take into account information obtained from other dimensions and to acknowledge that it may be difficult for families— as well as trainees—to begin a comprehensive interview focusing on areas of affect. Besides the specific responses to questions asked in these two dimensions, the interviewer considers the affect displayed by family members throughout the interview when he/she determines the rating scores. As usual with our approach, the McSiff concludes with a brief summary of the interviewer's assessment of the family, a request by the interviewer for the family to correct, amend, or validate his or her perceptions, and to thank the family for taking the time and effort to participate in the interview.

We drafted three versions of the McSiff accounting for different family constellations, including a nuclear family, couples only, and single-parent families. Our most recent version consists of one interview format applicable to any family constellation and uses skip-outs and notations to direct questions to family members. The McSiff begins with an orientation to the interview process, after which the interviewer obtains a list of problems identified by the family and the steps they have taken to resolve the problems. Following a discussion of the problems, the interview shifts to each of the McMaster dimensions in the following order: Roles, Behavior Control, Problem Solving, Communication, Affective Responsiveness, and Affective Involvement. Once the McSiff is completed, the interviewer codes responses on a separate data sheet based on notes and comments taken during the interview. The anchor points, levels of functioning, and principles of rating outlined in the MCRS manual guide the final rating of functioning. The rater uses the *same* form supplied in the MCRS manual to rate the six areas of family functioning and the overall level of family functioning. As the interviewer gains experience in clinical judgment and in conducting family interviews, there is less reliance on the McSiff when completing a family's assessment.

Strengths and Limitations

The McSiff, a structured interview based on a well-defined theoretical model, ensures that the interviewer elicits enough information about a family's functioning to rate each component of a family dimension as defined in the MCRS manual. Because the McSiff is designed to collect family information in a structured, comprehensive manner, it is transferable to other settings and does not rely on in-depth training. A variety of interviewers with no formal training in family therapy, and with little or no clinical experience with families (albeit experience in administering assessments and with clinical interviews), have been trained to reliably administer the McSiff. The McSiff, analogous to the widely used Structured Clinical Interview for DSM-IV, is structured so that the interviewer stays focused. Probes are included throughout the interview to ensure that the correct information is gathered. By asking the family for examples and using follow-up questions, the interviewer is able to specify which aspect of a dimension is causing a problem. The McSiff is a good teaching tool for learning the McMaster approach, for gaining experience in interviewing families, and for providing structure to a beginning clinician.

Families like the interview as each member gets to voice his or her opinion on many different topics and soon realize that the interviewer will solicit the opinion of each person. Family members are reassured that they will be heard and they begin to listen to each other. Because of the detailed questions and structure of the McSiff, a novice interviewer or beginning clinician may rely on the questions provided rather than listen to and engage with the family. If the interviewer is intent on a question and answer format (for example, not skipping any questions), the interview may sound rote and the family may get bored and be put off. Also, if an inexperienced interviewer administers the McSiff nonverbal cues and interactional processes may be missed.

These issues become particularly important if the McSiff is the first interaction the family has with the clinician, agency, or research staff. As an example, families presenting their problems in a clinical setting and looking for help can be put off if the interviewer relies too rigidly on the McSiff structure and does not pay attention to the immediate concerns of the family. In such cases it is important to listen to, and acknowledge, the family's concerns. We then explain to the family that we will return to address the problems but first would like a broader understanding of their family system. These limitations are not confined to the McSiff, but represent a beginning interviewer or clinician. If a trainee is interviewing the family, we often state so explicitly. More often than not, families respond in a positive manner even if the interview may take longer.

As noted, it is possible to complete all or parts of the McSiff in one session. Depending on the experience of the interviewer and the family's issues, two sessions may be needed to complete the entire interview. Even for complicated family problems and despite the therapeutic value found in many of these interviews, we recommend that no more than two sessions be used to complete the McSiff. The following case illustrates how a trainee used the framework of the McSiff to focus himself and the family. By adhering to the interview format, the trainee obtained a comprehensive picture of the family and addressed a pressing family issue that was being avoided.

Case Study—McSiff

The family is Mr. and Mrs. J, married for almost 50 years. The clinician saw Mr. J, age 78, to treat his depression and memory loss. After several months of treatment, the patient's depression resolved and his memory loss stabilized. However, the patient continued to be angry and complained about increasing arguments with his wife, age 80. The therapist asked if the patient and his wife would be interested in participating in a family assessment to see if they could pinpoint some of their problems. The husband and wife agreed to the interview and asked if their two adult sons could participate in the assessment as well. The summary of the J family is based on the clinician's knowledge of the family since Mr. J was in treatment.

> The husband, retired 12 years ago, had been a professional accountant with administrative responsibilities in a small firm; his wife was a homemaker. Their two sons were married, one with young children, a busy schedule, and family responsibilities. The older son was very involved with his parents, almost to the point of becoming a caretaker. He advocated for the patient and family, scheduled all visits, spoke with the clinician, and had attended the patient-clinician meetings.

After orienting the family about the family assessment, the therapist asked family members to list some issues that had become problems or difficulties within the family. According to Mr. and Mrs. J, problems actually began 10 to15 years ago when Mr. J retired. Both husband and wife were at home and began fighting. In the past 2 to 3 years, the situation escalated. Mrs. J felt that she did all the household tasks while her husband provided no help. She was energetic, spunky, a mover who got things done. Mr. J was slower, took his time, and liked to put things off. A major complicating factor in the case was that Mr. J was in the early stage of Alzheimer's disease. The memory problems evidenced by the patient and inherently associated with Alzheimer's were seen as recalcitrance by the wife and son. If the patient forgot to complete a chore, his wife thought he was just putting things off, or leaving the task to her. The patient, in turn, was reluctant to reveal his memory loss and, in trying to hide his deficits, became adept at making excuses. The patient ended up getting depressed, the arguments increased, the son became more enmeshed in the family system, and, at times, sided with his mother, which caused more anger and resentment in the family system.

The therapist summarized the problems as: (1) fighting between Mr. and Mrs. J, with an increase over the past two years; (2) difficulty associated with Mr. J's diagnosis of Alzheimer's disease; and (3) the son's involvement in trying to deal with his parent's issues. The family agreed on these problem areas and then proceeded with the interview.

Roles

The first dimension assessed in the McSiff is Roles. From the summary given above, it is clear that several components of this dimension were problematic. Role allocation, accountability, system maintenance and management, nurturance and support, and overall role functioning were all rated as problem areas. Mr. and Mrs. J's roles were traditional in the sense that he was the breadwinner while she took care of the house. They seemed comfortable and set with their roles while Mr. J was working, but once he retired Mrs. J was ambivalent. She constantly complained about her husband not being helpful, but she also would not let go of the chores for him to do as he saw fit. As a result, Mrs. J was often overwhelmed.

MCRS score using the McSiff – Roles = 3

Behavior Control

No sub-component of this dimension was rated as problematic.

MCRS score using the McSiff – Behavior Control = 5

Problem Solving

The family received mixed ratings on this dimension. Whether instrumental or affective, there was difficulty in communicating problems. The family also had problems in developing alternatives. Once a decision was made, however, they did act on it and monitored it. Their ability to evaluate the problem solving process varied. At times the sons' input helped in the decision making process but at other times, it complicated the matter for Mr. J felt he was outvoted.

MCRS score using the McSiff – Problem Solving = 4

Communication

This area of family functioning presented major problems for the J family. All sub-components of the dimension (amount of time spent talking, clear, direct, and overall communication) were problematic. Communication in this family was very poor. The patient did not want to voice his concerns regarding memory loss. When he did, his wife, and sometimes his son, blamed him for making excuses. The family could not talk clearly and directly among themselves. They did not take time to talk together, for each time they made the attempt, accusations and blaming quickly escalated to heated arguments.

MCRS score using the McSiff – Communication = 2

Affective Responsiveness

No sub-component of this dimension was considered problematic, although Mr. and Mrs. J acknowledged that their anger was escalating. Both were able to respond with a full range of emotions: fear, anger, happiness, pleasure, concern, sadness. When the interviewer asked questions, the patient and his wife were quite willing and able to give examples of when they felt certain emotions and what triggered them.

MCRS score using the McSiff – Affective Responsiveness = 6

Affective Involvement

Family members were neither appropriate nor effective in specific areas of this dimension. The couple, as well as their older son, had become overly involved with each other. Although the son tried to be helpful to his parents, his helpfulness became excessive. Both he and his mother would nag his father, become too close, and not give the patient enough space.

MCRS score using the McSiff – Affective Involvement = 3

Clinical Use

The therapist used the results of the McSiff to focus both himself and the family members on a number of important issues. Although Mr. and Mrs. J had poor communication skills and very different personality styles, they had managed to work out a system over the years that had kept them together as a family. That system became increasingly problematic when Mr. J retired several years ago. The more pressing issue for this family and the underlying catalyst for seeking help with family problems was dealing with the early stages of Mr. J's illness. Mr. J and his family had great difficulty in accepting his diagnosis of Alzheimer's disease.

Since their affective responsiveness was appropriate and in the healthy range, the therapist was able to have constructive family sessions in which all family members confronted their feelings of fear, anxiety, and anger over the looming illness. The clinician educated the family about Mr. J's depression, Alzheimer's disease, how the two illnesses contributed to Mr. J's problems, and how the family could set realistic expectations for themselves as the disease progressed. With the therapist's help, the family enrolled Mr. J in a senior day care center for two afternoons a week. The improvement in Mr. J and in the family as a whole was so marked that they decided to increase his participation to three days a week. This gave all family members much needed space, lessened the unhealthy over-involvement of the older son, and took some pressure off Mr. J from feeling like he had to conceal his forgetfulness and memory lapses.

During the holidays Mr. J did not attend the senior center for two weeks. His continuous presence in the house, the increased holiday stress, and more than the usual number of visitors had an immediate negative impact on the family's functioning. In a positive sense, however, the family realized in a subsequent family session how important the day care program was for each of them. They learned how to communicate their concerns in a direct and positive manner and how to focus on a particular problem or issue. Finally, they realized that their overall family functioning would likely change from time to time and it was up to each family member to communicate their concerns if and when changes occurred. They learned how to fight fair when they had an issue and to let things go that were not important.

The first two case studies presented in this chapter were managed by experienced clinicians with different backgrounds (one a trained family therapist, one a clinical social worker), while the last case was managed by a psychiatrist being trained in the McMaster approach. The following section highlights how the supervisor took advantage of the guidelines set up by the McSiff to teach a clinician how to assess a family's functioning and how to use that assessment when conducting family therapy.

Teaching Use

The therapist, relatively new at applying family therapy, used the model (with supervision) to stay focused on key problems, get input from each family member, and work together to resolve the issues. He used results from the McSiff to decide what specific components of a dimension were problematic. He recognized how the family was avoiding dealing with Mr. J's diagnosis of Alzheimer's and he used the McMaster approach to encourage each family member to state their feelings and concerns. Therapists in supervision learn how to focus on different aspects of a family's dynamics, how the family's functioning affects and is affected by a patient's illness, and how he or she can systematically address issues and problems that the family faces. In this case, the McMaster approach was useful in drawing out and having the family discuss an emerging family problem, the onset of a degenerative illness. They did so within the context of a family meeting. By using the McMaster framework, the family learned how they could address current and future problems.

Beginning therapists need a common set of guidelines to draw upon so they can frame their clinical discussions during supervision. The McMaster approach provides this common framework and the McSiff helps trainees become proficient in conducting family interviews and learning the fundamentals of the model. When using the McSiff, the trainee feels secure that he/she will not miss any important areas of family life, allays anxiety by providing structure when interviewing several family members at once, and keeps the therapist in control in what can become a highly charged situation. The McSiff provides a structured format, somewhat like a mental status examination of the family, which helps the trainee pinpoint family problems. The family often responds to a structured interview by calming down. Once the family understands the reasoning for the interview and is assured that each member will get a chance to air their opinion, they become interested in the process itself and begin to listen to each other. The family also responds to the clinician's interest in the total family system and often provides valuable insights on the family's functioning.

The McSiff helps trainees avoid getting bogged down in particular problems before understanding the family. Once they see the family's pattern of functioning in different areas of their lives, the trainee can address the broader, underlying questions. In the case presented above specific problems, such as the patient's poor excuses for doing work, the son's intrusiveness, and the wife's complaints could have all been addressed without tackling the main underlying issue, their complete avoidance of the onset and impact of a major health problem. By stepping back and looking at the total system, the therapist was able to gain a better understanding of the family and determine the most effective therapeutic path.

Concluding Remarks

The FAD, MCRS, and McSiff are the three assessment tools developed and used by our group for teaching, research, and clinical purposes. As the oldest and easiest to administer, the FAD is also the most widely used instrument of the three. Increasing use of the MCRS and the McSiff suggest the growing interest and needs of many clinicians to assess and treat families. Researchers use the MCRS and the McSiff to obtain objective views of a family's functioning. Trainee supervisors see the value of the McSiff as one way of helping therapists and interviewers maintain a focus on family issues. We do not see one instrument as being better than another, but as complementary. Clinicians and researchers need different tools to help map out family problems; these instruments provide a mental status examination of the family system through a subjective or objective perspective. While providing a framework with which to approach family assessment and treatment, these instruments do not replace good clinical sense. Just as a bad clinician disregards what the family says (or any input revealed by assessments), a good clinician will take these reports into account but will also exercise sound clinical judgment.

CHAPTER 6

Research Using
the McMaster Model

Background

Three major questions guided our research over the past several decades. First, we wanted to know if there were differences in family functioning between normal families and families in which one member has a psychiatric or nonpsychiatric, medical illness. Our clinical impression that there were differences needed to be examined systematically. Second, we wanted to test the assumption that a family's functioning had a measurable impact on a patient's course of illness. Third, we wanted to test the PCSTF, the family treatment approach that was based on the MMFF.[50] Before addressing these questions, we needed to develop a set of constructs that were reliable, valid, clinically meaningful, and empirically testable. Epstein and his colleagues embarked on a series of studies described in previous chapters. As we noted, clinicians and researchers worked together in an iterative process, testing, questioning, and refining concepts until satisfied with a prototype of a family functioning model, a treatment approach, and research assessments. These prototypes were used to address part of the first question listed above, that is, family functioning in normal families. Readers can appreciate the complexity of the issues involved when a series of studies was needed just to address what constitutes normality.[1,7,51,52]

Once we built the framework for a valid and reliable model, and instruments to assess the model, we were free to examine family functioning of families across a wide spectrum and in a variety of contexts. We compared family functioning in families in which a member had a psychiatric illness, a medical illness, or both. We analyzed the family's functioning in families with a member who had a specific illness (e.g., major depression, rheumatoid arthritis) or a specific clinical characteristic such as suicidality or stroke. We conducted both short- and long-term follow-up studies and examined the relationship between family functioning and course of illness. We examined different stages of the illness (acute, 6-, 12-, and 60-month follow-up) to look at questions that were cross-sectional in nature and we used several time points to analyze longitudinal issues. Our studies included families with a member hospitalized for an illness, family members treated as outpatients, and community controls. We compared family functioning across different cultural groups. Finally, we analyzed data by individual family member characteristics such as role (patient, parent, caregiver), gender, and marital status.

The knowledge that we gained from these studies, together with clinical insights derived from our experience with families, led us to several conclusions regarding families and their functioning that, we believe, have important clinical implications. In this chapter, we list the conclusions (see Table 6.1) and, after outlining basic principles of our research perspective, report on the studies from which we drew our conclusions. As we present our research program, it will become clear how we moved from reporting impressionistic observations in our earliest work to presenting quantifiable and more sophisticated analyses in later studies. Besides incorporating our own and others' research findings into our work, we also took advantage of new research techniques and methodologies as they developed in the field. Throughout all our research endeavors, we continue to keep a strong clinical-research connection by grounding our work with empirical validation and making sure that the conclusions we reach from our findings make clinical sense.[11]

After reviewing these conclusions in depth, we describe a series of treatment studies that we initiated using the McMaster approach, discuss our findings, and address research gaps, limitations of our work, and future directions.

Basic Principles

We begin by introducing our overall perspective of conducting research so that our methodological approach is clear.

1. *Subjective and objective perspective.* We view these perspectives as complimentary pieces of a puzzle rather than as opposing viewpoints. The FAD measures the family's perspective of their functioning while the MCRS and McSiff capture an outsider's (the clinician or the interviewer) rating. Depending on the research question, one approach

Table 6.1 Research Conclusions Using the McMaster Model

1. Systemic factors of the family system—such as structural, organizational, and transactional variables—are powerful determinants of the psychosocial development of family members.

2. A family characterized by dysfunctional family functioning does not necessarily indicate that all (or any) individual family member(s) has significant psychopathology.

3. The fact that an individual has a psychiatric illness does not necessarily mean that his or her family's functioning is dysfunctional.

4. Families with a member who has a psychiatric illness report significant impairment in their family's functioning, particularly at the acute stage of an illness episode.

5. Family functioning is related to a patient's course of illness, including the patient's suicidality, length of illness episode, and probability of recovery.

6. There is no one dimension or specific cluster of dimensions of family functioning that predicts healthy/unhealthy family functioning or that is consistently related to outcome of a specific psychiatric disorder.

7. Poor family functioning can manifest itself in any dimension. To date we have not found a prototypical family type that is representative of poor family functioning in any given disorder.

8. Families with a medically ill member generally report less problematic family functioning than families with a psychiatrically ill member, but more dysfunction than nonclinical families.

9. Family functioning is dynamic. A family's functioning may vary over time, by stage of family development, by stage of illness (acute vs. chronic), or by change in family role (e.g., patient, caregiver).

---

may be more or less appropriate. Most of our research findings are based on the FAD, as it is the oldest of our instruments and the easiest to use. Many of our more recent studies have included the MCRS (obtained by a clinician rating or through the use of the McSiff by a trained rater) and the FAD. By collecting both ratings we are able to compare the perspectives and address specific questions geared to a specific perspective. To date, we have found neither the FAD nor the MCRS to be a better or a more consistent predictor of illness course. Although we expect some correlation between subjective and objective ratings (i.e., particularly good or particularly poor functioning families), we do not expect that subjective and objective ratings will match completely.

2. *Cross-sectional vs. longitudinal analyses.* Both of these approaches to data analysis have strengths and weaknesses and can be reasonable choices depending on the questions being asked, the data that are available, and the time frame of the study. Our research encompasses both

types of analyses. In our more recent work, we emphasize course of illness questions and therefore have followed subjects through longer-term follow-up periods.

3. *Episodic vs. chronic illnesses.* Illnesses have different natural histories that may include acute, recurrent, and/or chronic stages. For example, some forms of depression may be chronic, while others may be episodic with periods of wellness interspersed with episodes of depression. Stroke may be conceived as an acute period of distress followed by a stage of adjustment. Dementia may be characterized as long, deteriorating, and chronic. Research questions may target the acute phase, short- or long-term adjustment to the illness, and various levels of adaptation. In all of these conditions, the natural history of the illness needs to be taken into account to understand the role of family functioning and its relation to expected outcome. We have examined both chronic and episodic illnesses as well as different lengths of follow-up periods. We are careful to include these details in each article as they circumscribe the conclusions we draw and often suggest a new series of research questions.

4. *Analyzing family functioning.* In the previous chapter we explained how scores are derived for each of the McMaster instruments. With the FAD, equal weight is given to each family member's perception, regardless of role in the family or patient–nonpatient status. With the MCRS, each family member's opinion is solicited, but in some areas of family functioning, more weight is given to the adult's perception (e.g., child development issues) than to the child's perception. In either case, each family receives a rating on each family dimension. However, because of the complexity in analyzing family functioning, we typically use several methods of analysis. We begin our analysis by looking at each of the six dimensions defined in the MMFF and the overall, general functioning score. We examine the family dimension scores as continuous measures and as dichotomous, using the established healthy/unhealthy cut-off points. We do so for both the FAD and the MCRS. If we are interested in comparing functional vs. dysfunctional families, we use the established cut-off scores of the overall, general functioning scale to divide the sample. In any analysis in which we are restricted to using one family functioning score (for methodological or design reasons), we usually choose the general functioning scale as it provides us with a snapshot of the family's overall functioning.

When possible, we prefer to use both subjective (FAD) and objective (MCRS) ratings to give us a more complete family picture. Although the MCRS interview and the FAD instrument yield one score per dimension for each family, the FAD scores can be broken down to obtain the perspective of each individual family member on each family dimension. This strategy provides us with the opportunity to compare patient vs. family perspectives (i.e., discrepancy scores) when one member is in an episode of illness. We also use individual scores to compare perspectives of family functioning by family role (e.g., husband, wife, caregiver, parent, child), gender, and marital status. Increasingly, we have moved towards initiating longitudinal follow-up studies that involve change in family functioning over time. First we examined change in family functioning over two or three points in time in a series of naturalistic studies. More recently, we have undertaken a series of long-term treatment studies that include multiple data points, multiple treatment arms, and several study phases. In these studies we are interested not only in how the family's functioning changes over time, but also in the effect that including a patient's family in the treatment process has on the course of the patient's illness or the adjustment of the patient to his or her illness condition.

We typically use FAD dimension scores to make statistical comparisons between or within families (or groups) and reserve FAD items for content analysis. This approach is particularly helpful when trying to understand and interpret cross-cultural comparisons. Clinicians use FAD items to initiate discussions on family agreements and differences, clarify issues, and demonstrate how members within one family can have several opinions on the same topic.

Because several statistical applications may be appropriate to address a research question, and because methodologies change over time, we do not specify a particular statistical technique to use when examining family functioning. Rather, we look for continuing advances made in the field of methodology so that we are able to tackle new research questions—or apply a new approach to an old question. In the review that follows it is clear how our methodology matured, enabling us to address increasingly difficult research questions over time.

5. *Causal direction.* The causal relationship between family functioning and course of illness is unclear. On one hand, it may be that a family member's illness negatively impacts on a family's functioning. On the other hand, problematic family relationships may precipitate the emergence of or exacerbate a medical or psychiatric illness, or may delay recovery from an illness episode. Viewed from another angle, one might argue that the perception of good family functioning is merely a reflection of a patient's recovery. Our clinical and research experience suggests that good family functioning may contribute to a patient's recovery, shorten the length of an episode, prevent or delay

recurrence or relapse—all increasing the "well-time" of a patient. Although we will present data to support these conclusions, we are careful not to infer causality.

Our interest in the causal link is less on what comes first (poor family functioning or an episode of illness) and more on how we can use the family's functioning to provide patients and family members the best possible treatment outcome. In addition to symptomatic improvement, quality of life and interpersonal relationships may improve. It may be that the best outcome is helping a family cope better or establish stability in the family.

These analytic perspectives are complex parts of any research undertaking, and are part of ongoing debates in the field of research methodology. We choose the best available methods to analyze our data and address research questions of interest. Because we are aware of the strengths and weaknesses of research designs or data limitations, we tend to be conservative in drawing conclusions and stating research and clinical implications. We view research as part of an ongoing process in which we continue to learn and build on previous work. As Lebow has suggested "Good research proceeds in a stepwise fashion, building a base of findings that may take decades to fully explicate."[53] We fully agree with this statement and try to take a hard and honest examination of our data. In the end, this approach helps us to adjust our thinking and develop a truer, more comprehensive and valid treatment and assessment model.

Early Studies

Our first major work on families began in 1955. In a series of studies based at McGill University, Epstein, Westley, and a group of researchers sought to discover which factors in families produced mentally healthy members. This was an extensive data gathering phenomenological exercise studying nonclinical families in great depth. The material that was gathered was replete with rich, anecdotal detail of a very broad range of family transactional processes and dynamics. The final report was completed in 1964 and published in *The Silent Majority*,[10] a volume of work that became the forerunner of much of our later research.

The instruments, hypotheses, and approaches of our studies in the late 1950s and early 1960s were considered high caliber at the time. Viewed from today's vantage point, the methodology is much less sophisticated than the studies that we are now involved in. Early researchers had the freedom to follow leads in almost any direction of family life when conducting family interviews. There were almost no limits on the range of data that could be gathered in these interviews. The research group was free to speculate, theorize, interpret, test ideas, and draw inferences. Using data that they were able to extract from these in-depth interviews, Epstein and his colleagues developed a classification system in which they described a series of dimensions of family life that seemed crucial in understanding a family's functioning. Studying these families in juxtaposition to treating families in clinics, they were able to discuss a critical gap in family systems theory, that is, normal family functioning.

One advantage of working with nonclinical and clinical families simultaneously was that it helped the researchers clarify concepts of normality and pathology through exposure to a wide range of family types and family functioning. Defining a workable and pragmatic conceptualization of the term "normal family functioning" involved much discussion and research that is summarized in Walsh.[52] Ultimately, Epstein and colleagues felt it useful to equate the notion of a normal family with that of a healthy functioning family. This basic and necessary conceptual development had both theoretical and practical consequences. It helped provide a basic framework within which to place family types and it helped in later establishing the idea of healthy/unhealthy cut-off points that could have meaning and relevance for both clinicians and researchers. It also led to an appreciation of the strengths that families had and how clinicians could use those strengths to improve a family's functioning. We sometimes use the terms functional and dysfunctional to make the same distinction between families.

A second advantage to working with clinical and nonclinical families was the ability to question long-held assumptions. For instance, it had been assumed in the family therapy field that ineffective families had more problems or stressors than families that functioned effectively. Our studies actually suggested that families encountered the same range of difficulties, but that families differed in the approach taken to resolve problems. Problems might refer to day-to-day issues, chronic stressors, or family crises. Families that were able to function effectively were able to solve their problems while families characterized by ineffective functioning dealt with their problems only partially or not at all.[54] For example, some families were able to recognize a problem but were unable to decide on appropriate actions to resolve the problem. Other families were not able to act on the proposed solution or were not able to even recognize a problem existed. It became clear that the process involved in problem solving actually is made up of several discrete steps. The steps that a family takes to manage the problem—including what and how they define the problem—became incorporated into the McMaster assessments of family functioning and in the PCSTF. The key became the manner or process in which families handle the problem.

As work continued with both types of families (clinical and nonclinical), clinicians and researchers were able to conceptualize desirable patterns of family functioning. Describing the family in terms of power allocation, division of labor, patterns of intrafamilial affective involvement and expression, and communication allowed for a clear representation of family organization. These family dimensions were first presented as a classification system called the Family Category Schema which evolved into the MMFF. We noted earlier that the final model had to have clear, measurable concepts so that we could tests our ideas empirically and provide a theoretical schema that was transferable to other researchers and clinicians. We began to test the model.

Several important findings emerged from our early studies. First, methods of allocating power and sharing tasks and responsibilities correlated with indices of emotional health of individual family members. Second, we found that the open expression of positive welfare emotions had an important effect on an individual's development while the uncontrolled expression of rage and hostility was destructive. Further, families that had developed techniques to openly express anger in a controlled, yet tactful fashion had positive outcomes. Taken together, these observations led to the formulation of one of the first conclusions based on empirical data.

1. **Systemic factors of the family system—such as structural, organizational, and transactional variables—are powerful determinants of the psychosocial development of family members.**

Clinical Implication. This conclusion is the basis of our rationale for providing family assessment and family treatment. It draws attention to the relationship between the individual and the family system. The conclusion suggests that the family—a major component of the social environment—may have as much to do with creating disturbances in the functioning of the family as does an individual's psychopathology. In addition, the functioning of a family influences an individual's behavior and feelings within the family. This conclusion is in accord with the tenet that the whole is greater than the sum of its parts. However, it is important to keep in mind that the statement also refers to the relative power of the variables. That is, emphasizing a family system does not negate the contribution of psychological, interpersonal, development, or other individual factors that are part of the system. In fact, the qualitative assessment of the data collected through family interviews underscored the importance of being able to distinguish a poor functioning family from the psychopathology of individual family members.

The psychopathology of a parent(s) in some families had minimal correlation with either the emotional health of the children or with the overall functioning of the family as a unit. A positive, loving, and supportive family environment blunted the potentially destructive effects of severe intrapsychic pathology in any individual family member. More important than any individual pathology, ". . . the way in which a family organized itself and functioned as a unit was both a consequence and a cause of the mental health or illness of family members."[10] The key factor to the family's functioning appeared to be the emotional climate maintained in the family system.

The combination of strong support, genuine concern and loving care, along with an absence of destructive comments or chronic hostility provided a foundation able to withstand strain from within or outside the family group and protected the ongoing relationships and development of family members. Any family system, *regardless of its composition,* was able to establish a healthy functioning family by maintaining a supportive environment that was satisfactory to all family members and at the same time allow for disagreements. For any family with children, the establishment and maintenance of appropriate adult–child boundaries was noted to be critical. Once we made a clear, conceptual distinction between a family's functioning and the psychopathology of individual family members, we were able to examine the data and come to two separate, but related conclusions.

2. **A family characterized by dysfunctional family functioning does not necessarily indicate that all (or any) individual family member(s) has significant psychopathology.**

Clinical Implication. The fact that a family's functioning is poor does not justify the assumption that individuals within the family are disturbed or pathological. It is the interrelationship within the family that is dysfunctional. Individuals making up the family system may all be healthy, but they cannot handle the family's problems. Also, the dysfunction may be due to a series of setbacks or changes within the family system (e.g., loss of job, death, divorce, marriage or re-marriage, retirement, ill health) that put undue stress on family interrelationships. The dysfunction may be temporary or permanent, and it may affect all parts of the family system or only a few areas of family life. A complete and thorough family assessment will help to determine the appropriate therapeutic intervention.

3. **An individual's psychiatric illness does not necessarily indicate that his or her family's functioning is poor.**

Clinical Implication. When the research group first drew this conclusion, it was in direct contrast to the prevailing assumption in psychiatry that if a patient was sick, it must be because the family was dysfunctional. It was felt that the family was the most likely cause to explain the patient's sickness. By combining clinical and research data, Epstein's research group showed that many families of patients with a psychiatric illness were able to cope quite well. There was no reason to blame the family or assume that the patient's illness was caused by the family or by the family's dysfunction. In contrast, by evaluating the family's functioning, a clinician could draw on, support, and reinforce the family's coping skills rather than undermine them. This theme is one of the major premises of the McMaster approach to treating families.

These first three conclusions were important in the sense that they set the stage for the clinical and research work that was to ensue over the next several decades. In fact, the clinical implications of these findings led to the formulation of the next research question: Could a therapeutic reordering of the organizational, structural, and transactional patterns bring about a healthy result in clinically presenting families? Clinical sense and anecdotal experience suggested that it was indeed possible to intervene therapeutically in a family's functioning and thereby affect an individual family member. In order to answer the research question, Epstein and his colleagues needed to focus as much as possible on one or another of the organizational or structural variables as they had defined them. They needed empirical validation of their clinical impressions and the conclusions that were drawn, a larger and more varied sample than their earliest studies, and replication of their findings with new groups of patients. Clearly, there was much work to be done.

Naturalistic Follow-Up Studies— Populations with Psychiatric Illness

The early studies from which these conclusions were drawn continued when Epstein and a core group of clinicians/researchers moved to McMaster University in Hamilton, Ontario. Drawing on the initial findings from McGill, and supplemented by studies done at McMaster, the group concentrated on developing, testing, and refining the model, treatment approach, manuals, and assessments. The iterative process between clinicians and researchers yielded clearly defined concepts, a step-by-step treatment manual, a self-report assessment, and a prototype for the objective, clinician rating scale. Although membership of the clinical/research team shifted during each move, Epstein kept the focus on developing the family therapy model as well as the family research and training programs. At each site the overall aims of the research remained clear: to understand how a family functions, how the functioning could affect the course of a patient's illness, how the illness could affect a family's functioning, and, ultimately, on how family interventions could help both patient and family members.

Building on previous work, the team that gathered at Brown initiated several studies of family functioning that addressed these questions in a variety of patient groups. In doing so, the new team of family researchers satisfied needs that had been identified earlier, namely, empirically testing the impressionistic findings that had led to the early conclusions, acquiring a large data base of patients and family members, and recruiting subjects diagnosed with medical and/or psychiatric illnesses. These studies provided quantitative support for the conclusions listed above and led to several findings that are discussed below. In addition, results from one set of studies generated questions and ideas that led to new, but related, clinical and research issues.

One of the first studies carried out by the Brown Family Research Program compared family functioning among families of a diverse group of psychiatric patients and a matched nonpsychiatric control group[55] (see Table 6.2). We used the FAD to examine the functioning of families in which one member was hospitalized with a diagnosis of a DSM-III disorder: major depression, schizophrenia, alcoholism, adjustment disorder and bipolar disorder (manic phase). DSM-III diagnoses were based on an independent chart review by three experienced psychiatrists. Patients were included after receiving one of the above diagnoses and were excluded if they met criteria for a concurrent psychiatric illness. Any discrepancy between the three reviewers was decided through consensus. Results of this study indicated that families of psychiatric patients reported significantly impaired family functioning when compared to nonclinical families. In general, the most consistent and severe impairments were found in the families of patients with major depression, alcoholism, and adjustment disorder. Families of schizophrenic and bipolar patients showed less significant disturbances. When we excluded the patient's score from the mean family score, there were no significant changes in the severity or in the pattern of impairment.[55] The conclusion we drew from this set of analyses was:

4. **Families with a member who has a psychiatric illness report significant impairment in their family's functioning, particularly at the acute stage of an illness episode.**

Clinical Implication. Although psychiatric illness does not automatically indicate dysfunctional families (# 3 above), it is also true that a significant proportion of families of psychiatrically ill patients report family problems, particularly at the acute phase of the illness. Family members may be under increased stress during an acute phase of an episode, they may become more aware of family issues and the interaction with a patient's course of illness, or they may be more likely to seek help for their families while attending to

Table 6.2 Family Functioning in Families With and Without a Psychiatrically Ill Member[55]*

	Schizophrenia 18	Major Depression 22	Bipolar Manic 15	Alcohol Dependence 19	Adjustment Disorder 12	Control 23
N of Families	18	22	15	19	12	23
Problem Solving						
Mean (sd)	2.18 (.50)	2.50 (.66)	2.38 (.50)	2.42 (.52)	2.28 (.35)	1.98 (.32)
% Unhealthy	44.4	72.7	53.3	63.2	58.3	26.1
Communication						
Mean (sd)	2.22 (.27)	2.50 (.42)	2.19 (.50)	2.44 (.33)	2.39 (.44)	2.08 (.34)
% Unhealthy	50.0	86.4	60.0	94.7	75.0	34.8
Roles						
Mean (sd)	2.31 (.27)	2.49 (.30)	2.44 (.33)	2.33 (.25)	2.36 (.41)	2.11 (.28)
% Unhealthy	44.4	68.2	66.7	47.4	58.3	26.1
Affective Responsiveness						
Mean (sd)	2.30 (.50)	2.58 (.57)	2.25 (.44)	2.28 (.57)	2.21 (.47)	1.93 (.46)
% Unhealthy	38.9	77.3	60.0	57.4	58.3	26.1
Affective Involvement						
Mean (sd)	2.08 (.48)	2.57 (.52)	2.13 (.34)	2.38 (.57)	2.46 (.58)	1.93 (.46)
% Unhealthy	50.0	86.4	53.3	79.0	83.8	26.1
Behavior Control						
Mean (sd)	1.94 (.45)	2.45 (.51)	2.11 (.49)	2.27 (.45)	2.18 (.50)	1.76 (.34)
% Unhealthy	44.4	81.8	60.0	73.7	75.0	30.4
General Functioning						
Mean (sd)	2.12 (.42)	2.53 (.62)	2.22 (.48)	2.40 (.41)	2.27 (.36)	1.79 (.39)
% Unhealthy	61.1	86.4	73.3	89.5	83.3	26.1

* Based on the self-report measure, FAD. Family scores, excluding the patient.

the patient's illness. The clinician can expect that families may evince more problems during times of crisis, but needs to be mindful not to make causal inferences. With the family's help, the clinician can distinguish between the family's reaction to the illness of a patient and the typical pattern of family functioning—either before the onset of illness or when the patient is not in episode. This does not imply that the therapist avoids any family problems in relation to the patient's overall course of illness, acute phase, or hospitalization. But in addition to what may or may not have precipitated the crisis, the therapist does need to be aware of what is representative of the family's long-term functioning.

Given the difficulties in family functioning at the acute stage of the illness, a logical question for the research team was to determine what happened to a family's functioning over time and in relation to the course of the patient's illness. Several studies looking at short- and long-term course of illness have helped us address these questions. Although most of our studies have focused on patients with a depressive disorder or bipolar illness, we have also examined family functioning in medically ill patients.

We followed a group of patients hospitalized with major depression (N = 28) and their family members over a 12-month period after discharge from hospital.[56] Families of the depressed patients were matched with nonclinical control families on family stage and socioeconomic status. With one exception (behavior control), families with a depressed member reported significantly worse family functioning at the acute stage of illness compared to the nonclinical families. By 12 months post-discharge, family functioning improved for the families in which the patient recovered from their depression. Despite improvement, families with a depressed member continued to report difficulties in three areas of family life (problem solving, communication, and general functioning). These ratings remained significantly different from the nonclinical families (see Figure 6.1). When we examined time to recovery, there was no difference between patients whose family functioning at the acute stage was good vs. those whose family functioning was poor. If family members saw improvement in their family's functioning, however, the patient recovered faster than if family members saw no improvement. The relationship between perceived improvement and recovery held for all dimensions, but reached significance in the areas of affective involvement and in the family's overall functioning.[56]

These findings provided empirical evidence of an association between family functioning and course of a depressive illness. The results provided us with questions for another study. We wanted to know if a family's functioning differed when a patient was diagnosed with major depression only versus if the patient was depressed and had a concurrent illness (either

FAMILY FAD SCORE – FOR PATIENTS AT ACUTE STAGE

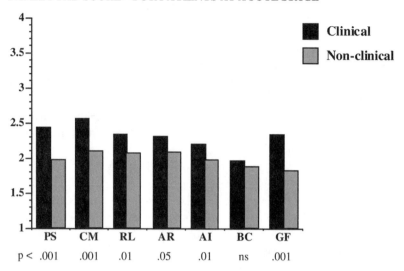

FAMILY FAD SCORE – FOR PATIENTS WHO RECOVERED

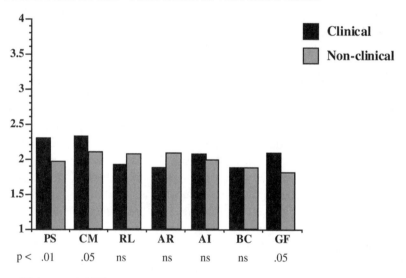

*Keitner et al, 1987

The higher the score the worse the functioning

Figure 6.1 Clinical Families at Acute and Recovery versus Matched Non-Clinical Controls.*
The higher the score, the worse the functioning.

medical or psychiatric). Additionally, we were interested to see how objective ratings of family functioning compared to subjective ratings—and how both were related to the course of illness. Finally, we wanted to explore these questions more systematically and with a different, and larger, sample. We recruited 78 patients hospitalized with a diagnosis of major depression. Data capturing depressive symptomatology, family functioning, and recovery status were collected at the acute, six- and twelve-month phases of this naturalistic study. Two experienced clinicians, blind to the family's functioning, confirmed the diagnosis of depression. Therapists trained in the McMaster approach provided objective family functioning ratings using the MCRS. The Modified Hamilton Rating Scale for Depression[57] was used to determine recovery status. Several research reports, focusing on different aspects of the study, were generated from this research.[58-63]

Like our earlier study, we found that families reported poor family functioning on several family dimensions at the acute stage of the episode. Despite improvement over time, families still perceived difficulties in their functioning at the six-month follow-up period. Communication, in particular, was rated poorly both subjectively and objectively (see Table 6.3). Families of patients whose depression was compounded by other illnesses reported worse family functioning than families in which the depressed patient had no concurrent illness. The differences reached significance only in the area of problem solving. Objective ratings suggested that the family functioning of patients with a comorbid illness was significantly worse in the area of behavior control compared to the family functioning of patients with major depression only. Of interest, correlation analysis showed better agreement between subjective and objective measures of family functioning when the patient's depression was compounded by other illnesses. It may be that when the number of problems reach a certain magnitude, it is easier to identify poor family functioning or, conversely, more difficult to deny it.[58]

When we examined the data at 12 months, patients whose family functioning was rated poorly at the acute stage by both subjective and objectives measures had a significantly poorer course, characterized by lower recovery rates and poorer overall functioning scores[63] (see Figure 6.2). Since we found that patients with a comorbid condition had a more difficult course and were less likely to recover than patients with major depression only,[59] we examined these and other factors, simultaneously, to determine the overall effect on course of illness. The final model suggested that the odds of recovering from a major depressive episode requiring hospitalization was .94 (i.e., patients had a 50–50 chance of recovery). In order of importance, the five factors significantly associated with a patient's increased likelihood of recovery were: a shorter length of hospital stay, an older age at depression

Table 6.3 Subjective and Objective Ratings of Family Functioning with a Depressed Member[58]

Subjective Ratings – FAD

Families with good Functioning (n=22)	Acute phase x̄ (sd)	Follow-up phase 6 Months x̄ (sd)	12 Months x̄ (sd)
Problem Solving	1.94 (.29)	1.91 (.26)	1.98 (.37)
Communication	2.07 (.32)	2.05 (.37)	2.04 (.36)
Roles	2.11 (.26)	2.07 (.23)	2.09 (.31)
Affective Responsiveness	1.92 (.34)	1.89 (.37)	1.89 (.44)
Affective Involvement	1.89 (.42)	1.89 (.32)	1.88 (.35)
Behavior Control	**1.90** (.23)	1.82 (.35)	1.80 (.37)
General Functioning	1.71 (.24)	1.72 (.34)	1.78 (.34)

Families with poor Functioning (n=23)	Acute phase x̄ (sd)	6 Months x̄ (sd)	12 Months x̄ (sd)
Problem Solving	**2.36** (.34)	2.19 (.31)	2.04 (.28)
Communication	**2.49** (.26)	**2.38** (.31)	2.16 (.32)
Roles	2.25 (.31)	2.15 (.30)	2.04 (.28)
Affective Responsiveness	**2.38** (.48)	**2.24** (.47)	2.13 (.55)
Affective Involvement	2.17 (.32)	2.05 (.29)	1.98 (.39)
Behavior Control	1.98 (.34)	1.83 (.37)	1.77 (.29)
General Functioning	2.29 (.29)	**2.14** (.36)	1.95 (.32)

FAD score: the higher the score, the worse the functioning.
Bold number denotes unhealthy score according to FAD cutoffs.

Objective Ratings – MCRS

Families with good Functioning (n=10)	Acute phase x̄ (sd)	Follow-up phase 6 Months x̄ (sd)	12 Months x̄ (sd)
Problem Solving	5.50 (.85)	5.10 (1.20)	4.70 (1.16)
Communication	**4.70** (.95)	5.40 (.84)	4.40 (1.07)
Roles	5.40 (.97)	5.70 (.82)	5.00 (1.15)
Affective Responsiveness	4.90 (1.10)	5.33 (.50)	**4.60** (.84)
Affective Involvement	6.10 (.74)	5.70 (.95)	5.00 (1.25)
Behavior Control	5.80 (1.32)	5.50 (1.08)	5.40 (1.17)
General Functioning	5.40 (.52)	5.40 (.84)	4.90 (.99)

Families with poor Functioning (n=25)	Acute phase x̄ (sd)	6 Months x̄ (sd)	12 Months x̄ (sd)
Problem Solving	**3.28** (1.02)	**3.96** (1.37)	**3.60** (1.19)
Communication	**2.68** (1.03)	**3.44** (1.29)	**3.36** (1.08)
Roles	4.17 (1.40)	**4.44** (1.04)	**4.28** (1.21)
Affective Responsiveness	**3.32** (.95)	**3.76** (1.09)	**3.68** (.90)
Affective Involvement	**3.96** (1.24)	**4.60** (1.35)	**4.52** (1.26)
Behavior Control	**3.76** (1.69)	**4.52** (1.53)	**4.40** (1.55)
General Functioning	**3.20** (.76)	**3.88** (1.13)	**3.80** (.91)

MCRS score: the higher the score, the better the functioning.
Bold numbers denotes unhealthy score according to MCRS cutoffs.

Table 6.4 Risk Factors for Recovery at 12 Months of 65 Depressed Patients[60]

	Beta	SE	Exponential Beta	χ^2	p
Risk Factor					
Length of stay (days)	−.115	.056	.891	6.05	.01
Age of onset (years)	.057	.025	1.059	5.05	.03
FAD-General Functioning (1–4)	−1.779	.829	.169	4.61	.03
Number of previous hospitalizations					
(0 = none or one, 1 = two or more)	−1.799	1.026	.165	3.07	.08
Comorbidity (0 = no, 1 = yes)	−.978	.642	.376	2.32	.13

Model χ^2 (df = 5) = 28.7, L^2 = 61.27, p = .0001, R = .456, R^2 = .208 The risk factors associated with a better chance of recovery were: fewer days in hospital, older age of onset, better family functioning, fewer than 2 hospitalizations, no other comorbid psychiatric or medical condition.

onset, better family functioning, fewer than two previous psychiatric hospitalizations, and absence of a comorbid illness,[60] (see Table 6.4).

Since almost one-half of patients with a major depressive disorder will experience another episode in their lifetime,[64–66] we recontacted patients 5 years after they completed this study and 6 years after the index episode.

We already knew that, compared to patients with poor family functioning, patients with good family functioning at index were more likely to maintain their healthy functioning and recover from the depression within one year.[61] In addition, we found that improvement in family functioning in the first 6 months after discharge from hospital was strongly related to the patient's long-term course of illness.[62] With the exception of affective involvement, however, clinicians and family members differed in their assessment of which dimensions of family life improved significantly.

As data for these studies were being collected and analyzed, we reviewed another set of analyses which focused on comparisons between patients who were suicidal or nonsuicidal and their family members.[67,68] Family functioning was not significantly associated with suicidal behavior in patients hospitalized with major depression: there were no differences in family functioning between families with and without a member who attempted suicide. However, patients who attempted suicide saw their family functioning as significantly worse than patients who made no attempt. Also, compared to nonsuicidal patients and their family members, suicide attempters rated their family functioning significantly poorer than other family members. Suicide attempters also differed significantly from other family members when rating their family's functioning. Areas of functioning that were rated

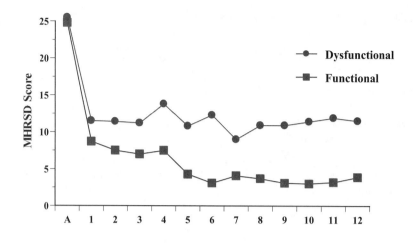

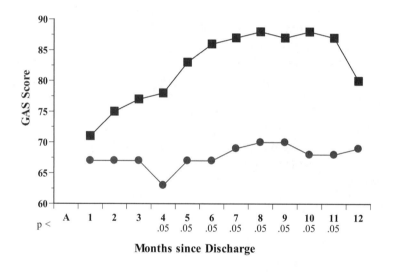

* Miller et al, 1992

Figure 6.2 Family Functioning Related to Depression (MHRS) and Overall Functioning (GAS) Scores Over TIme.*

significantly poorer by the suicide attempter group included problem solving, communication, roles, and general functioning (see Figure 6.3).

Although the findings from these two studies cannot be used to predict future suicidality, they suggest a probable link between family functioning and suicidality in depressed patients. The results indicate that a clinician

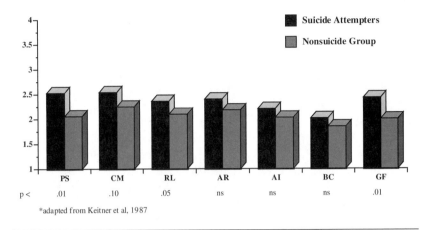

Figure 6.3 FAD Scores of Depressed Patients: Suicide Attempters versus Nonsuicide Group*

should assess the social environment of depressed patients and address any problematic family issues. In particular, it may be important for the clinician to understand the patient's view of his or her family's functioning, especially if it differs significantly from other family members. Results from these follow-up studies reinforced the conclusions that we drew from earlier work, but led us to another conclusion as well:

5.   **Family functioning is related to a patient's course of illness, including the patient's length of episode, recovery status, and suicidality.**

Clinical Implication. How the family understands and deals with the patient's illness has an impact on its course. Since the family may influence what happens to the patient, it may be important for the clinician to bring the family directly into the treatment process. If it is not possible for a family to engage in treatment (or the clinician feels it is unnecessary), a thorough evaluation of the patient and his or her family's functioning might at least help the clinician obtain a better grasp of the sources of strength and possible barriers to a patient's recovery. Because the patient's perspective may be distorted by the illness, a baseline evaluation with the entire family might be useful to the clinician in clarifying and obtaining additional information about the patient and his or her family environment. One or two family sessions might be followed by periodic family meetings as requested by the clinician, patient, or family members.

We have seen that good family functioning and/or improvement in family functioning is related to recovery for patients hospitalized with major depression. We also assessed family functioning in 199 outpatients who were

Table 6.5 Family Functioning in Acutely Depressed Inpatients and Chronically Depressed Outpatients[70]

FAD	Inpatient N = 197 (Mean, sd)	Outpatient N = 198 (Mean, sd)	p
Problem Solving	**2.36** (.55)	**2.45** (.57)	ns
Communication	**2.41** (.48)	**2.46** (.50)	ns
Roles	**2.37** (.43)	**2.43** (.41)	ns
Affective Responsiveness	**2.32** (.62)	**2.45** (.67)	.05
Affective Involvement	**2.20** (.51)	**2.25** (.46)	ns
Behavior Control	1.99 (.42)	1.93 (.40)	ns
General Functioning	**2.26** (.56)	**2.36** (.58)	.10

Bold numbers = unhealthy score

diagnosed with chronic major depression or double depression (i.e., patients whose dysthymia was exacerbated by a major depressive episode.[69] The baseline ratings of family functioning of this outpatient sample of clinically depressed patients were comparable to, or exceeded, the ratings of acutely depressed inpatients (see Table 6.5).

We analyzed data using patient scores only in two groups of the depressed outpatients, patients with chronic major depression vs. those with double depression. Patients with chronic major depression reported significantly worse family functioning in behavior control compared to patients diagnosed with double depression. At the end of 12 weeks of pharmacotherapy, these two groups of outpatients improved equally in their depressive symptomatology, but not in their perception of family functioning. Patients with double depression indicated less improvement in their perception of family functioning than did patients with chronic depression. Similar to our findings with inpatients, outpatients who recovered from their depression reported difficulties in their family's functioning, particularly in communication and general functioning, but also in problem solving and affective responsiveness.[70]

We pooled data from several research projects and re-examined the relationship between family functioning and psychiatric illness.[71] Families with a member diagnosed with a schizophrenic spectrum disorder, major depression, bipolar disorder, substance abuse, and adjustment disorder reported significantly higher levels of dysfunction compared to nonclinical control families in all family dimensions except behavior control. Families of patients with anxiety disorders and eating disorders also reported significant differences in family functioning from control families, but in fewer family dimensions. Unlike our earlier study that compared family functioning across several diagnostic groups,[55] Friedmann's report included patients with or without comorbid psychiatric illnesses. Patients and family members in all diagnostic categories consistently reported unhealthy functioning in problem solving, communication, affective involvement, and general functioning. Only families of patients with eating disorders reported areas of healthy functioning. Family dimensions which received the worst ratings differed by diagnostic group. That is, although a higher percentage of patients and family members reported most difficulties in the areas of communication and roles, patients within the schizophrenic spectrum reported more problems in the area of affective responsiveness. These findings are interesting because of the large sample size and the variety of diagnostic categories that are represented. Because patients may have had more than one psychiatric disorder, however, we cannot attribute specific areas of family dysfunction to specific illnesses.

Because it is common for patients to be diagnosed with more than one psychiatric or medical illness, we looked more closely at the relationship between concurrent illnesses and family functioning. We had already found that patients who had a primary diagnosis of major depression and a concurrent illness had worse family functioning and a smaller likelihood of recovery from depression than patients with no comorbid disorder.[58,59] We wondered if the kind or number of comorbid illnesses impacted on the likelihood of recovery from depression and on a family's functioning. We recruited 53 patients hospitalized with major depression and administered structured interviews to determine any coexistent Axis I (psychiatric illness) or Axis II (personality disorder). An internist, blind to the study hypotheses, reviewed each patient chart to determine the presence of any Axis III (i.e., medical) condition, including severity and chronicity. Depressed patients with no comorbid illness viewed their family's functioning better than depressed patients with a comorbid medical illness who, in turn, viewed their functioning better than depressed patients with another psychiatric illness or another psychiatric and medical illness. While family functioning scores improved by 6 months, patients still reported impairment in many family dimensions. Patients rated communication, roles, problem solving, and affective responsiveness as particularly difficult areas of family functioning.[62]

Although these studies provide additional support for the conclusions related to family functioning at the acute phase and over the course of the illness, we mentioned them for several other reasons. First, we found the comparability of scores of chronically depressed outpatients and acutely depressed inpatients interesting. Second, we wanted to point out that, depending on the study question and the population, different family dimensions may or may not prove significant. In one study communication and general functioning showed significant group differences. In another study problem solving was a particularly difficult dimension. Finally, we wanted to suggest different ways to approach data analysis and show how our thinking moved from the findings of one study to questions for another. For example, in an early study[55] we examined patients with different psychiatric diagnoses. In the pooled data analysis,[71] we used the primary diagnosis as the defining category. Results of these studies and reassessment of our patient population influenced our approach in the comorbid study. We used stricter criteria to define the primary and secondary diagnoses (through use of a structured interview and trained interviewers) and stricter criteria to arrive at the severity, chronicity, and diagnosis of the medical condition (through ratings made by an internist blind to psychiatric and family functioning ratings).

From the studies discussed above, as well as data analysis from all of our research, we suggest the following conclusion:

6. **There is no one dimension or specific cluster of dimensions of family functioning that predicts healthy or unhealthy family functioning, or that is consistently related to outcome of any disorder.**

Clinical Implication. Families are heterogeneous and, therefore, will have different strengths and weaknesses to work from. Since we have not found empirical evidence which points to any one dimension as a key that will unlock family problems, it is important that each clinician uses a systematic approach when conducting family assessments. In doing so, it will be less likely that the clinician takes a predetermined course based on his or her own bias (or favorite dimension) and more likely that he or she will find the strengths (and weaknesses) within each family system.

While these clinical studies were being conducted, we had the opportunity to work with colleagues from other cultures and other countries. When the McMaster approach was originally developed as a practical method of treating families presenting with a variety of problems we did not explicitly consider cross-cultural applications of the model and instruments. We found that the conceptual framework of the theory, model, treatment, and assessments did not preclude their use in other cultural settings. Once our ideas, research, and treatment approach were presented at national and international forums, clinical and research colleagues from around the world expressed an interest in learning more about the MMFF and PCSTF. We reported that the FAD has been translated into 20 different languages. The MCRS, McSiff, and the PCSTF are currently in the process of being translated into several languages (French, Hungarian, Italian, and Spanish).

Our research on cross-cultural family studies focused on depressed patients and their family members, because of our interest in this particular clinical area and the feasibility of collecting data rather than to any restrictions imposed by the model. In two studies we used the FAD to compare North American and Hungarian families with and without a depressed member.[72,73] We first translated and back-translated the FAD to ensure that the Hungarian FAD was reliable. In both cultural settings, families with a depressed member reported poorer family functioning than control families. The two depressed groups showed differences in their perceived family dysfunction that were more cultural than illness specific. In the control families, the two groups did not differ in their overall functioning nor in affective areas of family life. Differences were apparent in problem solving, communication, roles, and behavior control (see Table 6.6).

Results from these studies suggested that cultural values affect family life more than illness variables, and that apparent cross-cultural differences in family functioning could be captured using the FAD. Japanese colleagues[74] have since replicated our original studies with the FAD. We incorporated the ratings of perceived family functioning of depressed and nonclinical Japanese families with our own previously collected data.[75] While depressed

Table 6.6 Mean FAD Scores of Nonclinical and Clinical Families in Different Cultures[72,73–74]

Nonclinical Mean (sd)	Hungarian (N = 58)	Japanese (N = 27)	American (N = 95)
Problem Solving	1.71 (.30)[a]	1.97 (.33)[b]	1.86 (.34)[b]
Communication	1.84 (.41)[a]	1.96 (.32)[ab]	2.00 (.36)[b]
Roles	**2.37** (.30)[a]	1.97 (.30)[b]	2.06 (.29)[b]
Affective Responsiveness	1.93 (.54)[a]	2.14 (.39)[b]	1.90 (.48)[a]
Affective Involvement	1.96 (.30)[a]	**2.15** (.31)[b]	1.87 (.34)[a]
Behavior Control	**2.50** (.37)[a]	**2.02** (.30)[c]	1.74 (.31)[b]
General Functioning	1.77 (.39)[a]	1.82 (.27)[a]	1.71 (.36)[a]
Depressed Mean (sd)	(N = 62)	(N = 20)	(N = 118)
Problem Solving	1.84 (.39)[a]	**2.22** (.46)[b]	**2.36** (.48)[b]
Communication	2.04 (.39)[a]	2.16 (.34)[a]	**2.42** (.42)[b]
Roles	**2.34** (.28)[a]	2.11 (.29)[b]	2.32 (.40)[a]
Affective Responsiveness	2.16 (.54)[a]	**2.30** (.41)[a]	2.33 (.54)[a]
Affective Involvement	2.05 (.38)[a]	**2.22** (.28)[b]	2.19 (.42)[b]
Behavior Control	**2.57** (.32)[a]	**2.18** (.36)[c]	1.98 (.32)[b]
General Functioning	**2.22** (.42)[a]	**2.02** (.35)[a]	2.26 (.52)[b]

Numbers in bold denote unhealthy functioning. Different letters denote statistical differences. For example, Japanese and American families do not differ regarding their perception of problem solving, but do rate their problem solving as significantly worse than Hungarian families.

families in all three cultures experienced difficulties in their family's functioning, the nature of the family difficulties appears to be more specific to the culture than to the depression. Linking our findings from the cross-cultural work with our findings from years of research with a variety of clinical and nonclinical samples and settings led us to another conclusion.

7. **Poor family functioning can manifest itself in any dimension. To date we have not found a prototypical family type that is representative of poor family functioning in any given disorder or population group.**

Clinical Implication. It is very important to assess each family as a unique entity. Membership in a diagnostic category or cultural group does not predispose a family into certain types of weaknesses. The poor functioning shown by a family is based on the family, not on the illness or the ethnic category. Clinicians cannot presume a particular dimension is related to a particular illness or ethnicity. (We suspect these statements hold true for family type and social class as well, but have not systematically tested the assumption in a large scale community-based study.) This conclusion is similar to the previous one in that they both caution the clinician against taking short-cuts when conducting an evaluation.

Naturalistic Follow-Up Studies— Populations with Non-Psychiatric Illness

Although the bulk of our research has focused on patients with a psychiatric illness and their family members, we have also been interested in linking other chronic, debilitating, and relapsing, non-psychiatric illnesses with the family's functioning. As in studies with psychiatric populations, we felt that any illness, including a physical or non-psychiatric illness, could affect a family's functioning. The functioning of a family with a member who has a physical illness may, in turn, affect the course of the illness. In some cases (e.g., traumatic brain injury), the family may need to make radical adjustments in certain family dimensions, such as family roles or communication. In other cases (e.g., stroke rehabilitation), a family's functioning may be an important factor in treatment compliance. In all cases, it may be useful to conceptualize the family's functioning as an intermediate variable that acts between the stress of an illness and its medical impact on the patient, caregiver, and family members.

In one study, we compared FAD family functioning scores across different disability groups as well as between nonclinical and psychiatric populations.[76,77] When all of the disabled categories were grouped together, FAD scores were similar to the nonclinical control group. When we separated the groups into distinct disability categories, we were able to rank order the sample by the amount of perceived family dysfunction. Patients with lupus erythematosus or spinal cord injuries and their family members reported the most effective family functioning and were most similar to the nonclinical control families (see Table 6.7). Patients with rheumatoid arthritis and their family members ranked in an intermediate range, while those with multiple sclerosis (MS) or stroke were more likely to report less effective family functioning. Mean scores for these last two groups ranged between the mean scores of the nonclinical controls and the means for the psychiatric sample. Since cognitive disturbances are associated with both MS and stroke, it may be that cognitive and mental disturbances have the most deleterious effect on a family's functioning.

When we examined patients with a non-psychiatric disability, the role of the family caregiver was particularly relevant. One issue was how the caregiver functioned vis-à-vis the patient's illness, including his or her perception of burdens and rewards when caring for the patient. Another was how the family's functioning was affected by the illness, and whether the family made adjustments and maintained healthy functioning or became dysfunctional in one or more dimensions. Important factors we considered when looking at the relationship between family functioning and any non-psychiatric illness were the nature and severity of the illness and the length of time a family member assumed the caregiving role. In one study that focused on stroke patients,[78] we found no differences in family functioning scores between a community sample and a sample of stroke patients and their family members. A second study involving patients with a physical disability[79] also suggested no differences in perceived family functioning between the study sample and nonclinical controls.

Although caregivers of the disabled reported more anxious, depressive, and somatic symptoms, the level of symptomatology did not reach significance. When we controlled for duration of care giving, we found that those who provided care for a longer time reported significantly more family dysfunction than those whose caregiving was less than two years in duration (see Figure 6.4). Problem solving and communication were particularly prone to worsen and be less effective over time while type of disability did not account for deterioration in the family's functioning.

As noted earlier, one way to optimize patient care is by helping the patient adhere to treatment recommendations. We hypothesized that family functioning would directly and indirectly affect a patient's outcome by influencing his or her approach to treatment adherence.[80] We assessed a patient's treatment adherence as high or low and compared the adherence levels to the caregiver's perception of family functioning 5 months after a

Table 6.7 Family Functioning in Families with a Medically Ill Member

	Stroke	Lupus	Rheumatoid Arthritis	Multiple Sclerosis	Spinal Cord Injury	Cut-off Score*
Families	41	43	71	98	54	
Individuals						
Problem Solving						
Mean (sd)	1.95 (.45)	1.77 (.51)	1.88 (.43)	2.10 (.46)	1.90 (.44)	**2.20**
% Unhealthy	12.2	9.3	15.5	34.7	22.2	
Communication						
Mean (sd)	2.10 (.32)	2.08 (.44)	2.20 (.37)	2.21 (.47)	1.97 (.47)	**2.20**
% Unhealthy	31.7	37.2	47.9	56.1	27.8	
Roles						
Mean (sd)	2.15 (.27)	2.09 (.48)	2.22 (.35)	2.35 (.38)	2.15 (.38)	**2.30**
% Unhealthy	31.7	37.2	31.0	44.9	27.8	
Affective Responsiveness						
Mean (sd)	2.07 (.44)	2.02 (.56)	2.01 (.43)	2.24 (.53)	1.94 (.62)	**2.20**
% Unhealthy	26.8	32.6	26.8	51.0	33.3	
Affective Involvement						
Mean (sd)	2.04 (.42)	1.98 (.53)	1.98 (.44)	2.15 (.45)	1.83 (.45)	**2.10**
% Unhealthy	41.5	44.2	40.9	60.2	22.2	
Behavior Control						
Mean (sd)	2.01 (.35)	1.74 (.48)	1.88 (.43)	1.86 (.39)	1.76 (.42)	**1.90**
% Unhealthy	51.2	27.9	46.5	43.9	38.9	
General Functioning						
Mean (sd)	1.88 (.38)	1.83 (.46)	1.88 (.37)	2.05 (.48)	1.68 (.45)	**2.00**
% Unhealthy	53.7	44.2	35.2	55.1	29.6	

*FAD cut-off scores. Greater than or equal to cut-off = unhealthy family functioning.

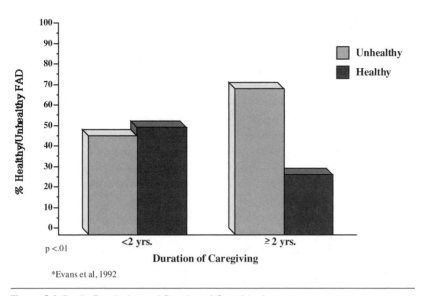

Figure 6.4 Family Functioning and Duration of Caregiving*

patient was discharged from a stroke unit. Families reporting good family functioning were more likely to report good treatment adherence. Differences were significant in problem solving, communication, affective involvement, and general functioning (see Table 6.8). Although treatment compliance is critical, other factors play a role in the rehabilitation of stroke patients. We examined stroke patients (N = 135) and their primary support persons in order to identify which factors interfere with optimal home care for patients who had undergone their first stroke.[81] Clinical, social, and family assessments (the general functioning scale of the FAD), collected at initial contact during hospitalization, were repeated at a 12 month follow-up visit. We divided the patients into whether or not they received successful home care and determined which factors best differentiated the groups. Depressive symptoms associated with the caregiver, lack of knowledge of stroke care, and poor family functioning all contributed to unsuccessful home care.

While the most direct method of affecting problematic family functioning may be addressing a family's issues through family therapy, alternate methods of treatment or counseling can also have a positive effect on a family's functioning. One study of stroke patients that did not specifically target family dysfunction or treatment using the McMaster approach nonetheless resulted in positive effects on the patient's family functioning.[82] Drawing on results of previous research, the study's focus was patient adjustment post-stroke as a function of caregiver knowledge, social resources, and family

Table 6.8 Relationship of Family Functioning to Treatment Adherence Ratings Five Months Post-Stroke[80] (N = 60)

Family Health		(n)	Adherence* High (30)	Low (30)	χ^2	p
FAD						
Problem Solving	Functional	(23)	28	10		
	Dysfunctional	(37)	22	40	7.05	.01
Communication	Functional	(28)	32	15		
	Dysfunctional	(32)	18	35	5.42	.02
Roles	Functional	(27)	23	22		
	Dysfunctional	(33)	27	28	.04	ns
Affective Responsiveness	Functional	(28)	25	22		
	Dysfunctional	(32)	25	28	.17	ns
Affective Involvement	Functional	(24)	33	7		
	Dysfunctional	(36)	17	43	15.6	.01
Behavior Control	Functional	(29)	22	27		
	Dysfunctional	(31)	28	23	.64	ns
General Functioning	Functional	(27)	30	15		
	Dysfunctional	(33)	20	35	4.31	.05

*percent of total sample

functioning. Targeting the caregiver, the three study conditions were: (1) routine clinical care of the patient (control group), (2) routine care of patient + two hours of educational classes for the caregiver, and (3) routine care of the patient + educational classes + seven individual counseling sessions. While perception of family functioning generally worsened over time, the deterioration in the two treatment arms was significantly less marked than in the control group. Furthermore, after an initial worsening in family functioning from baseline to 6 months, the subjects receiving education and counseling maintained or reported improvement in five of the seven areas of family functioning.

The control group reported continued deterioration in family functioning in all but communication while subjects in the education group fell in an intermediate position (see Table 6.9). In sum, we have found that families in which at least one member has a non-psychiatric, medical condition also have difficulties in one or more areas of family functioning. Family assessments may help to identify those families at risk who might benefit from early intervention.

8. **Families with a member who has a non-psychiatric physical illness generally report less problematic family functioning than families with a psychiatrically ill member, but more problematic family functioning than nonclinical families.**

Clinical Implication. Families of patients with physical illnesses may be vulnerable to stress or problems with family functioning, whether the illness condition is chronic, deteriorating, or waxes and wanes. Even though a family may appear to adjust to an acute crisis or hospitalization, the strain of caring for an ill family member may increase over time, thereby affecting the family's functioning, the patient's course of illness, and, possibly, other family members. Thus, in addition to treating a patient directly, a clinician may need to attend to symptom presentation in other family members (particularly the patient's caregiver), assess a family's functioning, and suggest a referral for family therapy if clinically indicated.

Several findings from studies we have done with physically ill, but non-psychiatric, patients mirror the results we have found in patients with a psychiatric illness. First, we found that differences in family functioning by illness condition are not statistically significant. Second, we found no empirical evidence that consistently links a specific family dysfunction with a specific non-psychiatric, physical illness. Finally, although there is support that healthy family functioning is associated with a better outcome for the patient, no individual family dimension stands out as the one, healthiest, or best, predictor of good family functioning.

There are at least two important differences in family functioning in our studies between families with a member who has a psychiatric vs. a non-psychiatric illness. First, in studies with psychiatric patients, the family's functioning was rated as significantly poorer than nonclinical control families. In contrast, perceptions of family functioning in families with a physically ill member were often similar to, or only slightly worse, than normal control populations at baseline. Second, family functioning often improves over time in families with a psychiatrically ill member whereas families with a physically ill member have reported deterioration in their family's functioning.

It may be that improvement or worsening in family functioning is related to a deteriorating versus an episodic course of illness rather than a psychiatric versus nonpsychiatric illness. Direct and indirect stressors of the physical illness may have negative effects on the family's functioning and circle back to affect the patient and other family members. The initial strength of a family's functioning may help to provide support to a patient and help him

Table 6.9 Comparisons of Study Intervention for Stroke Patients and Their Caregivers[82]

	Condition	Before Treatment	Time 6 Months After Stroke	1 Year After Stroke
FAD (N = 188)		(Mean, sd)	(Mean, sd)	(Mean, sd)
Problem Solving	Control	2.05 (.37)	2.27 (.35)	2.36 (.35)
	Education	2.03 (.40)	2.15 (.33)*	2.18 (.37)*
	Counseling	2.01 (.39)	2.11 (.39)*	2.11 (.44)*
Communication	Control	2.03 (.37)	2.32 (.35)	2.27 (.40)
	Education	1.98 (.39)	2.17 (.33)*	2.13 (.44)*
	Counseling	2.05 (.44)	2.15 (.37)*	2.08 (.40)*
Roles	Control	2.00 (.35)	2.23 (.42)	2.28 (.39)
	Education	2.01 (.33)	2.20 (.35)	2.26 (.39)
	Counseling	1.99 (.33)	2.22 (.39)	2.26 (.35)
Affective Responsiveness	Control	1.99 (.35)	2.18 (.37)	2.26 (.53)
	Education	2.00 (.36)	2.16 (.41)	2.21 (.39)
	Counseling	1.97 (.37)	2.17 (.37)	2.25 (.39)
Affective Involvement	Control	2.00 (.35)	2.19 (.36)	2.29 (.41)
	Education	2.00 (.36)	2.15 (.38)	2.14 (.44)*
	Counseling	2.01 (.37)	2.17 (.40)	2.15 (.45)*
Behavior Control	Control	2.04 (.36)	2.18 (.36)	2.22 (.44)
	Education	2.00 (.36)	2.17 (.35)	2.20 (.39)
	Counseling	2.01 (.47)	2.17 (.40)	2.07 (.35)*
General Functioning	Control	1.96 (.35)	2.21 (.40)	2.29 (.37)
	Education	1.92 (.47)	2.06 (.41)*	2.14 (.42)*
	Counseling	1.97 (.50)	2.06 (.44)*	1.94 (.42)*

*p < .01 from control.

or her adhere to a treatment regimen. On the other hand, if sustained caregiving is involved, it may become more difficult as the illness progresses or the family's resources become strained. The result may be a cumulative stress effect that begins to impinge on the family's functioning. One way to address these issues is to conduct a series of studies of family functioning in families with a member who has a deteriorating psychiatric illness (e.g., dementia, schizophrenia) and in families with a member who has an episodic yet chronic medical condition (e.g., diabetes, epilepsy).

The similarities and differences between populations with a psychiatric or non-psychiatric illness, along with insights gleaned from individual study findings, lead us to a final conclusion. Despite the large amount of empirical evidence we have accumulated to date, we continue to be impressed with the heterogeneity of families, their strengths and weaknesses, and differences in how each family views their family's functioning. Periodically, we have been tempted to suggest a prototype of family functioning for an illness (or life) stage or category. Although future research may prove otherwise, the data that we have collected do not yet support such a classification scheme.

9. **Family functioning is dynamic. A family's functioning will likely vary over time, by stage of family development, by stage of illness (e.g., acute vs. chronic), by change in family role (e.g., patient, caregiver), and by the changing composition of any individual family.**

Clinical Implication. While this may seem self-evident, the clinician should be careful about making assumptions regarding a family's functioning. Family circumstances and composition change over time, and functioning may shift as the family goes through different stages of development or a family member's illness course. There is no reason to assume that the family's functioning remains static as the family components change—such an assumption would be a contradiction of, not just the McMaster approach, but a central premise of systems theory.

Treatment Studies

At the beginning of this chapter, we noted three basic questions that drove our research. We wanted to know whether or not family functioning differed between nonclinical normal families and families in which one member had a psychiatric or medical illness and whether family functioning affected a patient's course of illness. Previous sections addressed the first two questions. The following section reports on progress made in addressing our third question, whether the family treatment approach we developed is helpful in improving a patient's outcome. We initiated four treatment studies to address this question and focused on families with a member diagnosed with major depression, bipolar disorder, or stroke.

In each of these studies, patients were hospitalized for their condition, recruited into the study, and randomized to different treatment conditions for their follow-up care after discharge from hospital. The amount and kind of treatment varied in each study, as did the number of months of patient and family follow-up. We provide details of the study design in order to highlight different ways of approaching research questions and to show how research methods may vary, depending on illness condition or study population. The underlying focus remains the same, that is, how to help patients and their family members improve their family's functioning and, ultimately, help improve the patient's course of illness. Data collection has been completed in two of the studies we discuss and some preliminary findings are presented. In two other studies, subject recruitment is ongoing and therefore analyses are not yet available.

Our first treatment study included 121 severely depressed patients and their family members. Two related research questions formed the basis of the study. First, we wanted to know if a therapist could enhance treatment effects in patients presenting with a severe depressive disorder by targeting and treating specific psychosocial deficits observed in the patient. Second, if we focused on two deficits, namely, cognitive distortion and family dysfunction, could we determine which patients were able to benefit from treatments that specifically address these deficits, namely, cognitive or family therapy respectively? The rationale in this study was to find a problem (i.e., the deficit) and correct it by applying a therapy that addressed the issues causing the problem. The family therapy component in this study was the PCSTF. One-half of the sample was randomized to a treatment that matched their deficit; the other half of the sample was mismatched to their treatment. There were four treatment arms: (1) standard medication management, (2) med management + cognitive therapy, (3) med management + family therapy, and (4) a combination of med management + cognitive therapy + family therapy. If evaluation at baseline suggested a need for family therapy (i.e., high family dysfunction), a match would be assigned to group 3 or group 4. Group 1 or 2 would be a mismatch for this patient. If a patient's assessment at baseline indicated high cognitive distortion, then group 2 or 4 would be a match; group 1 or 3, in which no cognitive therapy was offered, would be a mismatch.

Some preliminary findings are available from this study. First, although comparable to other studies of severely depressed patients, the overall recovery rate from depression for these patients (38/121; 38%) was relatively low. Second, matching treatments on the basis of poor family functioning or cognitive distortion did not increase treatment effectiveness. Third, patients with no improvement at discharge who received family therapy were likely to show more improvement by 3 and 6 months compared to patients who did not receive family therapy. Fourth, patients in the combined treatment condition were more likely to complete treatment, improve, or recover compared to the other treatment arms. The difference reached significance when the combined group was compared to the medication management group. Fifth, patients in the family therapy group and the cognitive therapy group had similar rates of retention, improvement, and recovery.

In two of the treatment studies we assessed a family's functioning subjectively (with the FAD) and objectively (with MCRS ratings). Both subjective and objective family ratings show an improvement over time from baseline through month 12 irrespective of treatment condition. However, while patients and family members rate their family's functioning as healthy at month 12, clinicians continued to rate the families' functioning in the unhealthy range (see Table 6.10). A second treatment study focused on patients diagnosed with a bipolar disorder. The aims of the study were to increase our knowledge of the effectiveness of treatments for bipolar disorder and determine whether adding a family therapy component to standard pharmacotherapy improved treatment response.[83] In this study design we compared medication management alone with two types of family therapy: individual family therapy using the PCSTF or a multi-family psychoeducational group.[84] Outpatient therapy continued for 28 months.

Although data analysis is not yet complete, we are able to report some overall trends. Fifty-eight percent of the patients met basic criteria for

Table 6.10 Family Functioning of Patients Hospitalized with Major Depression at the Acute Phase and at Follow-Up

	Acute	6 Months	12 Months
FAD (N = 71)*	x̄ (sd)	x̄ (sd)	x̄ (sd)
Problem Solving	**2.32** (.37)	2.08 (.31)	2.07 (.34)
Communication	**2.40** (.32)	**2.20** (.30)	2.15 (.31)
Roles	**2.35** (.34)	2.18 (.29)	2.16 (.34)
Affective Responsiveness	**2.28** (.47)	2.10 (.36)	2.09 (.42)
Affective Involvement	**2.16** (.35)	2.00 (.29)	1.96 (.34)
Behavior Control	**1.94** (.29)	1.79 (.25)	1.78 (.28)
General Functioning	**2.17** (.42)	1.97 (.35)	1.93 (.38)
MCRS (N = 74)**			
Problem Solving	**2.84** (.86)	**3.78** (1.13)	**4.15** (1.07)
Communication	**2.97** (1.03)	**3.81** (1.0)	**4.01** (1.10)
Roles	**3.08** (1.21)	**3.86** (1.06)	**4.34** (1.04)
Affective Responsiveness	**2.89** (1.00)	**3.47** (1.00)	**3.95** (1.01)
Affective Involvement	**3.58** (1.19)	**4.30** (1.03)	**4.58** (1.15)
Behavior Control	**3.51** (1.10)	**4.41** (1.03)	**4.81** (.93)
General Functioning	**2.94** (.99)	**3.80** (.99)	**4.20** (1.03)

*FAD score: the higher the score, the worse the functioning. Bold numbers = unhealthy.
**MCRS score: the higher the score, the better the functioning. Bold numbers = unhealthy

recovery, defined as a two-month consecutive period of patient scores < 7 on the Hamilton Rating for Depression Scale (HRS-D) and < 6 on the Bech-Rafaelson Mania Scale.[85,86] There were no differences in response rates by polarity at admission; nor were there differences in recovery from episode by treatment condition. Also, family functioning at index episode did not help in predicting response to treatment. When we stratified the sample by gender, males who were manic at baseline were significantly more likely to respond to treatment than males who were depressed. Further, married males were significantly more likely to respond to treatment than males who were not married. Neither the relationship between polarity and response to treatment, nor marital status and response held for female patients.[87,88] Also, family functioning and social support variables varied significantly by patient gender, albeit at 4 months rather than at the acute stage.

When we focused on family functioning ratings, the pattern of FAD and MCRS scores for patients with bipolar disorder paralleled the family functioning ratings for the depressed sample. That is, even though patients and family members report apparent difficulties in their family's functioning through 10 months, there is perceived improvement over time. Also, despite improvement in family functioning through 10 months post-hospitalization, clinicians' ratings remained in the unhealthy range (see Table 6.11).

Throughout this book we have tried to impress upon the reader our belief in using research findings to help us with our clinical work and to view the interplay between the two as a continuous learning process. Thus, even though the treatment studies of depressed and bipolar patients are still in the analysis stage, we were able to use the preliminary findings to move on to new research questions. For example, in the depression treatment study we were struck by differences in treatment compliance and response rates in patients receiving medication management only vs. patients receiving the combined treatment of medication management + cognitive therapy + family therapy. Our matching design enabled us to address questions that target patient and family deficits but, because of the randomization strategy we used, prevented us from assessing the additive effect of combining psychosocial treatments to standard pharmacological care. We initiated a new study so we could examine the effects of adjunctive therapy on the course of a depressive episode regardless of pre-treatment patient deficits.

Currently in the recruitment stage, the design of this study includes randomization to one of three treatment conditions: pharmacotherapy alone; pharmacotherapy + cognitive therapy; and pharmacotherapy + cognitive therapy + family therapy.[89] Like our previous treatment studies, we use the PCSTF as the family treatment component. Patients hospitalized with major depression and their family members are recruited to participate in a 24

Table 6.11 Family Functioning of Patients Hospitalized with Bipolar Disorder at the Acute Phase and at Follow-Up

	Acute	4 Months	10 Months
FAD (N = 38)*	x̄ (sd)	x̄ (sd)	x̄ (sd)
Problem Solving	**2.20** (.36)	2.13 (.38)	2.07 (.41)
Communication	**2.19** (.30)	2.18 (.31)	2.13 (.30)
Roles	**2.37** (.32)	2.28 (.31)	2.26 (.31)
Affective Responsiveness	2.18 (.50)	2.10 (.46)	2.12 (.51)
Affective Involvement	**2.15** (.38)	2.03 (.33)	1.98 (.33)
Behavior Control	**1.99** (.35)	1.86 (.28)	1.82 (.26)
General Functioning	**2.06** (.38)	**2.00** (.35)	1.94 (.32)
MCRS (N = 45)**			
Problem Solving	**3.29** (1.01)	**3.69** (.92)	**4.00** (1.11)
Communication	**3.02** (.99)	**3.58** (.92)	**3.89** (1.10)
Roles	**3.42** (1.08)	**3.82** (1.01)	**4.07** (1.01)
Affective Responsiveness	**3.04** (.80)	**3.69** (.92)	**3.93** (.86)
Affective Involvement	**3.93** (1.12)	**4.44** (.99)	**4.38** (.91)
Behavior Control	**3.91** (1.12)	**4.69** (.82)	**4.76** (.96)
General Functioning	**3.20** (.89)	**3.84** (.80)	**3.98** (.87)

*FAD score: the higher the score, the worse the functioning. Bold numbers = unhealthy.
**MCRS score: the higher the score, the better the functioning. Bold numbers = unhealthy.

week treatment trial following their discharge from hospital. We have completed one-half of our recruitment goal of 150 patients and family members and expect to meet our target within another year.

Besides initiating treatment studies with psychiatric populations, we have also embarked on treatment studies with patients who have a physical illness, but not necessarily a psychiatric illness. One of the challenges in conducting studies with patients who have a physical illness is the difficulty patients and family members have in attending in-person study interviews and/or in the amount of time they are able to concentrate on the interviewer's questions. Although these difficulties also arise with a patient who has a psychiatric illness, there may be a qualitative difference when the family member has a physical illness. For example, if the family under study has a member with a traumatic brain injury or stroke, it may not be possible for the patient to complete interviews (or assessments) or to come into the clinic to do so. We developed a new system, the Family Intervention: Telephone Tracking (FITT), which is a family oriented intervention for patients and family members (or caregivers) who are likely to need home care on a temporary or permanent basis.[90,91]

The intervention consists of a series of telephone calls to patient and family members/caregiver that has two components, one that is psychoeducational in nature and one that is oriented toward assessment and support. No treatment of psychiatric or family problems is provided. Rather, the interviewer supports patients and/or caregivers to use their own family relationships, capabilities, and resources to identify, address, or obtain assistance for any psychosocial, functional, or health problems that arise.[92] We have successfully used the FITT in a pilot study targeting stroke patients and their caregivers as they transition from the hospital setting to home care after discharge from the hospital. We delineated five areas that help identify problems associated with stroke patients and their family members. They are: family functioning, depressive symptomatology, neurocognitive functioning, functional independence, and physical health. Results from the pilot study have been promising. We found that, compared to standard medical care, patients and their caregivers participating in the FITT program significantly decreased their health care utilization, and improved both psychosocial functioning and family life.[93]

We have begun a prospective study that is focused on stroke patients and their caregivers. In the current study we included a longer follow-up period (18 months vs. the 6 month follow-up of the pilot study) so that we can assess long-term effects of the program. In addition, we hope to identify predictors of response to the FITT program as well as intermediate variables that predict treatment outcome. Patients are randomized to receive standard medical care with or without the FITT intervention. Over 200 patients and their caregivers have been recruited thus far; our target goal is 300 as a final sample size. We have developed FITT manuals as well as adherence and competency scales. The large sample in our ongoing study will help us validate and refine our instruments as needed. With the FITT system in place, and data being collected to refine and validate the manual and rating scales, we have the opportunity to expand our research into new areas of study. The focal areas that we identified for use with stroke patients can be adjusted to accommodate other serious illnesses in which a telephone intervention would be appropriate yet remain within the parameters of the model. The relative ease of the telephone intervention, the low costs associated with it, the savings in time allocation, and the ability to reach patients who may be temporarily housebound makes it an attractive alternative for several intervention strategies. Pilot studies have been initiated to test the FITT intervention with patients diagnosed with HIV and patients diagnosed with dementia and their caregivers.

Future Research

The field of family research continues to grow so fast that there are always more questions to ask, new areas of interest to investigate, and novel treatment applications or family assessments to be tested. There are also continuing developments in research design and methodology that can be used to address issues that have been neglected, reassess earlier findings, and bring new perspectives to old problems. The review of our research program has two main purposes. First, we wanted to look back at the work we have done over the past few decades, relate our empirical findings to the research questions that we set for ourselves, and draw the link between our research conclusions and the implications for clinical practice. Second, we intended to provide an understanding of our thinking and how we moved from early phases of our research—conceptualizing, developing, defining, and measuring constructs of family functioning and family treatment approaches—through testing our ideas in naturalistic studies, to our current work that evaluates the PCSTF in a variety of study populations and with a variety of research designs.

Plans for our future work continue to reflect our basic philosophy of moving our program forward by seeking to improve patient care with new clinical and research applications of the McMaster approach. As we noted, the process evolves on several levels at once. For example, work on the McMaster instruments, use of the McMaster approach with diverse patient populations, and development of new research questions relating to family functioning will form the basis of our research program for the next several years. While the FAD and the MCRS have been validated and the FAD used by colleagues throughout the world, the MCRS has been used less often. The MCRS is dependent on both knowledge and understanding of the McMaster model and, to some degree, on clinical skills needed to assess family functioning. We would like to increase the use of the MCRS since, as our research findings have shown, there is some discrepancy between subjective and objective family ratings. Because we view both perspectives as valuable and see them as an opportunity to learn more about the family, and possibly the course of an illness, we would like to examine this discrepancy systematically.

One way we have begun to address this issue is by developing the McSiff, the structured interview for paraprofessionals that yields an MCRS rating. We have collected data on over 200 families using the McSiff interview. In addition to acquiring a large data base of objective ratings of family functioning, use of the McSiff will allow us to pinpoint areas of family strengths and family weaknesses. We can then compare perceptions of the clinician with those of family members acquired through the FAD. Our plans are to use these data to validate the instrument, correlate the scores with our other assessments, and construct a reliable scoring system. The original McSiff consisted of three versions that reflected the traditional nuclear family, a single-parent family, and a couple with no children. By using a series of skip questions, we have consolidated these versions into one McSiff that can be used for any family constellation.[48] This new version is in use and available through our program, but still needs to undergo rigorous testing.

As mentioned in the previous section, we also developed the FITT, a telephone interview that may be used when patients or family members cannot easily leave their homes or come to the clinic/research setting. This instrument has shown promise in a pilot study involving stroke patients and their caregivers. Currently the FITT intervention is being used in three large funded research projects focused on stroke patients, patients with Alzheimer's disease, and drug abusing patients with HIV. Finally, as described in chapter 5, the FAD has been translated into 20 languages throughout the world. Although some are currently in the process of validation, most of the translated FADs have not yet been validated. Our family research group has worked closely with several colleagues to ensure accurate translation of the FAD. Success in recently completed work on the Italian, Spanish, Japanese, French, Hungarian, Slovenian, Croatian, French and Hebrew FADs has generated interest in providing translations in those languages of the MCRS and the McSiff. We anticipate that more researchers will take advantage of the expertise of the family research group and submit their back translations to obtain feedback from the developers of the instruments.

As we have developed a wider range of instruments to assess family functioning, we have also expanded our view of how the McMaster approach could be used when working with families with a variety of psychiatric and/ or non-psychiatric illnesses. We mentioned studies that include family functioning as one factor that may affect, or be affected by, patients with stroke, dementia, Alzheimer's disease, or HIV drug users. Two additional studies focus on the caregiver's role and his or her perception of family functioning vis-à-vis the rewards, burdens, and satisfaction associated with caring for a family member diagnosed with dementia and a family member who has a chronic mental illness.[94,95] Preliminary analyses in both studies suggested that caregiving was associated with increased burden, depressive symptoms, and impaired family functioning. Systematic analyses planned over the next year may help direct us to design new treatment studies that will take into account treatment needs of the caregiver as well as the designated patient.

We have begun work in the areas of epilepsy and nonepileptic seizures (NES) in the belief that the family functioning of the patient's family may have a direct or indirect effect on the patient's course of illness. This belief stems from our basic philosophy that, whether the illness is psychiatric or nonpsychiatric in nature, it is important to assess the social context in which the illness unfolds. Once we examine the relationship between family functioning and epilepsy and NES outcome, we will be in a better position to decide if family therapy would be a useful adjunctive treatment for patients with these disorders and their family members.

Finally, an area that has generated much interest among members of our research team has been psychosocial interventions offered to patients diagnosed with cancer. The diagnosis and treatment of cancer (as well as with the side effects of the treatment) is likely to have a profound impact on a patient and his or her family members, particularly a family's functioning and quality of life. In turn, evidence suggests that adjunctive psychosocial, behavioral, and educational interventions may help in the recovery or adjustment process for many cancer patients, including those who have undergone surgery. Since our model is structured, multi-dimensional, and systems-oriented, a short-term family treatment intervention may be useful in helping patients and families when one member is diagnosed with cancer. Because of this interest, we developed a multi-family group treatment program that incorporates elements of the McMaster approach in an intervention that will address issues and concerns of patients with prostate cancer and their spouse or significant other. In order to get feedback on our proposed treatment plan, we conducted a focus group with five men who had a prostatectomy one to six years previously and their partners. All couples expressed interest in our treatment as they dealt with profound changes in their family's functioning. After incorporating a few of their suggestions to our overall program, we are in the process of finalizing a proposal. If successful with this particular group of cancer patients, we plan on extending the intervention to patients with other types of cancer as well as other medical conditions.

Although we are extending our research to include patients with nonpsychiatric illnesses, we will continue our work with psychiatrically ill patients. In fact, including a variety of patient illnesses should help us to address one research topic that has been previously raised, namely, comorbidity and its relationship to a family's functioning. Our study on comorbidity mentioned in an earlier section included patients admitted to a psychiatric unit who had concurrent psychiatric and nonpsychiatric illnesses. We plan on obtaining another sample of patients admitted to the hospital with a nonpsychiatric physical illness who have a secondary diagnosis of major depression. The analyses for these studies are complicated and present major methodological issues to resolve. Nonetheless, they pose a set of new and interesting questions that may link physical and psychiatric disorders with family functioning and course of illness.

We derived a new set of questions from analyses generated by the longitudinal follow-up studies discussed earlier in this chapter. That is, once we moved from implementing cross-sectional research designs to conducting longitudinal follow-up treatment studies, we were struck by the inadequacy of standard definitions regarding illness course. For example, a patient with bipolar disorder may be symptom-free for eight weeks yet become symptomatic the following week, a typical pattern for this illness. Under these conditions, a patient who meets standard research criteria for recovery may not be considered well by a clinician. Relying on symptom change for a brief interval and ignoring other areas of dysfunction will not necessarily capture the turbulence of this illness. The inadequacy of outcome definitions is not limited to psychiatric illnesses. Outcome criteria for patients with epilepsy may include interictal level of functioning, comorbid mood or cognitive changes, as well as the more commonly used measure, absolute number of seizures during a specified time period.

Besides more accurately reflecting the clinical course of an illness, another reason to reassess parameters of outcome is to allow us to examine the link between fluctuations in the course of a patient's illness and patterns of his or her family functioning. Standard definitions of outcome (recovery, remitted, relapse) may not provide enough information about a patient's course of illness, the impact on families and their functioning, or the effect of family functioning on the illness. In addition, many illnesses (e.g., dementia, stroke) are marked by a deteriorating course. In the latter case, it may be more realistic to assess how families adjust to changing family conditions and how family therapy may help in the adjustment or coping process. Although many of our studies with depressed patients found that family members reported improvement in family functioning over time, at least two studies of caregivers reported worsening family functioning.[93,95] These studies involved patients with stroke and dementia, illnesses characterized by a chronic and deteriorating course.

If we examine patients with a variety of disorders and then examine the course of his or her illness and its relationship to family functioning, we may be able to compare and contrast patterns of similarities and differences between course of illness and fluctuations in a family's functioning. Whether the underlying illness is psychiatric or nonpsychiatric in nature, several of the disorders will likely share common course descriptors such as stable, remitting, episodic, acute, chronic, rapid cycling, fluctuating, and deteriorating. In addition, rather than merely assessing symptom change at two points in time, it may be more useful to include other measures relevant to course of illness—such as functional capacity, number of symptom-free days, proportion of time well or in pain, quality of life, and psychosocial sequelae associated with the illness. By widening the definition of illness outcome, we may be able to tease apart the relative contributions of social and biological determinants to a patient's course of illness.

Answers to these questions may help determine if adjunctive family treatment is indicated for a variety of disorders and, possibly, the best method to deliver it. Although the McMaster approach has been developed primarily for individual family treatment sessions, we have already noted how we have incorporated principles of this approach into new research designs and applications. For example, the FITT is a family oriented intervention that is based on the McMaster model and is currently being used with three different study populations: patients who have had a stroke and/or their caregivers, patients with dementia and their caregivers, and patients diagnosed with HIV. We used principles of the McMaster model in a multi-family psychosocial treatment of bipolar patients and their significant other and have adapted the multi-family approach for depressed patients in which several families meet together with two therapists for a limited number of sessions.[84] Finally, in our proposed adjunctive treatment for prostate cancer patients and their significant other, we suggest a sequence of 1 to 2 individual family sessions, followed by 2 weeks of telephone intervention and end with a brief series of multi-family group sessions.

This synopsis of our future work suggests three lines of research we would like to pursue, namely, refining the McSiff instrument and manual, widening our patient population pool, and developing new research questions, hypotheses, and family treatment applications. We need to test the McSiff, our objective rating of family functioning completed by paraprofessionals, against the FAD and the MCRS, and make adjustments as needed. The FITT intervention is being used in several ongoing studies. Although early analyses suggest its utility, we may need to revise and/or expand the manual before we provide widespread distribution. Second, we plan on expanding our recruitment to include a larger range of patients with psychiatric and nonpsychiatric illnesses as well as patients with comorbid conditions. Finally, we have generated a number of research questions that involves a wide array of patients, but concentrates on two major issues: new ways of looking at course of illness and fluctuations in illness course as it relates to a family's functioning.

Answers to these questions may suggest different applications of the McMaster approach for different populations. It may be that some aspect of the PCSTF needs to be modified, or that the McMaster approach has more (or less) utility for certain conditions. In general, we expect that patients with an illness characterized by progressive deterioration or a rapid, unpredictable course would have worse family functioning over time.

Conversely, patients with a non-deteriorating, more predictable course of illness with longer periods of wellness will report better family functioning. In either case, a family treatment approach such as the PCSTF may be useful in helping patients and their family members adjust their family functioning to cope with a family member's illness.

Limitations

Despite the amount of work we have done over the years, and the series of questions we have set for future studies, we are aware of limitations to our research as well as areas that we have only touched upon. One of the most basic issues remains the question of causality. The causal direction between family functioning and course of illness is unclear. Problems with understanding causal connections are not unique to family studies, but are common when any dynamic system is being investigated. We hope that our future research, as outlined above, will be useful in addressing some parts of this problem. Until we are able to be more precise, through advances in methodology or by identifying intermediate factors in the mechanisms of change in family functioning, we continue to need to be cautious whenever we discuss causality.

Other gaps in our research have more to do with time limitations and sample size than methodological restrictions. For example, we have not compared family functioning during different stages of family development so that we might see how strains and stressors affect a family's functioning over time, or within a particular life stage. Depending on developmental stage and composition of the family, family members may report problems in different dimensions of family life. Given a larger database, we would be able to examine family roles, gender differences, and child/adolescent perspectives in greater depth.

The reliability and validity of our research assessments have been well documented. Societal changes over the past three decades, however, have affected living arrangements, marital status, and women's roles. These changes may (or may not) have affected how family members view their families' functioning. A new sample of community controls would be useful to update our nonclinical population statistics, test for changes in perceived family functioning (including our healthy/unhealthy cut-off scores), and increase the diversity and applicability of our model and our assessments. We suspect that the test scores will not change noticeably for two reasons. First, despite societal changes, fundamental processes within the family have not changed. For example, even though a family constellation changes, problems still need to be solved, family members need to communicate with each other, roles need to be allocated, members need to respond and be affectively involved, behavior needs to be monitored. Second, the unhealthy cut-off scores established for the instruments were based on clinical assessments made by experienced clinicians and are not based on statistical means of a patient population. Nonetheless, because of the widespread clinical and research use of the McMaster instruments, it would be important to test these assumptions with a large, randomly selected community sample.

We have already noted that the translation of our instruments and manuals was not anticipated when they were first developed. We have worked with colleagues throughout the world to give feedback, suggest changes, and point out errors in translation. For the most part, however, with few exceptions the translated instruments have not been validated. As we reported, work is ongoing in several countries on translations, back-translations, and validation studies. We anticipate more work being done in this area and will try to keep readers abreast of new developments.

Summary and Conclusions

In this chapter we reviewed 50 years of our research. First, we examined differences in family functioning between normal control families and families in which one member has a psychiatric or non-psychiatric medical illness. Second, we analyzed how family functioning affected a patient's course of illness, and third, we provided preliminary data on treatment studies using the McMaster approach to family therapy. Before detailing our research findings, we listed the assumptions underlying our research, discussed our approach to different methodological issues, and provided a rationale for our analytic choices. We began with the early research studies in which we developed theoretical constructs and measures to assess family functioning. We summarized our early findings when we worked with clinical and nonclinical populations. From there we moved on to our naturalistic follow-up studies, first focusing on patients with a psychiatric illness and their family members. Next we discussed our research of patients with a nonpsychiatric, medical disorder. We listed conclusions drawn from our studies, presented evidence that led to these conclusions, and discussed the clinical implications that we took from our work. We presented a series of treatment studies that we initiated and provided preliminary findings of our work. We outlined our research program for the next few years and we noted limitations of our work.

In presenting our research findings we were struck by a number of factors. Throughout this book we reiterated our belief in the importance of assessing the social context in which the illness unfolds. We are convinced that a comprehensive clinical evaluation is necessary to capture the total environment of the patient. Moreover, as we have seen through our research, a checklist of symptom changes does not necessarily provide a complete understanding of the patient's illness, its course, and the fluctuation in family functioning that often accompanies the illness over time. We have been reminded again and again of the heterogeneity of families and the multidimensional aspects of the MMFF and the PCSTF. Our findings are consistent in that they do not focus on any one dimension as a predictor of risk, recovery, or relapse. Nor do we see a prototypical family that characterizes an illness type or a poor functioning family. These findings are supportive of the belief we held when we originally developed the McMaster model, namely, that no one dimension be viewed as the foundation for conceptualizing family behavior.

As we have shown, however, there are clear linkages between the family functioning of a patient and his or her likelihood of recovery from an illness episode. Good family functioning can increase the odds of recovery, shorten the time in episode, and improve the well-being of patients and family members. To date our preliminary analyses in the treatment studies have not shown a direct cause and effect between receiving family therapy and patient outcome. We look forward to exploring these datasets in more detail so that we can get a better understanding of how good family functioning affects patients. This knowledge will ultimately help us so that we will be able to provide better family interventions. Finally, through our completed studies and our proposed research we hope we have conveyed a sense of how the clinical and research elements of our program work together. The clinical component guides our research questions and helps us interpret data; the research side tests clinical assumptions that are made and moves us to generate additional questions. Weaving the two components together enables us to maintain a strong, coherent program.

CHAPTER 7

Frequently Asked Questions

We believe that the MMFF and the PCSTF provide structure and focus to guide a clinician to conduct a comprehensive evaluation and treatment for most families and family problems that he or she will encounter. We provided a complete and detailed explanation of our approach to family assessment, treatment, and research. However, whether in seminars, conferences, research meetings or professional correspondence, members of our group periodically receive questions that deal with the clinical, teaching, or research aspects of the McMaster approach. We thought it helpful to list some of the more frequently asked questions that we receive and how we respond to them. Hopefully, our answers will convey the meaning of the model in a practical sense as we address issues that arise routinely for clinicians, trainees, and researchers.

Some family members do not come in for family therapy, refuse to complete a FAD, or will not participate in the assessment in some other way. What can I do? How will this affect the treatment, assessment, research?

While we recommend that all family members participate in the family meetings, some will not be able to do so for a variety of reasons including temporary problems, scheduling or logistic problems, organizational issues, and clinical or behavior issues.

Examples of temporary or logistic problems might include sickness, work-related travel, being away at school, transportation issues, lack of childcare, work conflicts. These problems can be addressed by rescheduling, bringing young children/toddlers into the therapy room, or, if necessary, meeting without a family member. Sometimes family members have difficulty organizing themselves. If so, the issue could be identified as part of the presenting problem and addressed in treatment sessions. Finally, examples of clinical/ behavioral issues include a family member acting out, arriving at the meeting inebriated, or having an illness or symptom (e.g., aphasia from a stroke, psychosis) that precludes participation. In the case of these last examples, the clinician uses his or her clinical judgment to determine the risk of disruption to the family therapy process and whether or not the family meeting should be postponed.

Very often reasons given that a family member is unwilling to participate may be used by the clinician to assess and, possibly, improve the family's functioning. Depending on the particular circumstance, there are several ways to approach this problem. For example, the clinician can stress to the family that all members' input is valuable, each members' views will be heard, each family member's behavior affects the entire family, and the family's functioning affects each of them as individuals. For these reasons it is best for all to attend and participate. We find that if the clinician engages with all family members, explains that everyone will have a turn in expressing his or her opinion, and remains neutral while eliciting information, even family members who were initially hostile to, or threatened by the idea of family therapy become interested in giving their opinion and hearing what the therapist and other family members have to say. Once engaged, and able to listen to other viewpoints in a clinical setting, family members are able to become part of the therapeutic process.

A family member may choose to not attend the initial meeting or to refuse to engage in any therapy. In that event, it is up to the family members and the clinician to decide whether or not it is worthwhile to proceed with family therapy. It may be useful for the clinician to lay out the options that families have, including what issues might and might not be addressed realistically if a key family member does not participate. Since the McMaster approach is predicated on family members working together, it may be therapeutically useful to suggest that family members review what they would like to gain from family therapy. The clinician may point out explicitly that, for a variety of reasons, the family does not seem ready to engage in family therapy *at the time*. It is important that the therapist respects the family's position (even if he or she disagrees with the decision) so that the family feels comfortable reconnecting with the clinician at some future point. The clinician should be clear about the family's options, and be receptive if the family does decide to return.

If the family returns, and if much time has elapsed, it is important that the therapist conducts a completely new family assessment so that he or she does not make assumptions about the family's functioning based on a previous interview. Also, since the assessment interview sets up expectations for the treatment plan and begins the therapeutic process, it is worthwhile to address the reasons for previous reluctance to participate in therapy. We find that once families understand what is involved in family therapy, most choose to participate. Often families may decline family therapy but later (days, weeks, months) request it specifically.

From a research perspective, FAD ratings of a family can be obtained even if all family members do not complete the instrument. This is true because the total family score is an average of individual members' scores. If there are only two members in the family and only one completes a FAD, the case may need to be dropped from specific types of analyses (e.g., comparing a patient's perspective with a family member's perspective). On the other hand, some questions are analyzed using only an individual family member's score (e.g., patient's perception, father's perception, caretaker's perception). Finally, it is possible to obtain an objective rating (MCRS) of a family's functioning with a minimum of two family members. We use a family rating based on a single informant if a patient is unable to answer questions due to a medical or psychiatric condition or if a single parent with young children completes the assessment. These ratings can be used as long as the source of the family rating is clearly noted. Chapter 5 provides more details on uses of the instruments.

Is it all right to switch the order of assessing the family dimensions? Any suggestions about what should go first? Or last?

Based on clinical experience, the order in which to assess a family's functioning depends on the experience of the interviewer, his or her understanding of the MMFF, and his or her role as clinician, research interviewer, or trainee. The order becomes less important once the interviewer knows the model and is used to assessing each dimension. Until that time, it is better to use the same order to ensure that every dimension has been assessed. With practice, the clinician/interviewer moves to what feels most comfortable, viewing the assessment much like a family checklist of different areas of functioning. For an experienced clinician, the order may be determined by the family's responses to questions. Therapists begin the family interview with the Problem Solving dimension as this area of family functioning is concrete and the questions fit well after a brief discussion of the presenting problem. For example, a clinician begins by asking family members what brought them to seek help, including particulars about the immediate problem. Once the family has a chance to talk about the reasons for seeking treatment, the clinician suggests they return to discussing the problem, but first he or she needs to get more information about particular aspects of the family's functioning. At this point, the therapist can initiate the assessment by seeing how the family deals with problems in general, using the present-ing problems as a starting point. The therapist proceeds to other areas of the family's functioning as outlined in the MCRS. As long as the therapist is clear and direct about what he or she is doing and why, the family usually accepts the format.

For a trainee, research interviewer, or one with little clinical or inter-viewing experience, Roles may be an easier dimension to begin the interview both for family members and the interviewer. This is one reason why the McSiff begins with a very brief discussion about problems and then proceeds to the role dimension. Generally, we address the affective dimensions to-ward the end of the interview as it can be difficult for family members to discuss their feelings and difficult for a trainee to elicit responses or to man-age the situation if the family becomes distraught. Questions regarding sexual intimacy asked in the role dimension can be delayed until the end of a ses-sion after excusing children from the room.

Is it okay if you don't do an assessment using all dimensions?

For teaching purposes, a supervisor may ask the trainee to assess one, two, or three family dimensions rather than all six in a single session. Once the model is learned, and is being used for clinical purposes, the interviewer should assess all dimensions. We do not provide an overall clinical rating of the family unless we have assessed each dimension. Also, treatment is not initiated until a full assessment of the family has been completed.

It is possible to be more selective when conducting research. Very often researchers have limited resources and are unable to obtain complete as-sessments by experienced clinicians or complete FADs from family mem-bers. Alternatively, a researcher may purposely focus on only one or two dimensions of family functioning. If limited to one dimension, we ask fami-lies to give us an overall rating of their family (using the FAD General Func-tioning scale). If the rating for this dimension falls within a healthy range, education, advocacy, and support may be all that is needed by the family. If the dimension falls into a clinical range, a full assessment is necessary to determine which areas of family functioning are problematic and in need of clinical intervention. Colleagues found the General Functioning scale reliable and valid in a large study that analyzed family functioning in a com-munity sample of randomly selected families.[96] A weakness of this approach is the possibility of overlooking a problematic family issue by choosing se-lective dimensions of family life.

Which is better to use, the FAD, McSiff, or the MCRS? Do you need both family and clinician ratings?

It depends on what the question is, who is asking it, and for what purpose it is being asked. In chapter 5, we provided an in-depth discussion and examples of how clinicians, researchers, and teachers use each of these instruments to elicit information. Most of our research work has been done with the FAD, in part because it was the first instrument we developed to measure family functioning. Other factors that have made the FAD popular are its usefulness in providing a family's perspective, ease of administration, cost efficiency, and availability in several languages. When possible, we obtain subjective and objective measures so we can analyze which assessment is useful in predicting short- or long-term course, recovery, or relapse.

Experienced family therapists generally use the MCRS, often supplemented by periodic FADs given to family members. The McSiff is used most often by trainees, therapists new to the model, and experienced research interviewers. In sum, use of the instruments depends on: (1) whether the ratings of family functioning are for clinical, research, or training purposes; and (2) available resources, including experienced/trained personnel and time.

Can I get an average of family functioning by taking a mean of all the dimensions?

The General Functioning scale is the best indicator of average family functioning since it provides an overall family functioning rating. This is true if measured subjectively using the FAD or objectively using the MCRS. Because of the manner in which the ratings are obtained (either through specific items if using the FAD or clinical assessment if using the MCRS/McSiff), dimension scores should not be averaged.

Who can fill out the FAD form? Can children participate in the family assessment?

The FAD can be completed by anyone with an eighth-grade reading level. Our instructions suggest that any child 12 years and older is capable of completing the FAD, but many of our colleagues note that younger children are also able to do so. Some researchers have younger children complete the General Functioning scale only.

When conducting a clinical interview or the structured interview (the McSiff), the clinician asks for input from all family members using language that is age-appropriate. The therapist or interviewer may need to excuse children for questions directed to the parent or adult (e.g., questions regarding sexual satisfaction). The clinician should be respectful and let children know what is happening ("I would like to talk to your parents for a few minutes about adult matters. This has nothing to do with you and we won't talk about you unless you are here.") If the therapist wants to ask parents about their sexual relationship, this can be done at the beginning or end of a session or the children may take a break during the assessment. If no one is available to watch the children, the therapist may need to schedule a separate session for the adults/parents only.

What if a family member needs individual therapy in addition to family therapy?

Depending on the clinician's training and the individual's problems, the family member may be seen by the same therapist treating the family or may be referred to another clinician. In our program, we have worked with a variety of mental health professionals whose opinions differ with respect to treating family systems as well as a family member concurrently. While there are pros and cons for either position, several points should be kept in mind. First, the illness, severity, and specific situation will likely affect how the clinician sees the risks or benefits to treating both the family system and an individual family member. Second, if there is one treating clinician, he or she must feel comfortable with the arrangement and his or her ability to handle family as well as individual issues simultaneously. The family and the individual family member also need to find the arrangement acceptable; having an open discussion with the therapist and all family members will help to facilitate the decision.

If more than one therapist is involved in treatment, it is important that the therapies do not conflict or create confusion in the family or with the individual patient. Neither the patient nor the family should receive mixed messages about their therapy. Since the focus will likely differ, contact between therapists (even if minimal) becomes extremely important in order to keep the treatment on track, ensure that the individual is not set up against the family system, and help both the patient and the family progress in their treatment. Whether one or more therapists are involved, using a systematic family assessment and treatment plan become even more important for both the therapist and family members to follow.

Do I really need to have the whole family there? They just want couples therapy, the kids aren't involved.

If you meet with the couple and, after a complete assessment, agree about the identified problems, there is no reason why you cannot use the McMaster approach with couples.

Given that different family types and family constellations are common-place today, does the MMFF and PCSTF to assess and treat families still apply? Do you need to adjust for changes in family types or lifestyles?

While traditional nuclear families may have been the norm when Epstein and colleagues developed the model and treatment approach, these clinicians have treated a wide range of family types in a variety of developmental family stages. Because the McMaster approach was based on practical, clinical experiences of clinician/researchers, underlying assumptions of the therapy recognize the heterogeneity of families and the importance of treating each family as unique. In practice, the model focuses on getting families to identify *their* goals and on how to achieve them. As long as the goals of the treatment are not unsafe, the therapist can work with the family. The model is nonjudgmental with respect to different lifestyles and can be applied to blended-families, single-parent families, families with or without children, families with dual custody of children or families with same sex partners.

Once the therapist understands that the McMaster approach is viewed as treating a family system, then it is clear that healthy family functioning can be achieved irrespective of a family's composition. The clinician works with the family so that family members are able to establish and maintain a supportive environment. Family members learn how to deal with disagreements among themselves, including the possibility that they agree to disagree. Limitations in treating different types of presenting families may be a reflection of the interests, resources, and experience of the clinician rather than a lack in the model or treatment approach. Having said this, the McMaster approach and, indeed, family therapy is not indicated for all patients or all therapists. It is a powerful tool, however, that can help clinicians and family members deal with most of a family's problems.

Is family therapy an essential part of (psychiatric) treatment, or is it a luxury?

Evaluation of any patient should involve a complete biopsychosocial assessment of which the family is one component. An individual's problems can affect the family and the family's functioning can affect the individual. Further, what we recommend for one family may not work for another family. Therefore, we need to know how each family functions in order to arrive at the plan that is best for all concerned.

The treatment plan may or may not include family therapy. If family therapy is indicated, it is important that the family understand that without family therapy, treatment may not be successful. The assessment need not take long or be cumbersome (for patient or clinician), but it is important to obtain more than a description of symptoms (e.g., sleep, sadness) or to complete an illness checklist. We find that assessing the family saves time in the long run by addressing patient stressors, allying the family in a patient's treatment compliance and, at the least, providing the clinician with a more complete picture of the social context in which the illness unfolds. All of these factors may contribute to the clinical improvement of the patient.

How is the McMaster approach and McMaster therapy different from (or better than) other family treatments?

The McMaster approach requires a comprehensive and multi-dimensional assessment before any treatment is planned. This reflects our strong belief that any treatment begins with a complete understanding of the presenting as well as underlying problems and the context in which they occur. Our assessment is structured so that it is clear, directly related to the treatment model, and easily implemented by clinicians with different backgrounds, training, and experience. Besides being applicable to a wide range of family issues and its use by health professionals in many fields, the McMaster model is widely used by researchers.

As noted in the introduction of this book, we are less interested in providing a survey or a critique of family therapies and more interested in presenting a comprehensive explanation of the McMaster approach. Several sections of this book list specific points about the model and treatment that are unique to the McMaster approach or are fundamental to its practice. For example, in the McMaster model, the therapist uses a systems approach to work with the total family, emphasizes the responsibilities of each individual family member, finds strengths in the family in order to give positive feedback and empower group members, and works as a facilitator in the family therapy sessions. This approach differs from treatment models that are directive with the therapist delineating problems, deciding on therapeutic issues, and giving homework assignments. The McMaster model differs from postmodern approaches that emphasize individual feelings and input, downplay the responsibility that family members have regarding their own behavior, and diminish the clinician's role.

Rather than reviewing several models or schools of thought, a better strategy may be to become completely familiar with one or two approaches of family therapy, and use them as a basis for learning, comparing, and contrasting to other approaches. At this point we do not know, nor do we claim, that the McMaster approach is better than other family treatments. The studies to make these comparisons have not yet been done.

Why is the model so structured? When I use it, it seems too rigid and simplistic.

This question and comment often originate from a trainee or someone who is new to the model. A trainee may feel constrained by thinking about the next question to ask and feel inhibited about pursuing a comment from a family member, or picking up on a sudden thought/intuition. This feeling is common to many learning processes, including the McMaster approach; guidelines are often viewed as constraints until the student reaches a certain level of understanding. Rather than framed as a constraint, the structure of the model and the treatment plan can be viewed as a guide that actually helps one develop as a clinician. Once a therapist is familiar with the model and comfortable with the interview format, however, the structure is often seen as a family checklist (similar to a symptom inventory) and the interview as a valued working tool. From the point of view of families, individual members often find comfort in the structure and recognize that each question is asked of all families. They become less defensive when talking about their own families.

The clarity of the model, the instruments, and the treatment should not be confused with simplicity. The McMaster approach was developed to provide a systematic method of assessment and treatment in what is often a very complicated situation with several people participating at once. A comprehensive interview and useful therapy session requires much clinical knowledge and skill. The therapist's individual style, creativity, and personality become evident in how he or she engages with the family, listens to family members, facilitates discussions, and helps with family interactions and problem solving.

The approach was developed primarily to meet the needs of the family. In following the model, however, the needs of the clinician are met as well. The clinician follows the macro stages of the model, helping to keep him or her on track, but maintains a great deal of flexibility within the steps of the model. In our view, this systematic and comprehensive approach to evaluation and treatment of families helps the therapist become a better clinician.

Isn't the McMaster approach just an expansion of the problem solving methods used in behavioral or marital therapy?

The McMaster approach is much broader and, at the same time, more specific than behavioral therapies. It is broader in the sense that the model does not focus on any one dimension as the foundation for conceptualizing family behavior.[20] We have noted throughout this book that many family dimensions make up a family's functioning and we have provided a rationale as to why we focus on six particular areas (problem solving, communication, roles, affective responsiveness, affective involvement, and behavior control) that we feel are fundamental to understanding families (see chapter 3). The model is specific in the sense that each family dimension is delineated with key concepts that help the therapist focus and identify the strengths and weaknesses of the family system. For example, by careful probing of the family's communication patterns, role allocations, and affective responses, the therapist is able to obtain a comprehensive picture of the family's functioning, the perspective of each family member, and the barriers to a healthy functioning family.

One characteristic of the McMaster approach is the emphasis on obtaining a complete and systematic assessment of each family. This approach is tailored to individual needs of each family, and helps the therapist focus directly on problematic family issues. It does not prescribe a predetermined treatment module so popular with other models. Finally, the McMaster approach builds on strengths in the family system and makes family members responsible for changing the way their family functions.

The family came in with a crisis, so I took care of that rather than doing an assessment.

Although the McMaster model is not a crisis model per se, this is not to say that the model is inapplicable during a crisis. If a patient is suicidal, the clinician needs to tend to the patient's immediate safety, including hospitalization if necessary. Other examples of crisis intervention may include child/spousal abuse, fighting, substance abuse, and medical emergencies. In other words—by all means, it is always important to "stop the bleeding first."

In many cases, the clinician can use the principles of the model to help families deal with the crisis. For example, with the collaboration of family members, the therapist/counselor helps family members define the problem, discuss alternatives, and assign responsibility to family members. Once the crisis is settled, it is an opportune time to step back and complete a full family assessment on how the family handled the crisis. The severity of the crisis may be a useful gauge to determine the effectiveness of how the family functions. The crisis might also be a stepping-off point to assess how the family is doing generally and what they might do differently should another, similar, crisis arise. The therapist acts as a role model during the crisis by remaining calm and organizing, dealing with a difficult situation, and helping to decide on a plan from a number of alternatives.

In working with the family, the therapist will need to keep in mind several points, including the level of family crisis, if the family is in a chronic state of crisis, and what the family views as a crisis. In addition, it is important to know how the family functions on an everyday basis to see if the family generally functions well but has been temporarily upset by the crisis or whether the family has poor skills and difficulties even in their daily functioning. The clinician's options might include providing support by pointing out or calling attention to the family's strengths, or helping them with their weaknesses by working through the crisis and members' reactions to it.

Do I just keep adding problems as they come up?

It is possible to add problems to the list of issues that the family would like to address, especially if the assessment brings up a new issue or one previously unmentioned. Here a clinician's input may be valuable by helping the family assess priorities or identifying a more fundamental, underlying problem. From a list of seemingly unrelated problems, an experienced therapist may be able to extract one or two common themes or prominent issues.

In some families problems may continue to emerge during treatment. As long as previous issues have been worked on and resolved, it is all right to address new problems. However, we recommend challenging the family to discuss and problem solve around the issue. This can be a useful indication of their new capacity to address problematic areas within the family or be suggestive of areas that need more attention in the treatment process. The family may problem solve within a session with the therapist present or may attempt to resolve an issue on their own and report back in another session.

If new problems are substituted for older ones when the older ones have not yet been resolved, then the therapist should reassess the treatment as well as the transactional patterns occurring in session. It may be that the clinician has not clearly identified underlying problems or has not explained to the family the expectations in the therapy process. The first step might be to review the expectations of all, clarify the issues the family is working on, and see if there is a pattern or stumbling block which prevents the family from addressing the problems already delineated and not yet worked through. It may be that the family does not want to take responsibility for family problems or is afraid to do so and keeps presenting new problems as a defense against dealing with the problems agreed upon previously. One of the reasons we recommend limited number of treatment sessions is to emphasize the responsibility that the family has in changing their system and to de-emphasize reliance on a therapist to "fix" the system. The limit also puts pressure on the family and the therapist to be assiduous and active at every step during treatment. Finally, one way to help the family may be to space out the family meetings so that the family has time to work on solving the problems themselves.

How long do I keep seeing them?

It depends on the problems, the family, and the experience of the clinician. We have suggested one to two sessions to obtain a comprehensive assessment, followed by six to eight treatment sessions. Often the assessment itself is therapeutic. Many families need only two to three sessions in total to resolve the problems, help the family break out of a rut, and teach them to address new issues or view and act on their problems from a different perspective. On the other hand, some families may complete a full cycle of eight to twelve family therapy sessions over the course of six months to one year and still need to address additional problems. At this point the clinician decides if the family is stuck or making progress in their treatment, if another kind of therapy would be more useful (including adjunctive therapy), or if a consultation is advisable. Detailed guidelines in chapters 3 and 4 will help a clinician make these decisions and determine appropriate expectations for the therapist and for family members.

One sign that the family is ready to end treatment is when the family identifies a new problem, discusses alternatives for solving it, and puts a plan into action—with no input from the therapist. Not all problems warrant a therapist's involvement. If the family can discuss and resolve new issues as they learned in therapy, they are ready to stop treatment.

When do you know treatment is over?

When the family resolves the problems they have presented, no new issues are brought up by the family or clinician, or the family raises an issue and begins to solve it with no input from the therapist, the therapist's work is over. At first, it may be difficult for the therapist to sit back and allow this process to evolve. But when the work of the therapist is over, the treatment is over. The therapist may suggest a follow-up session after several months to check on the family, see if any new issues emerge, or see how the family functions when old issues resurface. The initiative for this session can come from the family or clinician.

When and how do you stop treatment if they are not doing their homework?

Before stopping treatment, the therapist first needs to understand why the family is not doing their homework. There may be several explanations. If an individual is too sick, he may not be able to do the homework. The homework may be too difficult for one or more family members, the work may not address the real problems of the family, there may be a misunderstanding of what was agreed upon in the contract, one or more family members may have changed their mind about the contract, or may have changed their mind about wanting help to change. The best approach is to ask the family directly what happened, why were they not able to fulfill what they had agreed upon.

Depending on the answer, the therapist can help the family set up a new contract. If the therapist feels the family is not ready to work on issues, it may be necessary to ask the family to stop treatment until they are ready or willing to commit to doing family work. The therapist should be clear, direct, and respectful of the family's wishes. Often asking the family to rethink if they want to engage in therapy is beneficial. The family must realize their own responsibility in working on family issues rather than expecting the therapist to fix them. If the therapist is working harder than the family in trying to solve problems, it may be time to reassess what the family expects from therapy. Three strikes and you're out may be a good rule of thumb to follow.

I think he or she needs to leave his or her spouse . . . can I say that?

The therapist does not advocate or prescribe separation or divorce. The premise of the McMaster approach is to help the family recognize problems, think about alternatives and solutions, confront the issues directly, and be responsible for their choices and actions. The therapist may point out four basic strategies open to the family. They may: (1) leave things as they are, (2) work on problems on their own, (3) use the family therapy sessions to work together and effect a change, or (4) separate. In presenting the options available to family members, the therapist tries to elicit specific advantages, disadvantages, and consequences of each option. The therapist is free to give his or her input on how the family presents to the therapist, including issues that have not been articulated by family members. With the help of the therapist, the family decides whether to pursue family therapy, stay in the marriage with no change, or change their marriage/living situation.

I sense an undercurrent of danger or violence in the family. What should I do?

Before any family therapy can proceed, the clinician first identifies the risk and makes an assessment of whether or not the danger is imminent. The clinician may need to be direct in pointing out safety issues for the spouse or children, especially if he or she denies evidence of danger. On the other hand, if the patient is depressed (or psychotic), he or she may present a distorted, negative picture of the family situation. A careful assessment of each patient's presentation and his or her psychosocial stressors will help the therapist determine which conditions apply.

If danger is not imminent, it is possible to incorporate specific conditions into the treatment contract that could help deal with the violence. For example, family therapy may proceed only if family members agree that there will be no violence while in treatment. One or more family members may need to obtain additional, individual help (e.g., abuse counseling) for the family therapy to proceed. The clinician may begin each session with a review of whether or not family members carried out what they agreed to do between sessions. This may be particularly critical if the clinician feels that an underlying potential for violence is part of the family system.

How do I avoid getting sucked into the family system?

Although it may be more common for students/trainees to become overly involved with the family, experienced therapists may also over-identify with one or more family members or with a particular family situation. How to recognize and deal with issues of counter-transference and boundary maintenance is an integral part of any therapist's training and is no different when applied in the family therapy setting. The therapist needs to be vigilant so as to respond to a family, an individual, or an issue in an objective, professional manner. By being aware of one's own issues and maintaining self-awareness, the therapist will be sensitive if he is too empathic when responding to individuals, starts taking sides in therapy sessions, or cannot maintain his objectivity. Once a therapist recognizes (or has doubts about) his feelings regarding a particular family or family member, he can take some actions. If it is possible to tape a session, a colleague or supervisor could provide feedback. A therapist may be able to step back and review his own taped session or peer review may be available to get other perspectives on the dynamics of the therapy sessions.

How do you divide up the attention between different family members?

The central role of a family therapist is to treat the family as a unit. In order to do so, the clinician needs to think systemically about the relationships within the family rather than thinking about individuals. If the therapist divides the session so that each member has an equal share of attention, then the therapist's likely focus is on individuals and individual problems rather than on the family system. One way to help a therapist think in systems is to figure out how an individual (or an individual's problem) impacts on the family system and how the family reacts to the individual (or his or her problem). The important point is that all family members need to feel that their perspectives have been heard and understood. The amount of actual time spent with each family member is of less importance.

What are your ethical obligations to a family versus an individual?

Unless there is a clear and present danger to an individual, the focus in therapy remains the system. If the therapist has knowledge that one family member is withholding information that might have an impact on another family member (drug use, spending money), the therapist tries to get the individual to disclose the information (in or out of session). If the disclosure does not happen and the therapist thinks it may be interfering with treatment, it is up to the therapist to stop the therapy so that he or she is not colluding in the process. In situations deemed basic to individual or family welfare (e.g., child/spousal abuse) the therapist can encourage the individual to disclose the information, making it clear that if the individual does not disclose the information the therapist is obliged to do so.

Under the guidelines of the McMaster approach, the therapist might convene a meeting to stop the therapy, saying a major premise is that the family needs to work together, and to communicate clearly and directly. As long as the family cannot be open and it affects the family's progress, it is best to stop treatment. The clinician makes it clear that she will be available if the family later decides to re-open the discussion.

When do you (if ever) invite members to a session who do not live at home?

An experienced therapist welcomes family members who would like to participate in the assessment and whose presence would likely contribute to an understanding of the family's functioning. The therapist assesses the appropriateness of whether other family members should participate in the treatment sessions. On one hand, perspectives of different family members can help provide a complete picture of the family's functioning. On the other hand, there may be boundary issues if all family members are a part of the treatment process.

Whether or not a clinician decides to include outside family members also depends on his or her experience. The key is to stay focused on the objectives of the treatment. It may be important to bring in other family members for the assessment only or to gather additional information, but then work with the core family once the issues are clarified. Over the years, we have invited relatives who live outside the household, family friends, and, on occasion, employers to attend family therapy sessions. If others are invited to participate in family meetings, it should be by mutual agreement, be clear why they have been invited to the session(s), and what the goal of the meeting is.

How much time do you spend on the presenting problem? Do you assess problem solving then or is that assessed at a separate time?

Enough time so that you feel you understand the problem, but not so much time that you find yourself trying to deal with it. As stated earlier, the family may need to talk about the problem—the reason why they are there—and the therapist needs to listen to what they are saying. Once the therapist understands, identifies, and restates the problem, then it is time to move on to the assessment. An experienced interviewer following the MCRS would move directly to the problem solving dimension, while an interviewer administering the McSiff would address the problem solving dimension somewhat later in the interview.

Very often a trainee (or novice therapist) gets stuck by letting the family rehash the problem using numerous examples or by trying to follow-up on an issue/topic that seems interesting. In either case, the result is the same. The session becomes unfocused, and the family loses interest or lacks engagement with the treatment. Until the therapist gains experience, she may need supervision so that she does not become either too superficial or too detailed.

The remedy is for the therapist to stay focused, listen to what the family is saying, observe the interactions of family members, and continue the assessment letting the family know that they will return to the problem when the full assessment has been completed. It is important to give feedback to the family about how the therapist hears and understands the problem—both to obtain validation from family members, as well as to engage them. The family will take the clinician's lead. If the therapist is clear about what he or she is doing and explains the need for a full assessment, the family generally is satisfied.

For example, a therapist might listen to a presenting problem and then summarize as follows before going on to the full assessment:

> If I have it right, things first changed when your daughter had a head injury. This was devastating to each of you individually and led to a number of changes in the family.
>
> [To the mother]: You chose to go back to school, at least partially to get away from it all and focus on something else.

[To the father]: You felt distanced as your wife spent more and more time studying, so your response was to spend more time at work. The effect of all of this has been that family matters have been left on the shelf, household tasks aren't being addressed, and problems are not being solved. We will revisit this set of problems that brought you in here, but first I want to ask you some questions about how your family functions. Is that ok with you . . . ?

Once the assessment begins and family members see that they each will have an opportunity to express their feelings and their views of the family issues, they come to an appreciation of the assessment and of what the clinician is doing. The pace of the interview is set by the needs of the family. By the end of an evaluation, the clinician will have a clear and concise understanding of the presenting problem as well as an understanding of each of the dimensions of the MMFF and the transactional pattern that maintains or perpetuates the problem. Specifically, the therapist will: (1) be able to describe a history of the problem in succinct terms, (2) discuss its impact on the family, (3) recognize specific family dimensions affected by the problem, and (4) understand what the family has done when attempting to solve the problem as well as the outcome of those efforts.

Therapists (clinicians, counselors) often have a checklist that they refer to (or that they have memorized) when conducting evaluations. There is a similar process when assessing families—the checklist is provided by the six dimensions of family functioning and one overall rating.

If they want to talk about a serious problem, should I interrupt to complete my assessment?

Listen enough so that the family knows you have understood, you feed back your understanding, and then go back to the assessment with a plan to address the problem along the way. It may be helpful to let the family know that it is important to gain an understanding of the problem within the context of their family's functioning.

What is the evidence that the McMaster approach is useful?

Throughout this book we have discussed how the McMaster approach is useful in clinical, teaching, and research work. In chapter 4, we demonstrated how a community practice and health services group successfully implemented the McMaster model and treatment approach as part of its community outreach program. In chapter 5, we delineated how each of the instruments is used for clinical, research, and teaching purposes. We provided examples of cases and how they were useful to a clinician, a researcher, and a trainee. The examples were drawn from a variety of disciplines, including family therapists, social workers, psychologists, and psychiatrists. In chapter 6, we summarized our research findings, documenting our work in populations with medical or psychiatric illness.

Evidence from our studies suggests that family functioning is related to course of illness, including poor outcome, recovery, suicidality, caregiver strain and burden, and comorbid illness. Predictive ability of the course or outcome of an illness has enormous implications regarding how best to utilize shrinking resources, including which patients or families to target for early intervention strategies, and which treatment option might work best for the short- and long-term course of illness. Despite the apparent relationship that we have found between family functioning and course of illness, we have not found a significant direct effect of PCSTF on remission or recovery in depression or bipolar disorder in the preliminary analyses of our treatment trials. We have found, however, that family therapy does have a positive effect on a family's functioning when one family member has a mood disorder.[97]

We are in the process of untangling the relationship between family functioning and compliance issues, coping mechanisms, quality of life, supportive interventions, and adjustment to a family member's illness. It may be that, rather than having a direct effect on a patient's illness, family treatment has powerful indirect effects. Family therapy may be more useful in helping a family adjust to a diagnosis (as described in chapter 5) or in helping family members cope with a chronic medical or psychiatric condition, particularly when the biological substrata of the conditions are the definitive variables.

In addition to our own work, we receive requests for information about our program and instruments, as well as inquiries about new uses of the McMaster model on a continuous basis. About one half of the requests we receive in the Family Research Program are from clinicians/therapists/counselors who practice in the community and are interested in the practical aspects of the treatment model. Another half is from clinician/researchers who incorporate components of the model into various parts of their clinic or research program. Some of the topics that have been or are being explored through use of the McMaster model (by means of the FAD, MCRS, McSiff, FITT or PCSTF) include: assessing at-risk children and their families throughout regional school systems; predicting successful family adoption; assessing families who provide foster care; learning how families respond to unemployment, civil war, forced migrations and adjustment to new living conditions (including new countries); comparing ethnic groups who have settled in different countries.

In preparing this book we surveyed several databases to see how clinicians and researchers are using the McMaster instruments. We accessed over 150 published articles and numerous unpublished theses that reference the McMaster approach, treatment, or specific assessments. We divided the publications into seven broad areas and include them in Part II (see Related Articles) as a list of additional readings. We were impressed with the broad range of areas that are represented and hope researchers find this listing useful.

CHAPTER **8**

Conclusions

We began this book by recognizing the renewed interest in understanding and practicing family therapy by psychiatrists, pediatricians, psychologists, social workers, psychiatric nurses, mental health professionals, pastoral counselors and, of course, family therapists. The McMaster family therapy approach that Epstein and colleagues first put into motion in the 1960s was, in hindsight, more consequential than they realized at the time. Components of the McMaster approach have been used over the past fifty years in a variety of clinical and nonclinical settings, its instruments have been translated into 20 languages, and its use in research is evident in the large bibliography we have compiled on a wide range of topics. We presented detailed guides for understanding and implementing the McMaster approach in earlier sections of this book.

Two overarching themes dominate the work that has been done over the past four decades and continue to direct us in our current thinking. First, the early developers of the model understood that their way of thinking about families, their inclusion of the family as an integral part of a patient's care, and their method of implementing family therapy was radical for psychiatry. It was not just the use of a systems approach and a systematic method of assessing and treating families that was a departure from the usual care of patients. Specific aspects of the McMaster approach itself were innovative when the model was introduced and remain novel today. Second, while the comprehensive method of evaluating and treating families was certainly innovative, the programmatic approach these developers took in integrating the clinical, teaching, and research components of the model was an equally important contribution to the field of behavioral health in general, and to family studies in particular.

Clinical

Two important innovations of the McMaster approach are the explanation and expectations set by the therapist at the beginning of treatment, and the thorough assessment of the family system before the start of any therapy. In addition, the clinician's role as a therapist is de-emphasized while his or her role as collaborator, educator, and facilitator is enhanced. Because of the shift from the traditional role of a clinician, family members become active participants in the family therapy, learn to recognize issues that create problems in the family's functioning, and to increase their ability to address and solve problems themselves as a family unit. Without dismissing or overlooking a family's weaknesses or pathology, the therapist draws on the family's strengths, emphasizing healthy aspects in the family system and using family members as a valued resource. Each family member is asked for his opinion about family issues, suggestions about how to resolve differences, and reactions to the therapist's input. The openness between the clinician and family members adds to a sense of empowerment that the family gains as they progress in their treatment.

In this book we tried to capture the clinical methods of implementing the McMaster model, including the innovations mentioned above, by providing a detailed description and guide to the MMFF and the PCSTF. We outlined the philosophy behind the McMaster approach and provided examples of family functioning, family dysfunction, problems in identifying issues, and common errors of inexperienced, as well as experienced, clinicians. Early in this work we cautioned that merely reading this book will not enable someone to conduct family therapy, but that it will provide a detailed and systematic guide for the assessment and treatment of families. We repeat this caution. Also, we would like to reiterate that the clarity of the model and treatment plan should not be confused with simplicity. As we noted in chapter 2, it took some time for Epstein to rethink his approach to patients and families and to apply the model faithfully. Each time he did so, he was struck by its effectiveness; each time he tried to cut short the process (e.g., by a cursory family assessment, by skipping a step), he was struck by how the treatment later stalled.

Although we emphasized thoroughly assessing the family and following the guidelines of the PCSTF, clinical judgment is an intrinsic part of the McMaster approach. The treatment cannot be conducted in a paint-by-numbers mode, but requires an empathic and evolving connection with family members. Therapist skills and the McMaster treatment model form an integral approach when working with families.

Teaching

Besides the clinical approach to treating families, we highlighted the teaching and research components of our program. We explained our thinking and rationale for developing the treatment model and traced its roots from the early experimental days at McGill University (Montreal), through the development of the model and instruments at McMaster University (Hamilton, Ontario), to our current location at Brown University (Providence, Rhode Island). We provided a training chapter that detailed how we set up and developed family training programs in a community setting, an academic clinical/research program, and psychiatric residency training. The training program incorporates two rating scales (the adherence and competency scales) used to help assess areas that may be difficult for the trainee to master and to help us evaluate training. We gave details of our training program so colleagues who establish their own family program can avoid some of the pitfalls we encountered.

In chapter 5, we provided examples of the instruments developed for the McMaster model and how they may be used in teaching the model to new or experienced therapists. We suggested how some therapists use the FAD to teach family members about different family members' perspectives on several areas of family life. We discussed the McSiff as a particularly useful instrument to help a less experienced clinician or a paraprofessional learn how to assess a family, and how to obtain information necessary for an objective rating of the family's functioning. Throughout this book we emphasized our strong belief in a continuous learning process embedded within our program. We continually learn from and elicit feedback from our colleagues, our students, and the families we treat.

Research

Another important principle that we tried to maintain over the years is to keep a strong link between our teaching, clinical practice, and our research. This linkage serves several purposes. We continually question assumptions that we make about families and their treatment, and we learn how our research findings fit into clinical practice. Our research questions must make clinical sense for us to pursue them; our findings are interpreted clinically and are not just post hoc explanations of statistical outcomes. Finally, the clinical/research link helps us to ask and answer new questions and explore new areas of research.

Throughout our work on the McMaster approach, our clinical work stimulated our research questions and our research findings influenced our clinical practice. We described this interaction throughout the book when we discussed the historical development of the model, the theoretical constructs from which we developed our assessments, and the early pilot studies that helped us define both clinical and research concepts. In chapter 5, we explained how we use family assessments (whether subjective or objective measures) for research purposes. In chapter 6, we focused on our research findings, summarized some of our early work, and provided empirical evidence in our studies of patients with psychiatric illness, medical illness, and comorbid illnesses. We described family functioning for different diagnostic groups as well as different stages of the illness. We tested assumptions of the model in different patient populations and we provided empirical results for several study comparisons related to a family's functioning. Finally, we included preliminary analyses of treatment studies in which the McMaster family therapy was one of the treatment arms being tested.

Part II includes the assessments we developed when applying the McMaster approach, whether for clinical use, teaching, or research. We hope these instruments will be helpful no matter which component of the McMaster approach is used.

PART **II**

Family Assessment Device
Version 3

Nathan B. Epstein, MD Lawrence M. Baldwin, PhD Duane S. Bishop, MD

Instructions:

This assessment contains a number of statements about families. Read each statement carefully, and decide how well it describes your own family. You should answer according to how you see your family.

For each statement there are four (4) possible responses:

Strongly Agree (SA)	Check SA if you feel that the statement describes your family very accurately.
Agree (A)	Check A if you feel that the statement describes your family for the most part.
Disagree (D)	Check D if you feel that the statement does not describe your family for the most part.
Strongly Disagree (SD)	Check SD if you feel that the statement does not describe your family at all.

These four responses will appear below each statement like this:

41. We are not satisfied with anything short of perfection.

___ SA   ___ A   ___ D   ___ SD   _____

The answer spaces for statement 41 would look like this. For each statement, there is an answer space below. Do not pay attention to the blanks at the far right-hand side of each space. They are for office use only.

Try not to spend too much time thinking about each statement, but respond as quickly and as honestly as you can. If you have difficulty, answer with your first reaction. Please be sure to answer *every* statement and mark all your answers in the space provided *below* each statement.

1. Planning family activities is difficult because we misunderstand each other.
   ___ SA   ___ A   ___ D   ___ SD   _____

2. We resolve most everyday problems around the house.
   ___ SA   ___ A   ___ D   ___ SD   _____

3. When someone is upset the others know why.
   ___ SA   ___ A   ___ D   ___ SD   _____

4. When you ask someone to do something, you have to check that they did it.
   ___ SA   ___ A   ___ D   ___ SD   _____

5. If someone is in trouble, the others become too involved.
   ___ SA   ___ A   ___ D   ___ SD   _____

6. In times of crisis we can turn to each other for support.
   ___ SA   ___ A   ___ D   ___ SD   _____

7. We don't know what to do when an emergency comes up.
   ___ SA   ___ A   ___ D   ___ SD   _____

8. We sometimes run out of things that we need.
   ___ SA   ___ A   ___ D   ___ SD   _____

9. We are reluctant to show our affection for each other.
   ___ SA ___ A ___ D ___ SD _____

10. We make sure members meet their family responsibilities.
    ___ SA ___ A ___ D ___ SD _____

11. We cannot talk to each other about the sadness we feel.
    ___ SA ___ A ___ D ___ SD _____

12. We usually act on our decisions regarding problems.
    ___ SA ___ A ___ D ___ SD _____

13. You only get the interest of others when something is important to them.
    ___ SA ___ A ___ D ___ SD _____

14. You can't tell how a person is feeling from what they are saying.
    ___ SA ___ A ___ D ___ SD _____

15. Family tasks don't get spread around enough.
    ___ SA ___ A ___ D ___ SD _____

16. Individuals are accepted for what they are.
    ___ SA ___ A ___ D ___ SD _____

17. You can easily get away with breaking the rules.
    ___ SA ___ A ___ D ___ SD _____

18. People come right out and say things instead of hinting at them.
    ___ SA ___ A ___ D ___ SD _____

19. Some of us just don't respond emotionally.
    ___ SA ___ A ___ D ___ SD _____

20. We know what to do in an emergency.
    ___ SA ___ A ___ D ___ SD _____

21. We avoid discussing our fears and concerns.
    ___ SA ___ A ___ D ___ SD _____

22. It is difficult to talk to each other about tender feelings.
    ___ SA   ___ A   ___ D   ___ SD   _____

23. We have trouble meeting our bills.
    ___ SA   ___ A   ___ D   ___ SD   _____

24. After our family tries to solve a problem, we usually discuss whether it worked or not.
    ___ SA   ___ A   ___ D   ___ SD   _____

25. We are too self-centered.
    ___ SA   ___ A   ___ D   ___ SD   _____

26. We can express feelings to each other.
    ___ SA   ___ A   ___ D   ___ SD   _____

27. We have no clear expectations about toilet habits.
    ___ SA   ___ A   ___ D   ___ SD   _____

28. We do not show our love for each other.
    ___ SA   ___ A   ___ D   ___ SD   _____

29. We talk to people directly rather than through go-betweens.
    ___ SA   ___ A   ___ D   ___ SD   _____

30. Each of us has particular duties and responsibilities.
    ___ SA   ___ A   ___ D   ___ SD   _____

31. There are lots of bad feelings in the family.
    ___ SA   ___ A   ___ D   ___ SD   _____

32. We have rules about hitting people.
    ___ SA   ___ A   ___ D   ___ SD   _____

33. We get involved with each other only when something interests us.
    ___ SA   ___ A   ___ D   ___ SD   _____

34. There's little time to explore personal interests.
    ___ SA   ___ A   ___ D   ___ SD   _____

35. We often don't say what we mean.
___ SA ___ A ___ D ___ SD _____

36. We feel accepted for what we are.
___ SA ___ A ___ D ___ SD _____

37. We show interest in each other when we can get something out of it personally.
___ SA ___ A ___ D ___ SD _____

38. We resolve most emotional upsets that come up.
___ SA ___ A ___ D ___ SD _____

39. Tenderness takes second place to other things in our family.
___ SA ___ A ___ D ___ SD _____

40. We discuss who is to do household jobs.
___ SA ___ A ___ D ___ SD _____

41. Making decisions is a problem for our family.
___ SA ___ A ___ D ___ SD _____

42. Our family shows interest in each other only when they can get something out of it.
___ SA ___ A ___ D ___ SD _____

43. We are frank with each other.
___ SA ___ A ___ D ___ SD _____

44. We don't hold to any rules or standards.
___ SA ___ A ___ D ___ SD _____

45. If people are asked to do something, they need reminding.
___ SA ___ A ___ D ___ SD _____

46. We are able to make decisions about how to solve problems.
___ SA ___ A ___ D ___ SD _____

47. If the rules are broken, we don't know what to expect.
___ SA ___ A ___ D ___ SD _____

48. Anything goes in our family.

  ___ SA   ___ A   ___ D   ___ SD   _____

49. We express tenderness.

  ___ SA   ___ A   ___ D   ___ SD   _____

50. We confront problems involving feelings.

  ___ SA   ___ A   ___ D   ___ SD   _____

51. We don't get along well together.

  ___ SA   ___ A   ___ D   ___ SD   _____

52. We don't talk to each other when we are angry.

  ___ SA   ___ A   ___ D   ___ SD   _____

53. We are generally dissatisfied with the family duties assigned to us.

  ___ SA   ___ A   ___ D   ___ SD   _____

54. Even though we mean well, we intrude too much into each others lives.

  ___ SA   ___ A   ___ D   ___ SD   _____

55. There are rules about dangerous situations.

  ___ SA   ___ A   ___ D   ___ SD   _____

56. We confide in each other.

  ___ SA   ___ A   ___ D   ___ SD   _____

57. We cry openly.

  ___ SA   ___ A   ___ D   ___ SD   _____

58. We don't have reasonable transport.

  ___ SA   ___ A   ___ D   ___ SD   _____

59. When we don't like what someone has done, we tell them.

  ___ SA   ___ A   ___ D   ___ SD   _____

60. We try to think of different ways to solve problems.

  ___ SA   ___ A   ___ D   ___ SD   _____

Instructions on How to Score the FAD

The McMaster Family Assessment Device (FAD) is designed to measure family functioning as described in the MMFF. It is made up of 7 scales, one measuring overall family functioning, and one for each of the 6 dimensions of the model. Each FAD item belongs to only one of the scales. Some items describe healthy functioning while others describe unhealthy functioning. Table 1 (below) indicates the items for each scale, classified according to whether they describe healthy or unhealthy functioning. Negative items are transformed on the scoring sheet as explained below.

Table 1 Assignment of Items to Scales

	Problem Solving	Communication	Roles	Affective Responsiveness	Affective Involvement	Behavior Control	General Functioning
Healthy Functioning Items	2*	3	10	49		20	6
	12	18	30*	57		32	16
	24	29*	40			55	26
	38	43					36
	50	59					46
	60						56
Unhealthy Functioning Items		14	4	9	5	7	1
		22*	8*	19	13	17	11
		35*	15	28	25	27	21
		52	23	39	33	44	31
			34		37	47	41
			45		42	48	51
			53		54		
			58*				

In Table 1, items marked with an asterisk are seven items added after the original report. They increase the reliability of the scales and do not affect their intercorrelation with other scales.

To score the FAD, code all responses as follows:

Strongly agree	= 1
Agree	= 2
Disagree	= 3
Strongly disagree	= 4

The FAD scoring sheet is used to score an individual's responses. The first step is to score all of the answers in the columns to the extreme left. The negative items are transformed by subtracting them from 5 and entering them in the second column headed TRANSFORMED SCORE. On the right-hand side of the scoring sheet are seven columns of boxes, one column for each of the seven scales. The scale to which an item belongs is indicated by the column in which the box aligned with the item falls. The item scores (transformed scores for unhealthy items) are next transferred to their appropriate boxes. To calculate a scale score, simply add the scores in each column and divide the sum by the number of items in the column that were answered. A family score is the average of all individual scores. The scale scores will range from 1.00 (healthy) to 4.00 (unhealthy). *If more than 40% of the items for a scale are missing, a scale score is not calculated. It is designated missing.*

FAD Scoring

McMaster Model Dimensions

Response	Trans-formed Score	Problem Solving	Com-muni-cation	Roles	Affective Respon-siveness	Affective Involve-ment	Behavior Control	General Function-ing
1. 5 – ___ = _____								_____
2. _____		_____						
3. _____			_____					
4. 5 – ___ = _____			_____					
5. 5 – ___ = _____				_____				
6. _____								_____
7. 5 – ___ = _____						_____		
8. 5 – ___ = _____			_____					
9. 5 – ___ = _____				_____				
10. _____				_____				
11. 5 – ___ = _____								_____
12. _____		_____						
13. 5 – ___ = _____					_____			
14. 5 – ___ = _____			_____					
15. 5 – ___ = _____			_____					
16. _____								_____
17. 5 – ___ = _____						_____		
18. _____			_____					

McMaster Model Dimensions

Response	Transformed Score	Problem Solving	Communication	Roles	Affective Responsiveness	Affective Involvement	Behavior Control	General Functioning
19.	5 – ___ = ___				___			
20.	___						___	
21.	5 – ___ = ___							___
22.	5 – ___ = ___		___					
23.	5 – ___ = ___			___				
24.	___			___				
25.	5 – ___ = ___					___		
26.	___							___
27.	5 – ___ = ___						___	
28.	5 – ___ = ___				___			
29.	___			___				
30.	___			___				
31.	5 – ___ = ___							___
32.	___						___	
33.	5 – ___ = ___					___		
34.	5 – ___ = ___			___				
35.	5 – ___ = ___		___					
36.	___							___
37.	5 – ___ = ___					___		
38.	___	___						
39.	5 – ___ = ___				___			
40.	___			___				
41.	5 – ___ = ___							___
42.	5 – ___ = ___					___		
43.	___			___				
44.	5 – ___ = ___						___	
45.	5 – ___ = ___			___				
46.	___							___
47.	5 – ___ = ___						___	
48.	5 – ___ = ___						___	
49.	___				___			

McMaster Model Dimensions

Response	Trans-formed Score	Problem Solving	Com-muni-cation	Roles	Affective Respon-siveness	Affective Involve-ment	Behavior Control	General Function-ing
50. _____ ---------- _____								
51. 5 – ____ = _____ --- _____								
52. 5 – ____ = _____ ------------ _____								
53. 5 – ____ = _____ -------------------- _____								
54. 5 – ____ = _____ -- _____								
55. _____ --- _____								
56. _____ --- _____								
57. _____ -- _____								
58. 5 – ____ = _____ -------------------- _____								
59. _____ ---------------------- _____								
60. _____ ---------- _____								

Sum of Responses	_____	_____	_____	_____	_____	_____	_____
Number of Questions Answered	_____	_____	_____	_____	_____	_____	_____
Scale Score	_____	_____	_____	_____	_____	_____	_____

Family Assessment Device – General Functioning Scale

1. Planning family activities is difficult because we
   misunderstand each other.
   ___ SA ___ A ___ D ___ SD _____

2. In times of crisis we can turn to each other for support.
   ___ SA ___ A ___ D ___ SD _____

3. We cannot talk to each other about the sadness we feel.
   ___ SA ___ A ___ D ___ SD _____

4. Individuals are accepted for what they are.
   ___ SA ___ A ___ D ___ SD _____

5. We avoid discussing our fears and concerns.
   ___ SA ___ A ___ D ___ SD _____

6. We can express feelings to each other.
   ___ SA ___ A ___ D ___ SD _____

7. There are lots of bad feelings in the family.
   ___ SA ___ A ___ D ___ SD _____

8. We feel accepted for what we are.
   ___ SA ___ A ___ D ___ SD _____

9. Making decisions is a problem for our family.
   ___ SA ___ A ___ D ___ SD _____

10. We are able to make decisions about how to solve problems.
    ___ SA ___ A ___ D ___ SD _____

11. We don't get along well together.
    ___ SA ___ A ___ D ___ SD _____

12. We confide in each other.
    ___ SA ___ A ___ D ___ SD _____

FAD General Functioning Scoring

1. 5 – _____ = _____

2. _____

3. 5 – _____ = _____

4. _____

5. 5 – _____ = _____

6. _____

7. 5 – _____ = _____

8. _____

9. 5 – _____ = _____

10. _____

11. 5 – _____ = _____

12. _____

$$\text{Total} \frac{\_\_\_\_\_}{12} = \_\_\_\_\_$$

A score of 2.00 or above indicates problematic family functioning. The higher the score, the more problematic the family member perceives the family's overall functioning.

McMaster Clinical Rating Scale

Nathan B. Epstein, MD Lawrence M. Baldwin, PhD Duane S. Bishop, MD

Introduction

Since the McMaster Model Clinical Rating Scale (MCRS) evaluates families according to the MMFF, a rater must be familiar with the model in order to obtain an accurate rating. By itself, this manual does not provide an adequate introduction. It contains brief descriptions of the MMFF dimensions, anchor point descriptions for the dimensions, and rating guidelines for using the scale. In order to obtain the necessary information to rate the family's functioning, a clinician assesses the family as outlined in previous chapters. The MCRS rating can be made by either the clinician doing the assessment or by an observer. Ratings made without complete information are likely to be wrong and should be avoided.

The MCRS assesses six dimensions of family functioning: (1) Problem Solving, (2) Communication, (3) Roles, (4) Affective Responsiveness, (5) Affective Involvement, (6) Behavior Control, and one overall rating, General Functioning. Each dimension is rated on a seven-point scale with 1 indicating severely disturbed functioning and 7 indicating superior functioning. A rating between 1 and 4 on any scale indicates that an individual within the family or the family as a whole is likely to need clinical help. A rating between 5 and 7 on any scale indicates that disturbances in that area are minor and not likely to require clinical help. Each of the six sections in this manual describes the rating of one of the dimensions of the MMFF. All sections have the same organization beginning with a definition of the concepts involved in that particular dimension. Next, we list a description of family characteristics at three levels of functioning: severely disturbed (1), nonclinical (5), and superior (7) followed by a set of principles for rating the family along the 7-point scale.

Ratings should be made carefully but not obsessively. The rater should have the meaning of a dimension clearly in mind before starting. If the family is clearly disturbed, the descriptions for the 1 and 5 ratings are reviewed before making the rating. If the family is clearly functioning well, the 5 and 7 anchor descriptions are reviewed before making the final rating. If it is unclear where the family should be rated, all 3 anchor descriptions are reviewed. In cases where there is insufficient data to make a rating, a notation is made in the appropriate place on the rating form. While the anchor point descriptions act as markers for the scale, the rater interpolates from them to arrive at ratings for the family. The principles for rating each scale help guide such decisions. Ratings assess the *family system's functioning* for a given dimension. One or two family members may have difficulty with a dimension while the family as a whole functions very effectively. Other members often compensate for individual problems. Ratings focus on the family system *as a unit* and not on individuals or on a summary of individual characteristics.

Problem Solving

Family problem solving refers to the family's ability to resolve problems to a level that maintains effective family functioning. A family problem is an issue which threatens the integrity and functional capacity of the family and which the family has difficulty resolving. Families can have ongoing difficulties that do not threaten them in this way; such difficulties are not considered in rating family problem solving. Family problems can be divided into two types: Instrumental and Affective. Instrumental problems are concrete and mechanical such as provision of money, food, clothing, housing, transportation. Affective problems are emotional, such as disruptive anger or depression. Families with instrumental problems rarely, if ever, deal well with affective problems that comprise the more basic nature of instrumental problems. However, families with affective problems may deal adequately with instrumental problems.

The MMFF delineates seven steps in problem solving:

1. Identification of the problem
2. Communication of the problem to appropriate resources
3. Formulation of alternatives

4. Decision to take a particular action
5. Action
6. Monitoring results of the action
7. Evaluation of the problem-solving process

   Families differ in their problem solving effectiveness. The differences can be viewed along a continuum. A healthy family has few, if any unresolved problems, and quickly and systematically deals with those that arise. Toward the disturbed end of the continuum, a family's problem solving behavior is less systematic and the family accomplishes fewer of the problem solving steps. At the extreme of the disturbed end of the continuum, a family is unable to identify problems, and consistently denies or mislabels them, so that they remain unresolved and generate much conflict.

Description of Anchor Points:

Characteristics of families that fall at the three anchor points on the Problem Solving scale are:

Severely Disturbed
1. The family does not recognize that problems exist.
2. The family is unable to correctly identify problems. This may involve projection, displacement or distortion.
3. The family is vaguely aware of problems, but engages in no discussion of them, thus precluding formal identification of problems.
4. The family endures long-standing instrumental problems even though resources are available to solve them.
5. The family cannot attempt to solve problems without generating much conflict.

Nonclinical/Healthy
1. The family allows no disruptive instrumental problems to go unresolved.
2. The family allows few affective problems to go unresolved. Most (70–80%) are resolved quickly and efficiently.
3. One or more family members notice problems when they arise, though they may occasionally mislabel the problems.
4. When a family member identifies a problem, she or he communicates it to the others.
5. For most problems (70–80%) family members propose specific alternative solutions, and choose among them.

6. The family solves 70–80% of its problems quickly and effectively: it solves the remaining 20–30% satisfactorily but the process is relatively inefficient/haphazard.
    This may be due to:
    a. a lack of awareness of how a problem is solved
    b. a willingness to allow resolution to take too long
    c. the non-participation of some family members

Superior

1. The family quickly recognizes that a problem had developed.
2. The family accurately identifies the problem.
3. Through discussion, the family clearly defines alternatives and decides on a course of action.
4. After acting, the family regularly evaluated its success.
5. The family is flexible: it adjusts approaches and solutions to different situations.
6. The family has a history of dealing successfully with problems.

Principles for Rating:

1. The fewer unresolved problems, the healthier the family.
2. The more problem solving steps accomplished, the healthier the family.
3. We rate a healthy or nonclinical family at 5 or higher.
4. We always rate a family with unresolved instrumental problems at 4 or lower.
5. If a family's competence in problem-solving varies greatly, we rate how well the family deals with its most potentially disruptive problem.

Communication

Communication is defined as the exchange of information among family members. As in problem solving, two major areas, Instrumental and Affective communication, are considered. Though affective communication in particular may include gestures, we limit ourselves to considering verbal expression almost exclusively, because it is the least ambiguous. In both of these areas we evaluate the quality of the communication along two continua. On the clear-to-masked continuum, messages run from clear to camouflaged, muddied, or vague. A message is clear when it is concise, relevant, and consistent with other information. It is masked when it lacks these qualities. On the direct-to-indirect continuum, we consider for whom the message is intended and to whom it is spoken. When these are the same person, the message is direct. When the speaker does not address the person for whom the message is intended, communication is indirect. When the intended recipient fails to receive the message, the communication is masked. These two continua are independent, so four styles of communication are possible:

1. Clear and direct
2. Clear and indirect
3. Masked and direct
4. Masked and indirect

When non-verbal messages directly conflict with verbal messages, there is either masked or indirect communication. These are the only circumstances in which we take note of non-verbal messages.

A healthy family is one that communicates in a clear and direct manner. As we move toward pathology, communication becomes less clear and direct. In a very disturbed family, communication is neither clear nor direct. Difficulties may enter not only in the sending of messages but also in receiving or interpreting them. It is important to make the distinction between affective communication and affective responsiveness, or the ability to respond with feelings. Please refer to the definition of Affective Responsiveness before rating Communication.

Description of Anchor Points:

Severely Disturbed

1. The family does not communicate. Rather there is:
   a. Silence
   b. Chaotic talking
   c. Irrelevant talking
2. Instrumental messages are masked, so that the content cannot be understood by other family members.
3. Instrumental messages are indirect, so that even clear content goes to inappropriate family members.
4. A family's affective communication is masked.
5. A family's affective communication is indirect.
6. Messages are communicated clearly and directly by ordinary standards, but some members of the family still do not hear or perceive what is being said.

Nonclinical/Healthy
1. All of the information necessary for instrumental functions is communicated clearly and directly.

2. In most situations (70–80%) where communication of affect is required, it is clear and direct and received appropriately.
3. Only in the remaining 20–30% of situations are messages either inadequately clarified or inappropriately directed.
4. If a message is unclear, an attempt is made to clarify it.
5. Communication may sometimes be inefficient or inadequate, but not to the extent that it is disruptive.

Superior
1. A family transmits messages when they are called for.
2. All messages (instrumental and affective) are clear and direct, and there is no misunderstanding.
3. If the recipient of a message does not completely understand it, he or she immediately asks for, and receives, clarification.
4. Messages are transmitted concisely and efficiently.

Principles for Rating:
1. The more often communication is masked, the lower the rating.
2. The more often communication is indirect, the lower the rating.
3. The more often masked messages cause miscommunication, the lower the rating.
4. Masked and/or indirect communication about instrumental issues is rated lower than if the difficulties occur when communicating affective issues.
5. Communication problems restricted to a single-family member are less serious when they are compensated for by good communication of other family members.
6. The more communication problems interfere with other aspects of family functioning, the lower the rating.

Roles

Family roles are the repetitive patterns of behavior by which family members fulfill family functions. Rating a family on the Role dimension involves assessing how well family functions are fulfilled. The most basic of these are the Necessary Family Functions. They form the basis for Necessary Family Roles. These break down into five groupings:

1. Provision of Resources. This includes providing money, food, clothing, and shelter.
2. Nurturance and Support. This includes providing comfort, warmth, reassurance, and support for family members.

3. Personal Development. This includes physical, emotional, educational, and social development of the children, and career, vocational, psychological and social development of the adults.
4. Maintenance and Management of the Family System. This includes the following:
   a. Decision-making Functions. Usually a parental role, these include the settling of disagreements and assumption of leadership.
   b. Boundaries and Membership. Dealing with extended families, taking in of boarders, controlling family size, and dealing with external institutions and agencies, such as church and government.
   c. Behavior Control Functions. These include maintaining discipline and enforcing behavioral standards.
   d. Household Finances. Dealing with monthly bills, banking, income tax and other household money-handling.
   e. Health-Related Functions. Dealing with illness, health maintenance, and compliance.
5. Adult Sexual Gratification: This includes degree of satisfaction with the couples interactions.

In addition to assessing how well the necessary functions are fulfilled. Role Allocation and Role Accountability must also be considered in rating the Role dimension. Role Allocation is concerned with a family's pattern of assigning tasks, and embraces a number of issues:

1. Is the assignment implicit or explicit? How is it accomplished?
2. Does the person assigned a task or function have the skill necessary to carry it out?
3. Is the family member given the power necessary to complete the job?
4. Can reassignment take place easily?
5. Are tasks allocated to the satisfaction of family members, or are some members overburdened while others avoid or are denied responsibilities ?
6. Do family members cooperate and collaborate?

Role Accountability is concerned with family members' sense of responsibility for the task they are assigned, and the monitoring and corrective mechanisms which assure task completion.

1. Are individuals made to feel responsible for tasks or functions?
2. Does the individual concerned honor that responsibility?
3. Is the fulfillment of that responsibility monitored by other family members?

4. Do family members move to correct situations where tasks are not being performed?

In a healthy family, all the necessary functions are fulfilled and allocation of tasks is reasonable and does not overburden anyone. In a severely disturbed family, one or more of the necessary functions are not adequately discharged.

Description of Anchor Points:

Severely Disturbed:
1. One or more of the first four necessary functions (Provision of Resources, Nurturance and Support, Personal Development, Maintenance and Management of the Family System) are consistently not accomplished.
2. Adult Sexual Gratification is a source of major conflict.
3. Assignment of tasks does not take place or is totally ineffective.
4. Assignment, when it occurs, is to individuals who cannot reasonably be expected to complete the task.
5. The family fails to ensure that tasks are carried out, and fails to ensure that individuals have a sense of responsibility for tasks.
6. Tasks are distributed inequitably among family members.
7. The family is unable to compensate for disruptions in role functioning.

Nonclinical/Healthy:
1. All of the first four necessary functions are carried out.
2. Most roles (70–80%) necessary to the first four functions are handled efficiently and effectively.
3. The remaining (20–30%) of roles are inefficiently or ineffectively handled, but this does not significantly disrupt family function.
4. Responsibility for tasks is, for the most part, felt and met.
5. Task distribution is reasonable.
6. The family is adequately able to compensate for disruptions.

Superior
1. All the necessary functions are carried out smoothly and efficiently.
2. Roles are clearly assigned.
3. Roles are appropriately assigned.
4. Responsibility is easily and firmly established, and little or no reinforcement or reminding of family members is required.
5. Task distribution is reasonable and acceptable to all family members.

6. The family is well able to compensate for disruptions in its normal functioning, and members are able to adapt their roles as change or crisis demand.

Principles for Rating:

1. In order to be rated 5, a family almost always adequately discharges the first four necessary functions. In rare cases, the family may still rate 5 in the presence of disturbed adult sexual gratification. (Low frequency of sexual activity might not constitute a disturbance if both partners clearly express satisfaction with the arrangement). Usually, however, a disturbance in adult sexual gratification will require rating of 4 or less.
2. If more than 30% of the role assignments are unclear or inconsistent, the rating must be 4 or less.
3. If more than 30% of responsibility for tasks is unspecified or disputed, the rating must be 4 or less.
4. If any family member takes on an excessive number of assignments in the areas of the first four necessary functions, the rating must be 4 or less.
5. If any family member takes inappropriate responsibility for assignments in the areas of the first four necessary family functions, the rating must be 4 or less.

Affective Responsiveness

Affective Responsiveness is the ability to respond to a range of stimuli with the appropriate quantity and quality of feeling. There are two general classes of affect to consider:

1. Welfare emotions: affection, warmth, tenderness, love, consolation, happiness and joy.
2. Emergency emotions: anger, fear, loneliness, anxiety, sadness, disappointment and depression.

In order to rate a family on Affective Responsiveness, it is necessary to assess each individual member's capacity to experience the full range of emotion and to assess whether the emotions they experience are situationally appropriate. Having assessed the individuals, the rating is made for the family system. An emotional response may be inappropriate in several different ways. A person may experience an abnormal emotion for a given situation.

Alternately, the emotion may be normal in type, but its intensity or duration may be unusually great or small.

A healthy family can and does have the capacity to respond with the full range of emotions. As we move toward the disturbed family, emotions may be inappropriate in type, intensity, duration or quantity. Severely disturbed families experience very constricted or highly excessive amounts of affect, most often poorly controlled and/or integrated. These are often inappropriate to the pertinent stimuli. Since this is such a subjective matter, there is considerable personal, and much cultural variation in what is considered to be an appropriate response. Raters must take this into account when assessing families from cultures other than their own.

Description of Anchor Points:

Severely Disturbed
1. Any of the following general patterns are present:
   a. Severe restriction of emotion.
   b. Constant overproduction of emotion.
   c. Chaotic liability of emotions, random mood swings.
2. Affective responsiveness is disturbed in the areas of both emergency and welfare emotions.
3. The majority of family members, including one or both parents, have difficulty with their affective responsiveness.
4. Affective experiences disrupt general family functioning.

Nonclinical/Healthy
1. The types of emotions experienced are appropriate to the situation, though the intensity or duration of the response may, at times, be inappropriate.
2. No single family member experiences consistently inappropriate affect in more than one emotional area.
3. Less than half of the family experiences impaired responsiveness in any one affect.
4. To the extent that inappropriate responsiveness exists for some family members, it is compensated for by the rest of the family.

Superior
1. All family members experience both welfare and emergency emotions in the appropriate situations nearly all of the time.
2. The range of emotions experienced reinforces family functioning.
3. On the occasions when an inappropriate response occurs, the family compensates for it and there is not disruption of family functioning.

Principles for Rating:

1. In order to rate a family's affective responsiveness, we must assess each member on the full range of both welfare and emergency emotions.
2. Inappropriate welfare or emergency affective responsiveness in a family member may or may not disrupt family functioning. Only if family functioning is disrupted a score of 4 or less be given.
3. The more family members experience inappropriate responses, the lower the rating of the family.
4. The more that inappropriate responsiveness disrupts family functioning, the lower the rating of the family.

Affective Involvement

We define affective involvement as the extent to which family members show interest in, and place value on, each other's activities and concerns. We look at how much, and in what way, they show interest and invest themselves in each other. Affective involvement may range from non-existent to extreme, and health lies in the middle of the spectrum.

Most Disturbed
- Lack of Involvement: No interest or involvement displayed and/or experienced.
- Symbiotic Involvement: Extreme and pathological interest and/or investment in others. Symbiotic involvement is seen only in very disturbed relationships. In such relationships, both persons have marked difficulty in differentiating themselves from each other.

Intermediate
- Involvement Devoid of Feeling: Some interest and/or investment in each other, but this is primarily intellectual in nature.
- Narcissistic Involvement: Concern for other family members is primarily a reflection of or secondary to the concern felt for oneself.
- Over-involvement: Excessive interest and/or investment in each other without the loss of individual differentiation.

Healthy
- Empathic Involvement: Interest and/or investment in each other for the sake of the other.
- Children's ability to empathize develops with age. This must be taken into account when rating families with young children.

Description of Anchor Points:

Severely Disturbed

1. In families characterized by lack of involvement, the following are found:
   a. Family members are so uninvolved with each other that there is no collaboration.
   b. Family members do not show any interest in each other.
   c. Individuals "do their own thing," "go their own way," with little or no comment from or interaction with others.
   d. Involvement that does take place is often forced by instrumental necessity.
   e. Meaningful relationships are with people from outside the family.
   f. Family members spend little or no time with each other.
2. Symbiotic involvement is present when there is sharing of delusions and/or cognitive difficulties such as poor reality testing, looseness of association, or tangential ideas. One or more of the following is likely to be found in families with symbiotic involvement:
   a. Any attempt at separating the symbiotic dyad leads to catastrophic reactions.
   b. Other family members do not intrude upon or force separation of the dyad (or triad)
   c. There is lack of personal privacy within the dyad.
   d. Independent decisions are rarely made.

Nonclinical/Healthy

1. There is involvement and it is non-symbiotic.
2. Family members spend some of their time discussing personal interests.
3. Family members spontaneously show an interest in other family members.
4. An overall family pattern of over-involvement, narcissistic involvement, or involvement devoid of feeling may occur briefly and sporadically in response to crises or particular events, but it is not the norm.
5. Family members indicate that others in the family take a genuine interest in them.
6. Some individual family members may consistently show some overinvolvement, narcissistic involvement, or involvement devoid of feeling, but they are in the minority.

Superior
1. All family members demonstrate, recognize, and accept empathic involvement with each other.
2. There is respect for individual privacy and activity.
3. Family members show a genuine interest in each other's activities.

Principles for Rating:
The chart below shows the range of ratings applied to families that display particular types of involvement.

	1	2	3	4	5	6
Symbiotic Involvement	_____					
Lack of Involvement	_____					
Narcissistic Involvement		_____				
Involvement Devoid of Feelings		_____				
Over Involvement			_____			
Empathic Involvement					_____	

The following rules may be helpful in making ratings:

1. The more the family shows non-empathic involvement, the lower the rating.
2. The more the style of affective involvement impairs general family functioning, the lower the rating.
3. The more the style of affective involvement generates conflict, the lower the rating.
4. The more the style of affective involvement inhibits normal development of family members, the lower the rating.
5. A family in which a parent shows pathological involvement is rated lower than one in which the pathological involvement noted is that related to behavior of the children.

Behavior Control

We define behavior control as the way in which a family expresses and maintains standards for the behavior of its members, particularly as regards:

1. Physical danger.
2. Psychobiological needs and drives, including eating, sleeping, eliminating, sex and aggression.
3. Social behavior, both within and outside the family.

There are four possible styles of behavior control:

1. *Rigid Control:* Little room for negotiation or change of standards regardless of the context.
2. *Flexible Control:* reasonable standards and flexibility with room for negotiation and change depending on the context.
3. *Laissez-faire Control:* no standards are adopted and total latitude is allowed regardless of context.
4. *Chaotic Control:* there is random shifting of standards so that family members do not know which will apply in a given situation.

In general, flexible behavior control is the most effective, and should be rated highest. It is followed by rigid and laissez-faire in that order. Chaotic is most pathological, and calls for a very low rating. In assessing thus function of the family, we make some allowance for the age of the family members. Note also that actual enforcement of behavioral standards, such as punishing a child, is considered to fall under Maintenance and Management of the Family System in the Role Dimension.

Description of Anchor Points:

Severely Disturbed:
1. Family members behave in ways that significantly risk physical harm to themselves or others.
2. Family members have bizarre, anti-social or immoderate patterns of eating, sleeping, eliminating, sexuality or aggressiveness. Examples: alcoholism, drug abuse, incest, sexual perversion or promiscuity, anorexia nervosa, child or spouse abuse.
3. Family members' behavior betrays their significant lack of respect for each other.
4. Family members do not agree among themselves on rules for behavior.
5. The family frequently predictably shifts among laissez-faire, flexible, and rigid styles of behavior control (chaotic control).
6. The family has reasonable clear standards, but no effective follow through, with the result that standards are not adhered to.
7. There is significant conflict as a result of behavior control problems.

Nonclinical/Healthy:
1. The family is adequately concerned with the physical safety of members.

2. Family members may disagree as to what standards apply, but these disagreements are clearly limited, and in any given situation there is a final, acceptance of a set of standards.
3. Behavior control deviates from a flexible pattern. However, this deviation does not lead to disruption of family functioning.
4. The family may not follow through enforcing all rules, but does so in the important areas of family life.
5. Family members know what the standards for behavior are.

Superior:
1. Generally, a flexible style of behavior control predominates.
2. Standards are generally clear even though their interpretation may vary according to context.
3. Standards are based on respect for others, inside and outside of the family.
4. More rigid behavior control may be invoked in dangerous situations.
5. Children participate in the issue of behavior control.

Principles for Rating:

1. The expectations for behavior of parents and children is taken into account in rating the family.
2. When the behavior control function of the family does not effectively deal with the behavior of one of the parents, the family is rated lower than when a child's behavior is not effectively handled.
3. Where children take advantage of parents' failure to support each other in administering the rules, the rating is lower.
4. The ordering of styles of behavior control from the most effective to the least effective functioning is: flexible control, rigid control, laissez-faire control, chaotic control.
5. Families in which control is significantly chaotic are rated 1 or 2. Chaotic control exists when standards and thus behavior are unpredictable. Family members lack consensus about standards and/or undercut each other in the enforcement of standards, or sometimes enforce standards and sometimes do not.
6. Although flexible control is generally most effective, rigid behavior control is at times appropriate for young children who have not yet reached the age of reason.
7. Rigid behavior control can be appropriate in some dangerous situations.

Clinician/Rater Family Assessment after the Interview

Family Name/ID:_____ Rater ID:_____

Please be sure to rate all seven categories, but only one rating per category is allowed:

	Very Disturbed				Non-Clinical	Superior	Insufficient Information
Problem Solving	1	2	3	4	5	6	7	II
Communication	1	2	3	4	5	6	7	II
Roles	1	2	3	4	5	6	7	II
Affective Responsiveness	1	2	3	4	5	6	7	II
Affective Involvement	1	2	3	4	5	6	7	II
Behavior Control	1	2	3	4	5	6	7	II
General Functioning	1	2	3	4	5	6	7	II

If uncertain about any of the ratings, please check the dimension and briefly explain the reason of the uncertainty.

___ Problem Solving _____

___ Communication _____

___ Roles _____

___ Affective Responsiveness _____

___ Affective Involvement _____

___ Behavior Control _____

___ General Functioning _____

If there were any additional questions that needed to be asked in any of the dimensions, please make a note below:

Problem Solving _____

Communication _____

Roles _____

Affective Responsiveness _____

Affective Involvement _____

Behavior Control _____

General Functioning _____

McMaster Structured Interview
of Family Functioning

Duane S. Bishop, MD   Nathan B. Epstein, MD
Gabor I. Keitner, MD   Ivan W. Miller, PhD
Caron Zlotnick,PhD   Christine E. Ryan, PhD

Name	Age	Role: Parent/Child/Other
Interviewer _____ Date_____		
Family Surname_____		
Family Constellation:		

Instructions

The McSiff has been designed to assess basic components of six dimensions of family functioning: problem solving, communication, roles, affective responsiveness, affective involvement, and behavior control. The interviewer's task is to question, review and explore each dimension in enough depth to obtain sufficient information so that a clear and reasonable rating can be made of the family's effectiveness in handling components of each dimension.

Explore Fully

It cannot be emphasized strongly enough that the interviewer should probe, explore, discuss, and question to assure that data are obtained in enough detail that ratings and coding are accurate and reliable. Disagreements should be explored. Open interaction and exchange between family members should be fostered. If any response is unclear, the interviewer checks with family members to obtain an answer the family can agree upon. The interviewer may ask for examples in order to clarify if he or she is unclear as to what the family member said or if the intent of the family member's statement is unclear.

When a parent or any of the older children disagree about answers to a question, the interviewer notes who disagrees. If family members appear to disagree with a statement, they can be asked, "You seem to see this differently. What is your view about it?" or "How do you see it?" The interviewer can make notations at any point when the information is unclear or unusual in order to review the questionnaire after the interview. If questions are unanswered it is assumed that the information could not be obtained. The interviewer notes his/her impressions and reasons why the information could not be obtained, including whether or not it was applicable.

As much time should be taken as is needed to complete the interview without getting bogged down by incessant details or examples. A second or even third appointment may be necessary, depending on the family and the problems raised. At the end of each *dimension* the interviewer tells the family that the questions will shift to another family area. At the end of each *section* (indicated by prompt boxes used for interviewer ratings) the interviewer summarizes the findings, gives feedback to the family and checks that the correct information has been obtained.

Format

The following list includes a number of format conventions used in the McSiff.

1. The interview schedule contains *major headings.* An example is **3a Orientation**. These headings break the interview into sections dealing with orientation and with each dimension of the MMFF: Roles, Behavior Control, Problem Solving, Communication, Affective Responsiveness, Affective Involvement.

2. Statements made by the Interviewer during the course of orienting the family, reorienting them, or introducing them to a new area are in **bold print**. An example is **"OK, let me explain what I expect to do. I'm interested in understanding how you and your family function . . . "**

   Instructions for the Interviewer to follow are set in italics. An example is: *Interviewer Instruction: direct the following questions to the parents.*

3. Some questions need to be asked in *every* interview. They focus on specific content areas within each dimension. They are in bold print and are designated with an asterisk " * ".

4. Under the required questions, there are *probes* and other <u>queries</u> that may be used as a follow-up if appropriate. They are meant as guides to aid the Interviewer in exploring an area in more detail.

   Example: **Do jobs get done?**
   Probe : **If not, what happens?**

5. There are blank spaces throughout the schedule, where responses of family members can be noted. Notes may be used if a response is unusual, unclear, or noteworthy. The more detail, the easier it will be to make decisions about coding or clinical/research issues.

6. Interviewer Ratings are placed at the end of a section in a boxed area (prompt boxes) where the Interviewer makes a determination about the presence or absence of family problems in a specific component of family functioning. There are two situations in which such ratings are required. They are:
   (a) subsection ratings—ratings to assess a *component* of a dimension, for example, whether or not the family has difficulty in handling problem identification (a component of problem solving) or role allocation (a component of roles)
   (b) dimension ratings—ratings to assess the *entire* dimension and indicate whether or not there are problems in that dimension.
   The Interviewer reviews these ratings and completes the same scoring sheet used in the MCRS. It is important to note that the scoring sheet is the same for the MCRS and the McSiff; the difference be-

tween the two is based on the experience of the interviewer with the McMaster approach—whether the family information is obtained in a clinical interview or through the structured interview.

7. There are two *Coding Grids* in the interview schedule (in Roles and in Affective Responsiveness) that help the interviewer organize a series of questions in a systematic way. The rater asks suitable questions and indicates who (mother, father, child) is involved in a particular task function. Examples from the Roles grid are "Who buys the groceries?" and "Who does household chores." Examples from the Affective Responsiveness grid are "Do you feel joy/pleasure/anger and Can you give me an example of when you felt joy/pleasure/anger?"

8. Throughout the interview there are notations in the left margin that indicate the type of family composition to which the successive questions apply.

C = Couple: family composition is couple only
F = Family: family composition includes parents and child/children
S = Single: family composition is single-parent and one or more children

Example:
After discussing a problem list, the Interviewer asks:

(C,F,S)   *Who first noticed the problem?

This question applies to all families regardless of the family constellation and is indicated by the notation (C,F,S).

To explore personal development of the entire family, the Interviewer asks:

(F)   Are you both equally involved in bringing up the children?

This question applies to a two-parent family with one or more children and is indicated by the notation (F).

1. ORIENTATION

Interviewer Instruction—*Ask the family the following:*

(C,F,S)

> **I'd like to start by asking each of you what you think we are going to do today. Does anyone have any ideas?**

Interviewer checks with each family member and feeds back a synopsis of what the family said.

Examples:
- You thought I was going to ask questions about your family and how it works.
- You thought we were going to talk about Sue's problems and I was going to give you help with them.

> **OK, let me explain what I expect to do. I'm interested in understanding how you and your family function. Often the way a family works affects each person in the family and what goes on with one family member affects the others. For these reasons, I would like to understand your family. I'm going to ask a variety of questions and I'll be jumping from topic to topic. I'll let you know what I'm thinking at each step so please correct me if you think I'm getting the wrong impression. It is also important that we be honest and straightforward with each other. OK?**

Interviewer Instruction—*Check with each family member before proceeding.*

1a. **Introduction:**

(C,F,S)

> *** Do you feel there are any areas or issues that are problems or difficulties for you as a family?**

* List Problems 1. _____

2. _____

3. _____

4. _____

(use back of page if more and note here)

Interviewer Instruction—*Check the list with each member of the family. Do they agree; would they like to add to the list?*

For each problem ask:
 * **Have you discussed the problem?**
 1. _____
 2. _____
 3. _____
 4. _____

 * **Did you take any action to deal with the problem?**
 If yes: What did you do to try and deal with the problem?
 1. _____
 2. _____
 3. _____
 4. _____

 * **Was the problem resolved/sorted out?**
 If not, why not? What prevented resolution?
 1. _____
 2. _____
 3. _____
 4. _____

2. ROLES
Under this heading the interviewer is looking at the repetitive patterns of behavior by which family members fulfill family functions.

The focus is on:
   a. how well family functions are fulfilled
   b. how family tasks are distributed
   c. if the tasks are distributed equitably
   d. the extent to which individual members have a sense of responsibility for their tasks

2a. Orientation
I'm now going to ask some questions about how jobs around the house get divided up and how well things are done.

2b. Provision of Resources
   Interviewer Instructions—*Ask the family:*

(C,F,S)

* In terms of day-to-day organization I would like to know first, who is involved in the following family jobs and second, how satisfactorily each job is performed?

Interviewer Instruction—*Check off the appropriate person on the grid and note if task is not being satisfactorily carried out. If not applicable, put NA.*

	M(1)	F(2)	C1(3)	C2(4)	C3(5)	0(6)	N/A (9)	
Grocery								1//____
Shopping								2//____
Menu Planning								3//____
Cooking								4//____
Clothes Shopping								5//____
Contributes Money**								6//____
Laundry								7//____
Cleaning								8//____
Yard work								9//____
Monthly Bills								10//____
Repairs around the House***								11//____
Dealing with Cars								12//____
Large Purchases								13//____
Decision to see Doctor/Dentist								14//____
Disciplining the Children								15//____
Deals with School								16//____

M = Mother/Wife   F = Father/Husband   C = Child
O = Other   N/A = Not Applicable
Index for Coding: ++ = Major Role Resource for that task
       + = Those who also assist

** If unemployed: How long? _____
        Previous work? _____
        Reason for not working? _____
        Other sources of money (e.g., disability, welfare, pension)
        _____

*** Adjust for apartment dwellers regarding repairs.

Interviewer Instruction—*Here you shift to role functions that are not on the grid. If any children are over 18 years and working ask:*
(F,S)

> * **Do children pay room and board? If Not, Probe: Why not?**

Interviewer Rating:

The family is adequately provided for in terms of food,   No   Yes   17// __6__
shelter, transport, clothing and money

*Comment:*_____

_____

2c. Role Allocation
(C,F,S)

> * **Do you discuss who is to do various jobs?** yes
>   *Probe If No:* **What stops you?** _____

> * **Do any of you feel overburdened by your jobs?** yes
>   *Probe If Yes:* **Who feels overburdened?**

>   *Probe if unclear:* **Do you each feel that jobs and tasks are fairly divided and that everyone has a fair share given their age, health and other involvements?**

> **Is anyone doing a job they should not be doing?**

> **Does anyone feel that they or others are doing too little?** yes

> * **Do you all accept your duties without arguing or complaining?**
>   *Probe If No:*   **Who argues/complains?** no
>   **What about?**

> * **Does the arguing or complaining cause a lot of problems for the family?**

> * **Does anyone refuse assigned duties?**
> *Probe If Yes:* **How is this dealt with?**

Interviewer Instruction: *Ask additional question if not clear or appropriate.*

Has anyone been ill or have there been other occasions when you had to change around jobs and roles?
Probe: How did that work out?

Interviewer Instruction: *Here you are interested in whether someone else took over the usual household functions—not with how they dealt with an illness problem specifically.*

(F,S)

As the children grow older or living conditions change do you alter the jobs people have?
Probe If No: What stops you from doing this?

```
Interviewer Rating:

The family effectively allocates roles?        No      Yes          18//3

Comment:_____
_____
_____
```

2d.   **Role Accountability**

(C,F,S)

* **Do you feel that jobs in the house are generally handled well by your family?**
If No: What is the problem?   *yes*

* **Does anyone in the house consistently not do his or her jobs?**
If Yes: Who? What is the problem?
Probe: Do they have the skills or ability to do the job?
Do they have time to do the job?
Do they take responsibility for household jobs seriously or not care?
[i.e. is the problem lack of skills, time or attitude?]

* **Do you check that jobs get done?**   *qu*
Probe If Yes: Who checks?
If a task is not carried out what happens?

Interviewer Rating:

The family maintains good role accountability?   No   Yes

19//__4__

*Comment:*_____

_____

_____

2e. **Personal Development**

In this area the focus is on:

a.   adult career related issues, health, and socialization

b.   child rearing, career development, and socialization

For adults career related issues should be major ones (Do I change my job, take more training, accept promotions if it includes a move?) and not everyday hassles that occur in work settings.

For questions concerning children, contact with the school was covered earlier in the grid of family tasks. The interviewer assesses how the parents handle tasks related to child issues.

The difficulty in interviewing is not to be superficial, but neither is it to explore every aspect of adult career issues and socialization, every aspect of child rearing, schooling and career development in children and child socialization. The interviewer reviews and questions to the point that it is clear whether or not there are major personal development issues that remain unresolved or whether there is some other significant problem in this area. Probes and suggestions for questioning are included as a guide.

Personal values may come into play in this component of family assessment. Difficulties in the area of personal development are those that jeopardize the maximal progression and development of the child or adult. If the child is extremely bright but not being encouraged to progress or to consider challenging career choices, this may or may not be a problem. Also, the family may feel that it's fine for a child to have no friends or one friend, whereas your own perspective may be different.

Interviewer Instruction: *Ask families with couples.*

(C,F)

> * **Do you discuss major career issues with each other? For example, changing jobs, promotions, and promotions if they mean moves, planning for retirement and long-term career goals?**

* Do each of you receive help from your partner in terms of these job related issues? *No*
> *Probe*: How is it <u>helpful</u>? What does your spouse do to help with that?

* Do you ever wish you could get more help in that area? *yes*
> *Probe if Yes:* What would you like your partner to do?

* How do you think you and your spouse are doing in terms of friends, activities, general outlook on life? Do you talk to each other about these issues? *NO*

Interviewer Instruction: *Ask single-parent only.*

(S)

* Do you discuss major career issues with anyone (issues such as changing jobs, promotions, job-related moves, planning for retirement and long term career goals)?

* How do you think you are doing in terms of friends, activities, your general outlook on life? Do you talk to anyone about these issues?

* If you have problems in these areas, do you get the help you need?
> *Probe if No:* What is the problem?
> *If Yes:* From whom?

* How do you feel you are doing in terms of bringing up the children?
> *Probe:* Do you feel you need any additional help?
> *If Yes:* What is it you feel you need most?

Do you have anyone around who can help provide that?
> *If Yes:* What prevents you from receiving help?
> *If No:* Do you know of any places you can go for that type of help?

Interviewer Instruction: *Ask family only.*

(F)

* Are you both equally involved in bringing up the children? *during*
> *If No:* Who is more involved?

* (If young children) Which of you would typically be involved in:
  • Getting them up and dressed?
  • Baths, shampooing their hair? *depends*

- Putting them to bed?
- Taking them out?
- Supervising their play?
- Talking to the children?

* (If school age children or older) Which of you are involved in:
  - Talking to the children?
  - Parent/teacher/school meetings
  - Discussions of career choice?

Interviewer Instruction: *It is important to determine the relative involvement of the parents. If one parent says that they get most involved, it is important to know whether the other one does or does not get involved. If not clear, explore with the following questions.*

To the parent who gets most involved,
> **Probe: Do you think there are problems with the way your spouse gets involved?**
> *If Yes:* **In what way?**   yes

Interviewer Instruction: *Ask the parent who is not involved:*
Do you also get involved in bringing up the children?
Do you think your involvement is reasonable, that you should be more involved, or less involved?
Do you see any problems with the amount that you are involved?
> *If Yes:* **What** _____
Do you see any problems with the way your spouse is involved?

Interviewer Instruction: *The following should be asked of children of an appropriate age. Then the parents' view should be sought.*
(F,S)

* **How do you feel you/your child(ren) are doing in terms of growing up?**
  > *Probe:* **If unclear, check how they are doing in terms of:**
  > **Schooling?** _____
  > **Friends?** _____
  > **Interest?** _____
  > **Taking responsibility?** _____
  > **Getting along in society?** _____
  > **Able to take on responsibilities suitable to their age?** _____

For appropriate ages check with children and/or parents:
   Are you/they thinking of leaving home, going off to
      school? _____
   Are you/ they handling dating in appropriate
      manner? _____
   Have you/they thought about a career/kind of work they
      would like? _____

   * Do the children get an allowance or pocket money?
      Probe If Yes: Who deals with that? Are there any difficulties?

Interviewer Rating:			
The family deals effectively with personal development? No	Yes	20//	4
Re Children	No Yes	21//	5
Re Adults	No Yes	22//	3

For couples #20 and #22 should be the same, #21 is coded not applicable (NA).

2f.   **Management of the System**
(C,F,S)

   * **If a decision is made and you disagree, who would usually have the**
      final word?   Miranda
         Probe: Is that always the case? _____ yes _____
         How does it vary? _____
         What happens? _____
         Are you comfortable with it being handled this way? _____

   Interviewer Instruction: *Ask each adult individually:*
   * **Do you have problems with your parents or extended family?**
      Probe if Yes: What are the problems?   no
      _____
      How much of a problem do they create for your family?
      _____
      Do they disrupt things? _____
      Who deals with the problems? _____

* Do you have problems with your (husband's/wife's/ex-spouse) parents or family? *no , Mirandas mum*

> *Probe if Yes:* What are the problems?

> _____

> How much of a problem do they create for your
> family? _____
> Do they disrupt things? _____
> Who deals with the problems? _____

Interviewer Instruction: *Ask single parent only.*

(S)

  * Do you have or have you had a close boyfriend/girlfriend or special relationship?

> *Probe If Yes:* Who? _____
> Has it or did it create any problems? _____
> If Yes: What problems? _____

  * Does anyone else live with you?

> *Probe if Yes:* Who? _____
> How was it decided that they would? _____
> Has it created any problems? _____
> Are there any difficulties associated with their living
> with the family? _____

Interview Rating:

Maintenance and management functions are   *No*   *Yes* | 23// 4
handled well?

Comment: _____
_____

2g. **Nurturance and Support**
Interviewer Instruction: *Ask each individual the following:*
(C,F,S)

  * When things get to you, or you have a bad day, who do you go to?
> *Probe if no one:* Are there times that you would like to go to your
> partner/family member(s) but don't?
> *If Yes:* What happens? Why is that? _____

What prevents you from turning to your partner/someone in the family?_____

If all contacts for nurturance and support are outside the family ask why that is: _____

* **Is it helpful to talk to your partner/family members about things that are bothering you?**

   Probe: How is it helpful? _____

   If Not: Why is that? _____

Interviewer Instruction: *If small children ask parent(s):*

(F,S)

   * **Who do the kids usually go to when upset?** _____

   * **Who usually responds and looks after the kids when they are upset?**
   _____

   Probe: How do you handle it if the child gets upset?_____
   _____

Interview Rating:

Are there provisions for nurturance and support?   No   Yes   24// *2*

*Comment:*_____

_____

2h.   **Adult Sexual Gratification**

Interviewer Instruction: *This part of the interview is completed without children present. Explore and probe to be clear regarding answers and make sure that they are not just being quickly given in order to avoid anxieties when discussing this topic.*

   Ask both couples and single parents, if he or she is involved in a relationship.

(C,F,S)

   * **Do you feel comfortable with the amount of affection you get (from each other)?**

   Probe if No: How would you like it to be different? ___ NO _____
   _____

* Are you satisfied with your sexual life? No
    Probe: **Would you change any aspects of your sex life if you could?**

_____

* Are you (both) happy with the frequency that you make love/have sex? no

* Do you feel that you can satisfy your partner? yes

Interviewer Instruction: *Ask each partner:*

* Do you feel satisfied by your partner? no

* Is it OK for you to say no? yes

Interviewer Rating:

There is a mutually shared adult sexual satisfaction? No Yes   25//3

*Comment:*_____

_____

_____

Interviewer Rating-Roles:

The family is effective in its role functioning?   No   Yes   26//___

Comment: _____

_____

---

3. BEHAVIOR CONTROL

The interviewer is looking at the way in which a family expresses and maintains standards of behavior for family members in the following areas:

a. physical danger
b. psychobiological needs and drives including eating, sleeping, eliminating, sex and aggression
c. social behavior, both inside and outside the family

Interviewer Instructions: *If children are older than eight years, adapt the questions for age appropriateness and begin with the section immediately following. If children are eight years or younger, review the children's section, modifying inquiries in order to ask the parents the questions and, where appropriate, skip sections.*

3a. Orientation
(C,F,S)

> * **I'd like to change focus now and review the rules and standards you have as a family.**

Interviewer Instruction—*Questions addressed to couples begin section 3b. When addressing children, ask for examples to be clear that they understand the questions asked.*

> * **OK. I'd like to start with the children—Is that all right?**

Interviewer Instruction—*Get agreement before proceeding.*

> * **I want to find out if you know what your mom or dad will allow you to do and what they won't let you do. Let me check some examples so I can be clear.**

> * **Do you know what time your mom or dad expect you to be in bed?**
> > *Probe if more than one child:* **Is that time the same for all of you?** _____
> > Is the bedtime kept to? _____
> > Are you allowed in other bedrooms? _____
> > If any of above is a problem, what happens when it occurs?
> >
> > _____

> * **Do you know what your mom or dad would consider dangerous if you did them?**
> > *Probe:* **What are they?** _____
> > *If No:* **What about things like crossing the road, running into the street, playing with matches, electric plugs or the stove?**
> >
> > _____

> * **Do your mom or dad have rules for things like that or other things they'd consider dangerous for someone your age?** _____
> > *If still No: Check with parents*

Is that true, or do you have clear ideas about what is dangerous for the children? _____

If Yes: What situations would you be concerned about?

_____

If No: Do you think you should have rules for dangerous situations? _____

If No: Why not? _____

OK—I'm going to shift to rules in another area.

* Do you know the rules for:
    The time you have to be in the house?
    How often you should bathe and brush your teeth?
    Whether you all have to eat together?

    Probe: Do you keep to it?

* Are people in your family allowed to hit each other?

    Probe: Do people ever hit each other?
    If Yes: Do they hit so hard that people get hurt?
    How often does that happen?

* Do you know when your mom or dad considers that kidding ends and sassing begins?

* Are there things that people in your family do that you feel are really wrong?
    If Yes: What are they? _____

* Interviewer Instructions—*Check if anyone is:*
    Using drugs? ____
    Drinking?   ____

Additional options or probes:
    Table manners?
    How much and what you eat?
    How loud you talk for example- can you yell and scream or do you have to whisper?

Interviewer Rating:

*The rules for children are appropriate given their ages
and circumstances?*   *No*   *Yes*   27//__6

Comment: _____
_____

* **Do you know what to expect if you break a rule?**
    If Yes: What _____
    If No: Why not? What happens? _____

* **Do you think that the punishment you get is reasonable given the rule you've broken?**
    If No: Is the punishment too strong? _____
         Too soft? _____
         Other: _____
    If unclear: **Does the punishment change depending upon which rule you break?**_____

* **Can you get away with things in your family?**
    If Yes: How often does that work/happen? _____

* **Is/Are your parent(s) too strict?**
    If Yes: What makes you think that? _____

Interviewer Instruction—*Ask children only if 2-parent family*
(F)

* **Do your parents agree on the rules?**
    If No: Who is stricter? ____ Mom ____ Dad

* **Who punishes harder?** ____ Mom ____ Dad ____ Neither

* **Does one of your parents ever say you can do something and the other says no?**
    Probe if Yes: How often? _____

Interviewer Instructions—*Direct the rest of the behavior control questions to the parent(s).*

(F,S)

* **Do you feel as parent(s) that I have gotten the correct picture?**
    If No: **Which part did you disagree with?** _____

Interviewer Instructions—*Determine if there are disagreements in the following areas:*

      Dangerous situation _____
      Eating, sleeping _____
      Toilet hygiene _____
      Parent/child interaction _____
      Sibling interaction _____
      Socialization _____

(F)

* **Do you generally agree as parents about the rules?**
    If No: **What happens when you disagree?**_____

* **Do you feel supported by your partner when disciplining the children?**
    If No: **What happens?**_____

Interviewer Instruction—*Ask each parent individually.*

(F,S)

* **Do you always punish them the same way? Are you consistent ?**
    If No: **What happens that you are not consistent?**

* **Do you change the punishment depending upon which rule is broken?**

* **As the children have grown older have you allowed them to do more and be more responsible for themselves?**

* **Do you make allowances for special situations/occasions?**
    If Yes: **How?** _____
    Probe If No: **Why not?** _____

Interviewer Rating:

The family is effective in the area of children's behavior control?   *No*   *Yes*

28// 4

Comment: _____
_____

3b.   **Reorientation**

   * **OK—I'm going to shift now.**

   Interviewer Instruction - *Include questions to couples here:*
(C,F,S)

   I want to get an idea of the expectations you have for each other and when there are problems, how you handle them.

   * **Do you feel anyone in the family**

   * **Drinks too much?**   no
        Probe If Yes: **Who?** _____
        What makes you feel that way? _____
        How do you deal with it? _____
        What do you do as a family to see that this does not happen?

   _____

   ***Eats too much?**   no
        Probe If Yes: **Who?** _____
        What makes you feel that way? _____
        How do you deal with it? _____
        What do you do as a family to see that this does not happen?

   _____

   * **Takes inappropriate risks, for example drives dangerously?**   no
        Probe If Yes: **Who?** _____
        What makes you feel that way? _____
        How do you deal with that? _____

* **Has anyone been in trouble with the law?** *no*
 Probe If Yes: Who? _____
 What were the circumstances? _____
 How do you deal with it? _____
 Probe: Does anyone do anything illegal? _____

Interviewer Instruction—*Direct to each partner:*

* **Does your partner ever embarrass you or put you off in public?**
 If Yes: In what way? _____ *no* _____

* **Do you feel comfortable the way everyone in the family treats each other in public?** *nt*
 If No: Why not? _____
 When that happens what do you do? _____

Interviewer Rating-Behavior Control:

The family is effective in the area of adult behavior control?   No   Yes   29// *6*

Comment: _____
_____

Interviewer Rating-Behavior Control:

The couple/family is effective in the area of behavior control?   No   Yes   30// ___

Comment: _____
_____

---

4. PROBLEM-SOLVING

The Interviewer focuses on the family's ability to resolve problems, and assesses the extent to which the family successfully carries out the various steps of problem solving for
 a. instrumental problems
 b. affective problems

4a.　Orientation
(C,F,S)

> * Are there any difficulties or issues that have come up that your family has dealt with in the past two to six weeks (or identify the last problem they can remember)?

Instructions to Interviewer—*If the family has difficulty give an example (car breakdown, major appliance failure, need to purchase large item, holiday plans, visitors for a week, someone upset, a bad report for a child). Give the family time and ask each individual to think of a problem.*

List Problems: _____

_____

_____

_____

If the family is defensive or can't respond, ask them to pick a problem they have solved well. When the family has outlined some problems identify an <u>instrumental problem</u> and ask the following questions.

4b.　Instrumental Problem Solving
If the family cannot come up with an instrumental problem, the Interviewer can introduce the questions with:

> **All families have practical problems that are part of life. Can you think of a practical problem that has occurred recently? Examples might be:**
> * **things break down in the house**
> * **the family needs to plan a vacation or make a big purchase**

Indicate instrumental problem being explored: _____

> * **When did you first notice the problem?**

> * **Who first noticed the problem/issue?**

> * **Is this the same person who usually notices such things?**
> *Probe:* **Did one person (in the family) pick up on the problem and then the other(s) recognize it as a problem?**

As appropriate:
>   **Did a few of you recognize it as a problem and then the rest see it as a problem?**
>   **Did no one notice it until someone else outside the family brought it to your attention?**

>   *** Is this the way problems usually get identified in your family?**
>   *If No:* **How is it different?**_____

Interviewer Rating:

Instrumental Problems *are correctly identified?*   *No*   *Yes*   31//__4__

Comments: _____

_____

4c.   **Communication of instrumental problems to the appropriate resource**

>   *** When you noticed the problem did you tell anyone?**   *no*

>   *** Who did you let know about the problem?**   *dad*
>   *Probe:* **Did you let anyone outside the family know about the problem?**
>   *If Yes:* **Who is that person?** _____
>   **Did you let the others know soon after noticing the problem?**

>   *** Is this usually the way you/ the family is told about a problem?**   *yes*
>   *If No:* **How is it different?** _____

Interviewer Rating:

Instrumental Problems *are communicated to the appropriate person?*   *No*   *Yes*   32//__3__

Comment: _____

_____

4d. **Development of Alternatives**

    * **What approaches did you consider to solve the problem?**

_____

_____

    * **Did you think of other ways to deal with the problem?**
        Additional Probes:
        Did you consider any other alternatives?
        Did any of you have ideas about how to solve the problem but did not share them?

> *Interviewer Rating:*
>
> *The alternative plan(s) of actions are suitable in terms of*
> <u>*instrumental problems?*</u>   *No*   *Yes*   33//4
>
> *Comments:* _____
>
> _____
>
> _____

4e. **Decisions and Action**
    * **How did you decide what to do?**_____

_____

    * **Did you come to a decision?**
        If No: **What stopped you?**_____

    * **Was the decision discussed (between both of you/with the person) who was affected by the decision?**

    * **Is this usually the way (you/the family) decides what to do?**
        If No: **How is it different?**_____

    * **Once you had decided on your course of action did you follow through?**
        If No: **What stopped you?**_____

    * **Do you usually follow through on your decisions?**

* How quickly was the problem solved?_____
    If slow ask: Why did it take so long?
    If the problem was not solved ask: why not?
    Do you usually solve a problem quickly?

Interviewer Rating:

The family is able to effectively decide and/or act on
instrumental problems?   *No*   *Yes*   34// 3

Comment: _____
_____

4f.   **Monitoring Action**

  * **How did you make sure the problem was acted on?**

  * **Did you check to see that things got done after you decided what to do about the problem?**
      If Yes: **Who checks to see that things get done?**_____

  * **Would you say this is typical of how you deal with most problems?**

Interviewer Rating:

The family effectively monitors <u>instrumental problem</u>
<u>solving</u>?   *No*   *Yes*   35// 4

Comments: _____
_____
_____

4g.   **Evaluating the success of instrumental problem solving**

  * **How well do you think you did with the problem?**

  * **Do you think it was the best way to deal with the problem?**

* Do you think that you have handled similar problems in the past more effectively?

* Did you learn anything from solving this problem that might help you with other problems in the future?

* As a family, did you discuss what in particular worked well for you or what did not work well in terms of handling the problem?

Interviewer Rating:

The family appropriately evaluates _instrumental problem solving?_   No   Yes   36// 3

Comment: _____

_____

Interviewer Rating:

The family is effective in their _instrumental problem solving?_   No   Yes   37// 3

Comment: _____

_____

4h.   **Affective Problem Solving**

Interviewer Instructions—*In the following section repeat the questions from above, but focus on affective/emotional problems. For affective problems introduce the questions with:*

Can you think of a problem that has occurred in the family that has involved feelings, for example someone has been upset or angry/excited about something?   dad not trying

Indicate _affective problem_ being explored: _____

* When did you first notice the problem?   mac + ch

* Who first noticed the problem/issue?_____ kids

* Is this the same person who usually notices such things?
> *Probe:* Did one person (in the family) pick up on the problem and then the other(s) see it as a problem?

As appropriate:
> Did a few of you in the family recognize it as a problem and then the rest see it as a problem? *UC?*

> Did no one notice the problem until someone else outside the family brought it to your attention? *no*

> * Is this the way problems usually get identified in your family?
>> *If No:* How was this situation different?_____ *ye*_____

Interviewer Rating:

<u>*Affective problems*</u> are correctly identified?   *No*   *Yes*   38//_*4*_

Comment: _____
_____

4i.   Communication of affective problems to the appropriate resource

> * When you noticed the problem did you tell anyone?

> * Who did you let know about the problem?_____
>> *Probe:* Did you let anyone outside the family know about the problem?
>> *If Yes:* Who?_____
>>> Did you let the other(s) know soon after noticing the problem? _____

> * Is this usually the way (you/the family) is told about a problem?
>> *If No:* How is this different?_____

Interviewer Rating:

<u>*Affective problems*</u> *are communicated to the*
appropriate person(s)?   *No*   *Yes*   39//4

Comment: _____
_____

4j.   Development of Alternatives

* **What approaches did you consider to solve the problem?**

_____
_____

* **Did you think of other ways to deal with the problem?**

Additional Probes:
   Did you consider any other alternatives?
   **Did any others have ideas about how to solve the problem and
   not share them?**

Interviewer Rating:

Alternative plan(s) of action are suitable in terms of
<u>*affective problem solving?*</u>   *No*   *Yes*   40//4

Comment: _____
_____

4k.   Decisions and Action

* **How did you decide what to do?**_____

* **Did you come to a decision?**_____
   If No: **What stopped you?**_____

* Was the decision discussed (between you/with the person(s)) who was affected by the decision?

* Is this usually the way (you/the family) decides what to do?
    If No: How is this different?_____

* Once you decided on your course of action, did you follow through?
    If No: What stopped you?_____

* Do you usually follow through on your decisions?

* How quickly was the problem solved?
    If slow ask: Why did it take so long?_____
    If problem was not solved, ask: Why not?_____
    _____
    Do you usually solve a problem quickly?_____
    _____

Interviewer Rating:

The family is able to effectively decide and/or act on
<u>*affective problems?*</u>   *No*   *Yes*   41// 5

Comment: _____
_____

4l. **Monitoring Action**

* **How did you make sure that the problem was known?**

* **Did you check to see that things got done after you decided what to do about the problem?**
    If Yes: Who checks to see that things get done? _____

* **Would you say this is typical of how you deal with most problems?**
_____

Interviewer Rating:

The family effectively monitors _affective problem solving?_   No   Yes

42//.3

Comment: _____

_____

4m. **Evaluating the success of affective problem solving**

   * **Do you think it was the best way of dealing with the problem?**

   * **Do you think you have handled similar problems more effectively in the past?**

   * **Did you learn anything from solving this problem that might help you to solve other problems in the future?**

   * **How well do you think you did with the problem?**

   * **As a family did you discuss what did or did not work well for you in terms of handling the problem?**

Interviewer Rating:

The family appropriately evaluates _affective problem solving?_   No   Yes

43//.3

Comment: _____

_____

Interviewer Rating:

The family is effective in their affective problem solving?   No   Yes

44//___4

Comment: _____

_____

4n.   **General recheck of problem solving**

   * **Just to review then: Do you feel most problems get dealt with quickly and efficiently in your family?**

   * **Are there any problems that keep coming up and do not get handled?**
        Probe: What are they? _____
                    What stops you from handling them? _____

Interviewer Rating-Problem Solving:

The family is effective in their problem solving?   No   Yes   45//___

Comments: _____
_____

Additional Comments on Problem Solving

_____
_____
_____

5.   COMMUNICATION
In this section, the Interviewer focuses on the family's ability to exchange both instrumental and affective information among its members. The Interviewer assesses:
   a.   the family's pattern of communication and
   b.   where it falls on the following two independent continua:
        • Clear—Masked
        • Direct—Indirect

   Interviewer Instructions—*The focus is on how information or messages are conveyed, and the way they are received and interpreted. When a family member demonstrates a problem in communication style, the Interviewer determines if the family is able to compensate for it or if the individual's communication problem interferes with the family's exchange of information.*

5a.   Extent of Communication
The Interviewer should be clear about the amount of time family members spend communicating. Generally, families indicate greater amounts of time communicating with each other than what actually occurs. There-

fore, probes and checks are needed to ensure you have a true picture when determining time. It may be helpful to have the family describe the family events and interactions of a typical day when beginning this section. The focus here is on personal and family issues. The interviewer needs to separate talking about world events from family and interpersonally oriented discussions. The estimated time in communicating should be for periods the family or you feel are spent in significant family talking.

(C,F,S)

* **How much time are you awake and together as a family/couple?** _____hrs./day *2hrs*

* **How much of this time is available and used to really talk as family members about personal and family issues.** ___30min___hrs./day

* **Are you satisfied with the amount of time?** *no*

Interviewer Instruction: *In order to assess whether or not the parental system spends their own time talking ask the following to the parents:*

(F)

* **How about the two of you—how much time do you spend talking with each other?** ___*3U*___hrs./day

* **Are you satisfied with the amount of time?** *no*

Interviewer Rating:

<u>Family Members</u> have a satisfactory <u>amount of time</u> <u>to talk</u> with each other?   No   Yes | 46//_2_

Comment: _____
_____

Interviewer Rating:

The <u>couple</u> talks a satisfactory amount with each other?
                                                 No   Yes | 47//_2_

Comment: _____
_____

For couples, #46 and #47 will be the same.

5b. Quality of Communication

(C,F,S)

F

   * Does (one of you/anybody) do most of the talking in your family?
      Probe If Yes: Who? _____

(F,S)   Does it interfere? _____ ho _____

(C,F,S)

   * Do you all talk to each other or do some of you not talk, or minimally
    talk, to each other?   no
       Probe If Yes: What happens? _____
       Why is that the case? _____

F, C

   * Do (any of) you feel you have trouble in the way you talk with each
    other?
       Probe If Yes: In what way? _____ fight _____

   * When talking about everyday issues do you feel that (your spouse/
    people in your family) understand what you are trying to say?
       If No: What happens that you don't? _____

FIC ?

   * (Do you/does your family) talk about feelings or moods very much -
    for instance if you're feeling happy or angry about something?
       If No: What stops you from telling (your spouse/others in the
       family) what you are feeling? _____ no

   * Do you talk straight-forwardly about feelings?
       Probe If Yes: Both good and bad feelings? _____ no _____

   * Do you have trouble understanding what (your spouse/others in the
    family) are trying to say about their feelings?   yes
       Probe If Yes: What is the problem or difficulty? _____
       Can you give me an example? _____
       _____

F, C

   * Do you listen to (each) other(s)?   NO

F C

   * Do you let (your spouse/others in your family) know that you've un-
    derstood what (he/she/they) have said?
       Probe If No: What stops you from giving family members an
       indication that you've heard and understood what they've
       said? _____
       If Yes: How do you do that? _____

* **If you don't understand what (your spouse/someone) is saying do you try to clarify it?**

* **Are there any topics that you don't allow (each other/members of the family) to talk about?**

F

    Probe: Do others agree that happens?_____

    Is it that (your spouse/the family) doesn't allow you to talk about that/them or that it is uncomfortable for you personally to talk about it? _____

    What makes it uncomfortable? _____

Interviewer Rating:

Communication is clear and not masked?   No   Yes   48// 4

Comment: _____

_____

---

f

* **Does (your spouse/other family members) ever answer for you?**   *no*

* **Does (your spouse/others) jump in or interrupt?**   *no*

Interviewer Instruction—*The next section is used to determine if indirect communication takes place, that is, do some family members talk about someone in their presence or through someone in order to get messages across. Examples include avoidance of speaking directly to an individual or locking out the individual for whom the message is intended.*

Overt examples of each are:

- Child looking at mother, "I just hate Dad. I don't care about him!"
- Father to child in mother's presence, "Sue, will you tell your mother to quit yelling."

f

* **Do (any of) you feel that (your spouse/others in the family) talk about you in your presence?**   *pro yes / kid*

    Probe: Can you tell me more about what you mean? _____

        Can you give me an example? _____

        Does it make you uncomfortable? _____

    If Yes: What is it that makes you uncomfortable? _____

Interviewer Rating-Communication:

The family is direct in their <u>communication</u>?   *No*   *Yes*   49// <u>2</u>

Comment: _____

_____

Interviewer Rating-Communication :

The family is effective and efficient in their
<u>communication</u>?   *No*   *Yes*   50//___

Comment: _____

_____

6. AFFECTIVE RESPONSIVENESS

The Interviewer assesses:
   a. the ability of each individual member to respond with a full range of emotions
   b. whether the emotions they experience are appropriate to the situation in both quantity and quality of affect

Interviewer Instructions—The focus is on what each individual person-
ally <u>experiences</u> rather than how they show or express it to others. Be
alert throughout the interview as situations and will often come up re-
lating to events in the interview (e.g., crying, responding to a members
tears, anger) or to historical material (bereavement, illness). The feelings
members experience at such times are useful.

Ask <u>each family member</u> the following question for each of the listed emo-
tions

welfare emotions: a. pleasure
                      b. tenderness/concern/affection

emergency emotions: a. anger
                      b. sadness/depression
                      c. fear

(C,F,S)

> * I want to check out how each of you individually responds in a number of ways. I'm interested in what you experience inside-not just what you let onto others.

Interviewer Instructions—*Use the questions on the next pages to determine problems in affective responsiveness (over responsiveness, constricted response, distorted response and note in grid).*

	Joy/Pleasure	Caring/Love	Anger	Sadness	Fear
Father/Husband					
Mother/Wife					
Child (1)					
Child (2)					
Child (3)					
Family					

Pleasure

(C,F,S)

> * Can you tell me about a time or experience that gave you a sense of pleasure?

> * What was it that particularly gave you pleasure?
> *Probes:* How did you experience it? _____
> How do you know it as pleasure? _____
> Are there other situations that lead you to feel the same way?
> _____
> *If Yes:* What are they? _____

> Do you feel that there are times that you experience too much pleasure-and you overreact to the situation? _____

> Do you feel there are times when you don't experience pleasure but you think you should? _____

Do you feel you experience pleasure differently that you think others do? _____

    If Yes: How? _____

Are you concerned about how you experience pleasure in some situations? _____

Tenderness/Concern

* Can you tell me about a time or experience where you felt tenderness or concern for someone else?

* What was it that led you to feel tenderness or concern?
    Probes: How did you experience the feeling? _____
    How did you know it was tenderness or concern? _____
    Are there other situations that lead you to feel the same way?
    _____

    If Yes: What are they? _____

Do you feel that there are times when you are overly concerned?
_____

    If Yes: Can you give me an example? _____

Do you feel there are times when you aren't as tender or concerned as you should be?
    If Yes: Can you give an example? _____

Do you feel you experience tenderness or concern differently than others?
    If Yes: How? _____

Are you concerned about how you experience tenderness or concern in some situations?
    If Yes: What concerns you? _____

* *If there has been no mention of concern for (spouse/other family members) ask:*

Do you ever feel concern or caring for (your spouse/other family members)?
    If No: Have you ever? _____

Anger

* Do you ever lose your temper?

* What happens to trigger it?

* Do you ever get angry?
  Probe: How do you experience the feeling of temper or anger?
  _____

  Are there other situations that lead you to feel the same way?
  _____

  If Yes: What are they? _____

Do you ever feel hurt or frightened before you get angry? _____

(To check for distortion or inappropriate affective response)

Do you feel you overreact with anger? _____
  If Yes: Can you give me an example? _____

Do you feel that there are times that you aren't angry but you should be?
  If Yes: Can you give me an example? _____

Do you think you experience anger differently than others? _____
  If Yes: How? _____

Are you concerned about how you experience anger in some situations?
  If Yes: What concerns you? _____

Sadness and Depression

* Are there situations where you feel sad or depressed?

* Can you give an example?
  Probes: Do you cry too easily? _____
  Do you cry when you feel you shouldn't? _____
  How do you know you're sad/depressed? _____
  How do you experience the feeling?_____
  What do you sense that tells you you're sad/depressed? _____
  Do you ever get angry before you get sad/depressed? _____

(To check for distortion or inappropriateness)

Do you feel you overreact with sadness or depression?_____
    If Yes: Can you give me an example? _____

Do you feel there are times when you aren't sad or depressed but you should be?
    If Yes: Can you give me an example? _____

Do you think you experience sadness and/or depression differently than others?
    If Yes: How? _____

Are you concerned about how you experience sadness and/or depression?
    If Yes: What concerns you? _____

Fear

* Do you ever get really frightened?

* Can you give me an example?
    Probes: Do you get terrified? _____
    How do you know you're frightened or terrified? _____
    How do you experience the feeling? _____
    What do you sense that tells you you're frightened? _____
    Do you experience another emotion and then get frightened?
    _____

(To check for distortion or inappropriateness)

Do you overreact and get terrified when you shouldn't? _____
    If Yes: Can you give me an example? _____

Do you feel there are times that you aren't frightened and should be?
    _____
    If Yes: Can you give me an example?_____

Do you think you experience fear in a way that's different than others?
    _____

Interviewer Rating–Affective Responsiveness:			
The family has an appropriate range of <u>affective responsiveness</u>	No	Yes	51// 5
<u>Welfare emotions</u> (pleasure, concern)	No	Yes	52// 5
<u>Emergency emotions</u> (anger, sadness, depression, fear)	No	Yes	53// 5

7. AFFECTIVE INVOLVEMENT
The Interviewer assesses:
   a. the extent to which family members show interest in each other
   b. the extent family members value each other
   c. how family members show interest and invest in each other

Interviewer Instructions—*The focus is not whether or not family members participate in others' activities, but whether they show interest and value each other. Ask the family members the following and be sure to clarify affective involvement issues for <u>each</u> family member.*
(C,F,S)

   * **What things are important to you?**

(*Interviewer can give examples such as hobbies, work, friends, special club, etc.*)
Alternative questions: **What interests you most?**
                   What hobbies or special interests do you have?

   * **(Does your spouse/who) pays attention to your interest in those things?**
       ***Probe:* How do you know (he/she/they) are interested?**
       ***Probe if no interest, or negative interest:* How would you like them to pay attention?**
(F,S)

   ***Are others in your family really interested in what you do?**
       ***Probe if Yes:* How do you know?** _____
       ***If No:* In what way do they show their interest?** _____
       Do you talk to each other about your interests? _____

* **Do you let each other know you are interested in them?**
  Probe: How do you know that? _____

Interviewer Instruction—*The Interviewer tries to tap if there is over-involvement or narcissistic involvement in the family with the following two questions:*

(C,F,S)

***Does (either of you/anyone) feel that (your spouse/another family member) is too close to, or too involved with them?**

* **Do you feel that (your spouse/others) ever becomes a nag about what is important to you or that they do not give you enough space?**
  Probe: What is it that they do that makes you feel that way?

  _____

* **Do you think (your spouse/others in the family) are genuinely interested in you or that (he/she/they) take an interest only because it is important to them?**

(Example: *They don't talk to you but they do brag to others about how well you're doing?*)

  Probe: What makes you feel that way? _____
  Can you give me an example? _____

Interviewer Instruction—*If the Interviewer has not obtained information from the children ask the following:*

(F,S)

* **What kinds of things do you like to do?**

* **Who shows an interest in that?**
  Probe: How do they show they're interested? _____

* **Do you wish people in the family showed more of an interest?**
  Probe: What makes you feel that way? _____

* **Do you feel that others really don't care?**
  Probe: What makes you feel that way? _____

* **Do you feel that people in the family don't give you enough space to do your own thing?**

* Does anybody in the family feel they are not as close to the others as they would like?
   Probe if Yes: What stops that from happening, what gets in the way? _____

Interviewer Instruction—*Ask the parents:*

* Do you feel the relationship(s) with your child/children is close enough?
   Probe if Yes: What makes you feel that way? _____
   If No: What makes you feel your relationship is not as close as you would like? _____

*Do you ever feel your relationship with your children is too close?
   Probe if Yes: What makes you feel that way? _____

Interviewer Instruction—*Other probes related to the above questions when two parents in the family:*
(F)

* Is that the same for both of you?
(S)

If different—How do each of you see the differences?

Interviewer Instruction—*Ask single parent:*

* Besides yourself, are there others closely involved with the children?
   Probe: Who?_____ _____
   How do they get involved? _____

Interviewer Instructions—*Ask the following of each member of a couple:*
(C,F)

* Do you feel your relationship with your spouse is close enough, not close enough or too close?
   Probe: If not close enough or too close: What is the problem? Can you give me an example? _____

* Do you feel your spouse genuinely cares for you?
   Probe if Yes: How does he/she let you know that? _____
   If No: In what way does he/she show that they don't genuinely care? Or in what way could he/she show you that he/she cares?
   _____

(A negative question but speaks to the absence of involvement)

Interviewer Rating–Affective Involvement:

This family has appropriate Affective Involvement:	No	Yes	54// __4__
Comment:_____			
_____			
The Family provides appropriate Affective Involvement for the <u>children?</u>	No	Yes	55// __5__
Comment:_____			
_____			
The <u>marital couple</u> have an effective Affective Involvement between each other?	No	Yes	56// __3__
Comment:_____			
_____			

For couples #54 and #56 are coded the same.

8. CLOSURE

The Interviewer summarizes his or her overview of the family. Check with the family that the correct information has been obtained.

(C,F,S)

Interviewer Instruction—*Ask the family:*

* Do you think I have a clear idea of how your family functions?
If No: **Where do you think I have gone wrong or what have missed?**
_____
_____

* Is there anything else you feel I should know about your family that we haven't covered?
If Yes: **What is it?** _____

1 = yes 2 = no
8 = does not apply
9 = missing

McSiff Coding Sheet

17 __6__
Provision of Resources

18 __3__
Role Allocation

19 __4__
Role Accountability

20 __4__
Personal Development
-general-

21 __5__
Personal Development
-children-

22 __3__
Personal Development
-adults-

RL

23 __4__
Maintenance &
Management

24 __2__
Nurturance & Support

25 __3__
Adult Sexual Satisfaction

same as
what
goes
next
page

26 __3.7__
Overall Role Functioning

27 __6__
Rules for Children

28 __4__
Behavioral Control
-children-

BC ✓

29 __6__
Behavioral Control
-adults-

30 __5.3__
Behavioral Control
-overall-

31 __4__
Identify Problems
-instrumental-

32 __3__
Communicate Problems
-instrumental-

33 __4__
Develop Alternatives
-instrumental-

34 __3__
Decision/Act on Problems
-instrumental-

PS ✓

35 __4__
Monitor Problems
-instrumental-

36 __3__
Evaluate Problems
-instrumental-

37 __3.5__
Instrumental Problem
Solving
-overall-

38 __4__
Identify Problems
-affective-

39 __4__
Communicate Problems
-affective-

40 __4__
Develop Alternatives
-affective-

41 __5__
Decision/Act on Problems
-affective-

42 __3__
Monitor Problems
-affective-

43 __3__
Evaluate Problems
-affective-

44 __3.0__
Affective Problem Solving
-overall-

45 __3.7__
Problem Solving
-overall-

46 __2__
Amount Time Talking

CM

47 __2__
Couple Time Talking

48 __4__
Clear Communication

49 __2__
Direct Communication

50 __2.5__
Communication
-overall-

51 __4__
Affective Response
overall-

52 __3__
Welfare Emotions

AR

53 __5__
Emergency Emotions

54 __4__
Affective Involvement
-overall-

55 __5__
Affective Involvement
-children-

AI

56 __3__
Affective Involvement
-couple-

Key: RL = Roles
CM = Communication

BC = Behavior Control
AR = Affective Reponsiveness

PS = Problem Solving
AI = Affective Involvement

Clinician/Rater Family Assessment after the Interview

Family Name/ID:_____ Rater ID:_____

Please be sure to rate all seven categories, but only one rating per category is allowed:

Put in graph

	Very Disturbed				Non-Clinical		Superior	Insufficient Information
Problem Solving	1	2	3	(4)	5	6	7	II
Communication	1	2	3	4	(5)	6	7	II
Roles	1	2	3	(4)	5	6	7	II
Affective Responsiveness	1	2	3	4	5	6	7	II
Affective Involvement	1	2	3	4	5	6	7	II
Behavior Control	1	2	3	4	5	6	7	II
General Functioning	1	2	3	4	5	6	7	II

If uncertain about any of the ratings, please check the dimension and briefly explain the reason of the uncertainty.

___ Problem Solving_____

___ Communication_____

___ Roles_____

___ Affective Responsiveness_____

___ Affective Involvement_____

___ Behavior Control_____

___ General Functioning_____

If there were any additional questions that needed to be asked in any of the dimensions, please make a note below:

Problem Solving_____

Communication_____

Roles_____

Affective Responsiveness_____

Affective Involvement_____

Behavior Control_____

General Functioning_____

McMaster PCSFT Adherence Scale

1. **Did the therapist meet with the entire family?**

1	2	3	4	5	6	7
Met with only one member		Met with marital couple only or two members absent		One family member absent		Entire family present

2. **Was the therapist active and directive?**

1	2	3	4	5	6	7
Not at all		Some activity		Considerable activity		Extremely active and directive

3. **Did the therapist actively attempt to engage the family in working *together* to explore therapeutic issues?**

1	2	3	4	5	6	7
Not at all		Some		Considerably		Extensively

4. **Did the therapist explain to the family his/her reasons for pursuing a particular topic?**

1	2	3	4	5	6	7
Not at all		Some		Considerably		Extensively

5. **Did the therapist communicate the goals and procedures of the session clearly and directly to the family?**

1	2	3	4	5	6	7
Not at all		Vague attempts		Clear communication		Very clear communication

6. **Did the therapist negotiate with the family assignments, changes in direction, or major emphases in a way that gives the family opportunity to have input?**

1	2	3	4	5	6	7
Not at all		Some		Considerably		Extensively

7. **Did the therapist summarize or encourage the family to summarize key issues discussed earlier in a previous session or in the current session?**

1	2	3	4	5	6	7
Not at all		Some		Considerably		Extensively

8. **Did the therapist convey his/her impressions and conclusions to the family for confirmation and feedback?**

1	2	3	4	5	6	7
Not at all		Some		Considerably		Extensively

9. **Did the therapist encourage the family's independence in dealing with their problems?**

1	2	3	4	5	6	7
Not at all		Some encouragement		Considerable encouragement		Extensive encouragement

10. **Did the therapist clearly label and define the current stage of treatment?**

1	2	3	4	5	6	7
Not at all		Vague attempts		Clearly defines stage of treatment		Exceptionally clear definition

11. **Did the therapist indicate that the responsibility for change is the family's?**

1	2	3	4	5	6	7
Not at all		Some indication		Considerable indication		Extensive indication

12. **Did the therapist define problems in operationalized, behavioral terms?**

1	2	3	4	5	6	7
Not at all		Some attempts		Operationally defined most problems		Operationally defined all problems in clear behavioral terms

13. **Did the therapist focus on problems defined in the assessment stage?**

1	2	3	4	5	6	7
Not at all		Some focus		Considerable focus		Extensive focus

14. **Did the therapist focus on affective as well as instrumental issues?**

1	2	3	4	5	6	7
Neglects affective issues completely		Under or over emphasis of affective issues		Appropriately balanced focus on affective and instrumental issues		Exceptional integration of affective and instrumental issues

15. **Did the therapist label unacknowledged affect in one or more family members?**

1	2	3	4	5	6	7
Not at all		Some		Considerably		Extensively

16. **Did the therapist label dysfunctional transitional patterns?**

1	2	3	4	5	6	7
Not at all		Some		Considerably		Extensively

17. **Did the therapist encourage the family to label their own behavior and affect.**

1	2	3	4	5	6	7
Not at all		Some		Considerably		Extensively

The following items are completed for an ASSESSMENT SESSION only

A1. **Did the therapist clearly define the goals of the assessment?**

1	2	3	4	5	6	7
Not at all		Some attempt to define		Considerable efforts to define		Extensive efforts to define

A2. **Did the therapist conduct a comprehensive assessment of family functioning before beginning treatment?**

1	2	3	4	5	6	7
No		Some attempt to assess		Considerable focus on assessment		Extensive focus on assessment

A3. **Did the therapist discuss and assess the family's presenting problem?**

1	2	3	4	5	6	7
Not at all		Some focus on presenting problem		Considerable focus on presenting problem		Extensive focus on presenting problem

A4. **Did the therapist assess the dimensions of the McMaster Model?**

1	2	3	4	5	6	7
Not at all		Some focus on dimensions		Considerable focus on dimensions		Extensive focus on dimensions

A5. **Did the therapist summarize the list of problems?**

1	2	3	4	5	6	7
Not at all		Some efforts to summarize		Considerable efforts to summarize		Extensive efforts to summarize

A6. **Did the therapist obtain the family's agreement concerning the identified problems?**

1	2	3	4	5	6	7
Not at all		Some efforts to obtain agreement		Considerable efforts to obtain agreement		Extensive efforts to obtain agreement

The following items are rated for a TREATMENT session only

T1. Was a major focus of the treatment session on reviewing tasks, their success and failure, and developing new tasks?

1	2	3	4	5	6	7
Not at all		Some focus		Considerable focus		Extensive focus

T2. Were the purposes of therapeutic tasks clear to the family?

1	2	3	4	5	6	7
Not at all		Somewhat Clear		Clear		Very Clear

T3. Were therapeutic tasks directed at increasing positive behavior?

1	2	3	4	5	6	7
Not at all		Some focus on increasing positive		Considerable focus on increasing positive		Extensive focus on increasing positive

T4. Did therapeutic tasks address dysfunctional transactional patterns?

1	2	3	4	5	6	7
Not at all		Some focus		Considerable focus		Extensive focus

T5. Did the therapist review previously assigned tasks?

1	2	3	4	5	6	7
Not at all		Some attention		Considerable attention		Extensive review and integration

T6. Did the therapist assign tasks to be completed outside the therapy session?

1	2	3	4	5	6	7
Did not		Some attempts to assign tasks		Considerable focus on assigning tasks		Extensive focus on assigning tasks

McMaster PCSFT Competence Scale

1. Collaboration
0 – Therapist does not attempt to set up a collaboration with family
2 – Therapist attempts to collaborate with family, but has difficulty
4 – Therapist is able to collaborate with family
6 – Collaboration is excellent: therapist encourages family as much as possible to take an active role in the session so they can function as a "team."

2. Feedback
0 – Therapist does not ask for feedback to determine the family's understanding of, or response to, the session.
2 – Therapist elicits some feedback from family, but does not ask enough questions to be sure the family understands the therapist's line of reasoning.
4 – Therapist asks enough questions to be sure that the family understands the therapist's line of reasoning throughout the session. The therapist adjusts his/her behavior in response to the feedback, when appropriate.
6 – Therapist is especially adept at eliciting and responding to verbal and nonverbal feedback throughout the session.

3. Interpersonal Effectiveness
0 – Therapist has poor interpersonal skills. Seems hostile, demeaning, or in some other way destructive to the family.
2 – Therapist is not destructive, but has significant interpersonal problems with one or more family members. At times the therapist appears unnecessarily impatient, aloof, insincere or has difficulty conveying confidence and competence.

4 – Therapist displays a satisfactory degree of warmth, concern, confidence, genuineness, and professionalism. No significant interpersonal problems.

6 – Therapist displays optimal levels of warmth, concern, confidence, genuineness and professionalism appropriate for this family in this session.

4. Pacing and Efficient Use of Time

0 – Therapist makes no attempt to structure therapy time. Session seems aimless.

2 – Session has some direction, but the therapist has significant problems with structuring or pacing (e.g., too little structure, inflexible about structure, too slowly paced, too rapidly paced).

4 – Therapist is reasonably successful at using time efficiently. Therapist maintains appropriate control over flow of discussion and pacing.

6 – Therapist uses time very efficiently by tactfully limiting peripheral and unproductive discussion and by pacing the session as rapidly as is appropriate for the family.

5. Establishing and Maintaining a Focus in the Session

0 – Therapist is unable to maintain a focus during session.

2 – Therapist is able to focus somewhat, but significant portions of the session are devoted to peripheral or unproductive discussion.

4 – Therapist is able to maintain focus and to refocus discussion when distractions occur.

6 – Therapist maintains focus throughout session and, when appropriate, labels any defocus that occurs and then successfully refocuses.

6. Clear, Direct Communication

0 – Therapist's statements to the family are unclear, vague and/or confusing.

2 – Therapist attempts to clarify his/her statements, but has significant difficulty communicating his/her ideas to the family.

4 – Therapist's statements to the family are clear and direct. The family appears to understand what the therapist means.

6 – The therapist is exceptionally skilled at clearly communicating his/her ideas to the family in a manner they can understand and accept.

7. Clarifying and Expanding Communication

0 – The therapist ignores or misperceives important communication between family members and/or between the family and the therapist.

2 – The therapist attempts to clarify communications in the session, but misses or mislabels subtle information.

4 – The therapist clarifies important communications during the session accurately.

6 – The therapist accurately clarifies communications during the session and correctly interprets the "meta communicational" aspects of the interaction.

8. Stimulating Transactions

0 – Therapist makes no attempts to stimulate transactions among family members.

2 – Therapist attempts to stimulate transactions among family members but has significant difficulty doing so or does so at inappropriate times.

4 – Therapist is successful in stimulating transactions appropriately.

6 – Therapist is exceptionally skillful at stimulating transactions among family members.

9. Labeling and Interpreting Transactions

0 – Therapist makes no attempt to label transactions.

2 – Therapist attempts to label transactions during the session, but has significant difficulty doing so (e.g., misses important transactions, mislabels transactions, focuses inappropriately on transactional patterns).

4 – Therapist appropriately labels important transactions during the session.

6 – Therapist is exceptionally skilled in labeling and interpreting transactional patterns and relates transactional patterns to family problems.

10. Task Setting

0 – Therapist does not assign tasks or assigns highly inappropriate tasks.

2 – Therapist assigns tasks that appear too easy or difficult and/or do not focus on identified problems.

4 – Therapist assigns tasks that address identified problems in an appropriate manner.

6 – Therapist assigns tasks that are especially relevant and on target.

11. Task Evaluation

0 – Therapist does not review assigned tasks.

2 – Therapist reviews assigned tasks, but fails to clarify adequately the reasons why the tasks went well or poorly.

4 – Therapist reviews assigned tasks and adequately explores reasons for poor or good performance by the family.

6 – Therapist reviews assigned tasks in an exceptionally skillful way (e.g. is able to relate performance on tasks to identified problems and broader family issues).

A.   Overall, how skillful was the therapist in this session?

0 – Poor
1 – Barely Adequate
2 – Mediocre
3 – Satisfactory
4 – Good
5 – Very Good
6 – Excellent

B.   How difficult was this family to work with?

0 – Not difficult, very receptive
1
2
3 – Moderately difficult
4
5
6 - Extremely difficult

McMaster Family Functioning
Concept Test

This test is designed to determine your understanding of the concepts and definitions presented in the MMFF. All answers, therefore, should be based on the model. The test consists of true-false, fill in the blank, and multiple-choice.

True-False

1. The affective involvement dimension is concerned with family cohesion and activity.
   True_____   False_____

2. Where there is little or no control of behavior, the style is said to be chaotic.
   True_____   False_____

3. "Rigid" refers to a transactional pattern.
   True_____   False_____

4. Life skills/personal development role functions include both child development and adult career development.
   True_____   False_____

5. The emphasis in behavior control is not solely on the manner in which adults set limits on their children's behavior.
   True_____   False_____

6. The communication dimension concentrates on verbal exchange.
   True_____   False_____

7. Depression and sadness are examples of emergency emotions.
   True_____   False_____

8. If a family can resolve affective problems, difficulties with instrumental problem solving are rare.
   True_____   False_____

9. "Complimentary" is a type of affective involvement.
   True_____   False_____

Fill in the Blanks

10. List six types of Affective Involvement:
    1. _____
    2. _____
    3. _____
    4. _____
    5. _____
    6. _____

11. When evaluating a family's style of behavior control, the _____ and _____ for acceptable behavior determine the style of behavior control.

12. The last three stages of Problem Solving are:
    a. _____
    b. _____
    c. _____

13. A young man comes home after given a ticket for speeding and says "All cops are clowns." This is an example of _____ and _____ communication.

14. The definition of Behavior Control refers to the pattern a family uses to handle behavior in the following three situations: _____, _____, and _____.

15. "Accountability" is an issue relevant to the _____ dimension.

16. Give a one-sentence definition for the following McMaster model dimensions:
    a. Communication: _____
    b. Roles: _____
    c. Affective Responsiveness: _____

17. What are three necessary Role functions? _____, _____, and _____.

18. Give a one-sentence definition of the following types of involvement:
    a. Narcissistic: _____
    b. Empathic: _____
    c. Lack of Involvement: _____

19. Describe briefly the first stage of Problem Solving. _____
    _____

Multiple Choice

20. A mother is annoyed at a teenage daughter for not tidying her room. With mother, father, and two children at the dinner table, she makes the following comment: "The kids are driving me nuts." This is an example of:
    a. clear and direct communication
    b. clear and indirect communication
    c. masked and direct communication
    d. masked and indirect communication

21. Provision of resources includes tasks related to:
    a. purchase of food
    b. maintaining the family car
    c. family income
    d. budgeting and money management decisions

22. Listed below are four stages of Problem Solving:
    a. identifying the problem
    b. deciding upon a suitable course of action
    c. developing alternative action plans
    d. communicating the problem to appropriate resources

    Which of the following sequences represent a correct ordering of the above items?
    1. a b c d   2. a d b c   3. a d c b   4. d a c b

23. Which of the following is not an aspect of Affective Responsiveness?
    a. range of feelings
    b. emergency feelings
    c. appropriateness of feelings
    d. how feelings are (verbally) expressed

24. Significant aspects of the first stage of Problem Solving include:
    a. who identifies problems
    b. whether the problem is accurately identified
    c. who decides the method by which the problem is solved
    d. the person to whom a problem is communicated

    1. a   2. b   3. c   4. d   5. a & b   6. a b d   7. a & c

25. The following comments can be attributed to scapegoating:
    a. it is a necessary role function
    b. it is an integrative function for the family system, but may be destructive to individuals
    c. the scapegoat is a passive victim
    d. all of the above

26. Affective Responsiveness is:
    a. a process dimension
    b. determined by affective involvement
    c. an individual control function
    d. a necessary for affective communication

27. Indicate which of the following is *not* involved in Role Allocation:
    a. appropriateness of roles
    b. implications or explicitness
    c. who is involved in the process
    d. effectiveness with which the task is carried out
    e. how roles are shared between family members
    f. all of the above

28. Which of the following statements are true?
    a. A family can have difficulty with affective communication while communicating quite well regarding instrumental issues.
    b. A family can have difficulty with both affective and instrumental communication.

  c. A family which functions poorly in the area of instrumental communication will rarely communicate well affectively.
  d. Affective responsiveness is not necessary for affective communication.

    1. a   2. b   3. a b   4. a b c   5. b c d

29. When handling dangerous situations, the pattern the family adopts is:
  a. the transactional pattern
  b. the role allocation pattern
  c. the behavioral control pattern
  d. the problem solving behavior pattern

30. Systems maintenance and management is:
  a. a systems concept related to maintaining homeostasis
  b. a role function
  c. a goal of family problem solving
  d. a leadership function
  e. all of the above

31. Which of the following dimensions have both instrumental and affective areas of consideration?
  a. Problem Solving
  b. Communication
  c. Roles
  d. Affective Responsiveness
  e. Affective Involvement
  f. Behavior Control

    1. a b   2. a b f   3. a b c   4. d e f   5. b c d
    6. all of the above

McMaster Family Functioning Percept Test

Read each statement, imagining that you have just heard someone use it to describe his/her family. Then decide which dimension of the MMFF is indicated by the statement.

PS = Problem Solving
CM = Communication
RL = Roles
AR = Affective Responsiveness
AI   = Affective Involvement
BC = Behavior Control

1. We get angry over small things.
   PS _____ CM _____ RL _____ AR _____ AI _____ BC _____ _____

2. If a crisis comes up, we have difficulty in organizing who does what.
   PS _____ CM _____ RL _____ AR _____ AI _____ BC _____ _____

3. We don't talk to each other when we are angry.
   PS _____ CM _____ RL _____ AR _____ AI _____ BC _____ _____

4. Our relationships tend to be businesslike rather than friendly.
   PS _____ CM _____ RL _____ AR _____ AI _____ BC _____ _____

5. There are some tensions and problems we can't seem to deal with.
   PS _____ CM _____ RL _____ AR _____ AI _____ BC _____ _____

6. The rules can be altered if there is good reason.
   PS _____ CM _____ RL _____ AR _____ AI _____ BC _____ _____

7. We often feel lonely even when we are together.
   PS _____ CM _____ RL _____ AR _____ AI _____ BC _____ _____

8. We agree on trip and holiday plans.
   PS _____ CM _____ RL _____ AR _____ AI _____ BC _____ _____

9. We usually get things done on time.
   PS _____ CM _____ RL _____ AR _____ AI _____ BC _____ _____

10. It seems like there are always too many people in the house.
    PS _____ CM _____ RL _____ AR _____ AI _____ BC _____ _____

11. Things around the house get fixed quickly.
    PS _____ CM _____ RL _____ AR _____ AI _____ BC _____ _____

12. We know what to do in an emergency.
    PS _____ CM _____ RL _____ AR _____ AI _____ BC _____ _____

13. It is difficult to talk to each other about tender feelings.
    PS _____ CM _____ RL _____ AR _____ AI _____ BC _____ _____

14. We know how family members will behave in most situations.
    PS _____ CM _____ RL _____ AR _____ AI _____ BC _____ _____

15. Tenderness takes second place to other things in our family.
    PS _____ CM _____ RL _____ AR _____ AI _____ BC _____ _____

16. Even though we mean well, we intrude too much into each others'
    lives.
    PS _____ CM _____ RL _____ AR _____ AI _____ BC _____ _____

17. We feel accepted for what we are.
    PS _____ CM _____ RL _____ AR _____ AI _____ BC _____ _____

18. Our house is well stocked with food and essentials.
    PS _____ CM _____ RL _____ AR _____ AI _____ BC _____ _____

19. Some of us can't be happy even when it's reasonable.
    PS _____ CM _____ RL _____ AR _____ AI _____ BC _____ _____

20. We enjoy talking about our personal interests.
    PS _____ CM _____ RL _____ AR _____ AI _____ BC _____ _____

21. Our household runs smoothly.
    PS _____ CM _____ RL _____ AR _____ AI _____ BC _____ _____

22. When you ask someone to do something, you have to check that they did it.
    PS _____ CM _____ RL _____ AR _____ AI _____ BC _____ _____

23. We share our happiness with each other.
    PS _____ CM _____ RL _____ AR _____ AI _____ BC _____ _____

24. We are too self-centered.
    PS _____ CM _____ RL _____ AR _____ AI _____ BC _____ _____

25. We avoid telling other family members about problems we see.
    PS _____ CM _____ RL _____ AR _____ AI _____ BC _____ _____

26. Our living conditions are comfortable.
    PS _____ CM _____ RL _____ AR _____ AI _____ BC _____ _____

27. We seldom try to go over how we resolved difficulties.
    PS _____ CM _____ RL _____ AR _____ AI _____ BC _____ _____

28. We have difficulties making clear to each other where and when to meet.
    PS _____ CM _____ RL _____ AR _____ AI _____ BC _____ _____

29. Sometimes we are quite careless.
    PS _____ CM _____ RL _____ AR _____ AI _____ BC _____ _____

30. We see crying as a sign of weakness.
    PS _____ CM _____ RL _____ AR _____ AI _____ BC _____ _____

31. We can be angry without losing respect for each other.
    PS _____ CM _____ RL _____ AR _____ AI _____ BC _____ _____

32. We resolve most emotional upsets that come up.
    PS _____ CM _____ RL _____ AR _____ AI _____ BC _____ _____

33. We are not satisfied with anything short of perfection.
    PS _____ CM _____ RL _____ AR _____ AI _____ BC _____ _____

34. We could not possibly exist without each other.
    PS _____ CM _____ RL _____ AR _____ AI _____ BC _____ _____

35. Some members are unhappy about where they are going in life.
    PS _____ CM _____ RL _____ AR _____ AI _____ BC _____ _____

36. It isn't always clear when we are being asked to do something.
    PS _____ CM _____ RL _____ AR _____ AI _____ BC _____ _____

37. We often feel we're being talked about, but we're not part of the discussion.
    PS _____ CM _____ RL _____ AR _____ AI _____ BC _____ _____

38. We trust each other.
    PS _____ CM _____ RL _____ AR _____ AI _____ BC _____ _____

Related Articles

The following is a list of published articles that have used the McMaster instruments in a variety of research settings. The list has been divided into the following categories: Studies of Patients with Medical Illnesses—Children and Adolescents (**A**), Studies of Patients with Medical Illnesses—Adults (**B**), Studies of Patients with Psychiatric Illnesses—Children and Adolescents (**C**), Studies of Patients with Psychiatric Illnesses—Adults (**D**), Cross-Cultural Studies (**E**), Instrument Development and Methodology (**F**), and Normals, Community Samples (**G**). Some articles listed in one category may also fall into an alternative category. These articles are indicated by a bold letter at the end of the listing signifying the alternative category.

A. Studies of Patients with Medical Illnesses— Children and Adolescents (**A**)

1. Ammerman R. T., Kane, V. R., Slomka, G. T., Reigel, D. H., Franzen, M. D., & Gadow, K. D. (1998). Psychiatric symptomatology and family functioning in children and adolescents with spina bifida. *Journal of Clinical Psychology in Medical Settings, 5*(4), 449–465. (C)
2. Aydin, B., Yaprak, I., Akarsu, D., Okten, N., & Ulgen, M. (1997). Psychosocial aspects and psychiatric disorders in children with thalassemia major. *Acta Pediatric Journal, 39*(3), 354–357. (C)
3. Bender, B., Milgrom, H., Rand, C., & Ackerson L. (1998) Psychological factors associated with medication nonadherence in asthmatic children. *Journal of Asthma, 35*(4), 347–353. (C)
4. Bihun, J. T., Wamboldt, M. Z., Gavin, L. A., & Wamboldt, F. S. (2002). Can the Family Assessment Device (FAD) be used with school aged children? *Family Process, 41*(4), 723–731. (G)
5. Fisiloglu, A. G., & Fisiloglu, H. (1996). Turkish families with deaf and hard of hearing children: A systems approach in assessing family functioning. *American Annals of Deafness, 141*(3), 231–235. (E)
6. Gowers, S. G., Jones, J. C., Kiana, S., North, C. D., & Price, D. A. (1995). Family functioning: A correlate of diabetic control? *Journal of Child Psychology Psychiatry, 36*(6), 993–1001.

7. Loder, R. T, Warschausky, S., Schwartz, E. M., Hensinger, R. N., & Greenfield, M. L. (1995). The psychosocial characteristics of children with fractures. *Journal of Pediatric Orthopedics, 15*(1), 41–46.(C)

8. Luescher, J. L., Dede, D. E., Gitten, J. C., Fennell, E., & Maria, B. L. (1999). Parental burden, coping, and family functioning in primary caregivers of children with Joubert syndrome. *Journal of Child Neurology, 14*(10), 669–672.

9. Magill-Evans J., Darrah, J., Pain, K., Adkins, R., & Kratochvil M. (2001). Are families with adolescents and young adults with cerebral palsy the same as other families? *Developmental Medicine and Child Neurology, 43*(7), 466 –472.

10. Max, J. E., Castillo, C. S., Robin, D. A., Lindgren, S. D., Smith, W. L., Sato, Y., et al. (1998). Predictors of family functioning after traumatic brain injury in children and adolescents. *Journal of American Academy of Child & Adolescent Psychiatry, 37*(1), 83–90.

11. Max, J. E., Robin, D. A., Lindgren, S. D., Smith, W. L., Sato, Y., Mattheis, P. J., et al. (1997). Traumatic brain injury in children and adolescents: Psychiatric disorders at two years. *Journal of American Academy of Child & Adolescent Psychiatry, 36*(9), 1278–1285. (C)

12. Pinelli J. (2000). Effects of family coping and resources on family adjustment and parental stress in the acute phase of the NICU experience. *Journal of Neonatal Nursing, 19*(6), 27–37.

13. Raiha, H., Lehtonen, L., Korhonen, T., & Korvenranta, H. (1997). Family functioning three years after infantile colic. *Journal of Developmental Pediatric, 18*(5), 290–294.

14. Riley, S. P., Greenstone, H., & Mainemer, A. (1997). A history of severe bronchopulmonary dysplasia contributes to functional difficulties and family distress at school age. *Pediatric Research, Part 2, 31*(4), 210.

15. Rivara, J. M., Jaffe, K. M., Polissa, R. L., Fay, G. C., Liao, S., & Martin, K. M. (1996). Predictors of family functioning and change 3 years after traumatic brain injury in children. *Archives Physical Medicine and Rehabilitation, 77*(8), 754–764.

16. Sawyer, M. G., Streiner, D. L., Antoniou, G., Toogood, I., & Rice, M. (1998). Influence of parental and family adjustment on the later psychological adjustment of children treated for cancer. *Journal of the American Academy of Child and Adolescent Psychiatry, 37*(8), 815–822.

17. Stancin, T., Taylor, G. H., Thompson, G. H., Wade, S., Drotar, D., & Yeates, K. O. (1998). Acute psychosocial impact of pediatric orthopedic trauma with and without accompanying brain injuries. *The Journal of Trauma, 45*(6), 1031–1038. (C)

18. Wade, S. L., Taylor, H. G., Drotar, D., Stancin, T., & Yeates, K. O. (1996). Childhood traumatic brain injury: Initial impact on the family. *Journal of Learning Disabilities, 29*(6), 652–661.

19. Wiegner, S., & Donders, J. (2000). Predictors of parental distress after congenital disabilities. *Journal of Developmental and Behavioral Pediatrics, 21*(4), 271–277.

20. Yeates, K. O., Taylor, G. H., Drotar, D., Wade, S., Klein, S., Stancin, T., et al. (1997). Preinjury family enviornment as a determinant of recovery from traumatic brain injuries in school age children. *Journal of the International Neuropsychological Society, 3,* 617–630.

B. Studies of Patients with Medical Illnesses—Adults (B)

1. Alexander, C. J., Hwang, K., & Sipski, M. L. (2002). Mothers with spinal cord injuries: Impact on marital, family, and children's adjustment. *Archives of Physical Medicine and Rehabilitation, 83,* 24–30.

2. Arpin, K., Fitch, M., Browne, G. B., & Corey, C. (1990). Prevalence and correlates of family dysfunction and poor adjustment to chronic illness in specialty clinics. *Journal of Clinical Epidemiology, 43*(4), 373–383.

3. Bernbaum, M., Albert, S. G., Duckro, P. N., & Merkel, W. (1993). Personal and family stress in individuals with diabetes and vision loss. *Journal of Clinical Psychology, 49*(5), 670–677.

4. Boettcher, A., Billick, S. B., & Burhert, W. (2001). Family functioning and depression in patients with medical illness. *Psychiatric Annals, 31*(12), 694–700. (D)

5. Browne, G. B., Arpin, K., Corey, P., Fitch, M., & Gafni, A. (1990). Individual correlates of health service utilization and the cost of poor adjustment to chronic illness. *Medical Care, 28,* 43–58.

6. Clark, M. S. (1999). The double ABCX model of family crisis as a representation of family functioning after rehabilitation from stroke. *Health and Medicine Psychology, 4*(2), 203–220.

7. Clark, M. S., & Smith, D. S. (1999). Psychological correlates of outcome following rehabilitation from stroke. *Clinical Rehabilitation, 13*(2), 129–140. (D)

8. Clark, M. S., & Smith, D. S. (1998). Factors contributing to patient satisfaction with rehabilitation following stroke. *International Journal of Rehabilitation Research, 21*(2),143 – 154.

9. Clark, M. S., & Smith, D. S. (1999). Changes in family functioning for stroke rehabilitation patients and their families. *International Journal of Rehabilitation Research, 22*(3),171–179.

10. Duckett, S. (1987). Family assessment device. *Archives of Physical Medicine and Rehabilitation, 36*(1), 85–93.

11. Evans, R. L., Bishop, D. S., & Halar, E. (1987). Family interaction & treatment adherence after stroke. *Archives of Physical Medicine and Rehabilitation,* (August), 68.

12. Groom, K. N., Shaw, T. G., O'Connor, M. E., Howard, N. I., & Pickens, A. (1998). Neurobehavioral symptoms and family functioning in traumatically brain-injured adults. *Archives of Clinical Neuropsychology, 13*(8), 695–711.

13. Hewitt, P. L., Flett, G. L., & Mikail, S. F. (1995). Perfectionism and relationship adjustment in pain patients and their spouses. *Journal of Family Psychology, 9*(3), 335–347.

14. Inoue, S., Saeki, T., Mantani, T., Okamura, H., & Yamawaki, S. (2003). Factors related to patient's mental adjustment to breast cancer: Patient characteristics and family functioning. *Support Cancer Care, 11*(3), 178–184.

15. Kosciulek, J. F. (1994). Relationship of family coping with head injury to family adaption. *Rehabilitation Psychology, 39*(4), 215–230.

16. Kosciulek, J. F., & Lustig, D. C. (1998). Predicting family adaption from brain injury-related family stress. *Journal of Applied Rehabilitation Counseling, 29*(1), 8–12.

17. Kreutzer, J., Gervasio, A., & Camplair P. (1994). Patient correlates of caregivers' distress and family functioning after traumatic brain injury. *Brain Injury, 8*(3), 211–230.

18. Kristjanson, L. J., Leis, A., Koop, P. M., Carriere, K. C., & Mueller, B. (1997). Family members' care expectations, care perceptions, and satisfaction with advanced cancer care: Results of a multi-site pilot study. *Journal of Palliative Care, 13*(4), 5–13.

19. Marlowe, S., Bishop, D. S., Gionta, D., & Albro, J. (1997). Psychosocial effects of fibromyalgia on couples. *Arthritis & Rheumatism.*

20. O'Farrell, P., Murray, J., & Hotz, S. B. (2000). Psychologic distress amoung spouses of patients undergoing cardiac rehabilitation. *Heart Lung, 29*(2), 97–104. (D)

21. Reeber, B. J. (1992). Evaluating the effects of a family education intervention. *Rehabilitation Nursing, 17*(6), 332–336.

22. Roy, R. (1990).Chronic pain and "effective" family functioning: A re-examination of the McMaster Model of Family Functioning. *Contemporary Family Therapy, 12*(6), 489–503.

23. Zarski, J. J., DePompei, R., & Zook, A., II. (1988). Traumatic head injury: Dimensions of family responsivity. *The Journal of Head Trauma Rehabilitation, 3*(4), 31–41.

C. Studies of Patients with Psychiatric Illnesses— Children and Adolescents (C)

1. Allison, S., Roeger, L., Dadds, V., & Martin G. (2000). Brief therapy for children's mental health problems: Outcomes in a rural setting. *Australian Journal of Rural Health, 8*(3), 161–166. (G)

2. Brent, D. A., Kolko, D. J., Birmaher, B., Baugher, M., & Bridge, J. (1999). A clinical trial for adolescent depression: Predictors of additional treatment in the acute and follow-up phases of the trial. *Journal of American Academy of Child and Adolescent Psychiatry, 38*(3), 263–270.

3. Byford, S., Harrington, R., Torgerson, D., Derfoot, M., Dyer, E., Harrington, V., et al. (1999). Cost-effectiveness analysis of a home-based social work intervention for children and adolescents who have deliberately poisoned themselves. *British Journal of Psychiatry, 174,* 56–62.

4. Cunningham, C. E., Benness, B. B., & Siegel, L. S. (1988). Family functioning, time allocation, and parental depression in the families of normal and ADDH children. *Journal of Clinical Child Psychology, 17*(2), 169–177.

5. Dare, C., & Key, A. (1999). Family functioning and adolescent anorexia nervosa. *The British Journal of Psychiatry, 175*(7), 89.

6. Goodyer, I., Nicol, A. R., Eavis, D., & Pollinger, G. (1982). The application and utility of a family assessment procedure in a child psychiatric clinic. *Journal of Family Therapy, 4*, 373–395.

7. Gowers, S., & North, C. (1999). Difficulties in family functioning and adolescent anorexia nervosa. *British Journal of Psychiatry, 174*, 63–66.

8. Harrington, R., Kerfoot, M., Dyer, E., McNiven, F., Gill, J., Harrington, V., et al. (1998). Randomized trial of a home-based family intervention for children who have deliberately poisoned themselves. *Journal of the American Academy of Child and Adolescent Psychiatry, 37*(5), 512–518.

9. Hoagwood, K., & Stewart, J. M. (1989). Sexually abused children's perceptions of family functioning. *Child and Adolescent Social Work Journal, 6*(2), 139–149.

10. Joffe, R. T., Offord, D. R., & Boyle, M. H. (1988). Ontario Child Health Study: Suicidal behavior in youth age 12–16 Years. *American Journal of Psychiatry, 145*(11), 1420–1423.

11. Kaplan, B. J., Crawford, S. G., Fisher, G. C., & Dewey, D. M. (1998). Family dysfunction is more strongly associated with ADHD than with general school problems. *Journal of Attention Disorders, 2*(4), 209–216. (G)

12. Kerfoot, M., Dyer, E., Harrington, V., Woodham, A., & Harrington, R. (1996). Correlates and short-term course of self-poisoning in adolescents. *The British Journal of Psychiatry, 168*(1) , 38–46.

13. King, C. A., Segal, H. G., Naylor, M., & Evans, T. (1993). Family functioning and suicidal behavior in adolescent inpatients with mood disorders. *Journal of American Academy of Child & Adolescent Psychiatry, 32*, 6, 1198–1206.

14. King, C. A., Hovey, J. D., Brand, E., Wilson, R., & Ghaziuddin, N. (1997). Suicidal adolescents after hospitalization: Parent and family impacts on treatment follow-through. *Journal of American Academy of Child and Adolescent Psychiatry, 36*(1), 85–93.

15. Kline, P. M. (1995). An exploratory investigation of family functioning for child inpatients: Implications for practice. *Child and Adolescent Social Work Journal, 12*, 423–434.

16. Martin, G. (1996). Reported family dynamics, sexual abuse, and suicidal behaviors in community adolescents. *Archives of Suicide Research, 2*(3), 183–195. (G)

17. Martin, G., Rozanes, P., Pearce, C., & Allison, S. (1995). Adolescent suicide, depression and family dysfunction. *Acta Psychiatrica Scandinavica, 92*(5), 336–344.

18. Maziade, M., Caperaa, P., & Laplante, B. (1985). Value of difficult temperament among 7-year-olds in the general population for predicting psychiatric diagnosis at age 12. *American Journal of Psychiatry, 142*, 943–946. (G)

19. McKay, J. R., Murphy, R. T., Rivinus, T. R., & Maisto, S. A. (1991). Family dysfunction and alcohol and drug use in adolescent psychiatric inpatients. *Journal of American Academy of Child & Adolescent Psychiatry, 30*(6), 967–972.

20. North, C., Gowers, S., & Byram, V. (1995). Family functioning in adolescent anorexia nervosa. *British Journal of Psychiatry, 167*(5), 673–678.

21. North, C., Gowers, S., & Byram, V. (1997). Family functioning and life events in the outcome of adolescent anorexia nervosa. *British Journal of Psychiatry, 171*, 545–549.

22. Oates, R. K., O'Tool, B. I., Lynch, D. L., Stern, A., & Cooney, G. (1994). Stability and change in outcomes for sexually abused children. *Journal of American Academy of Child and Adolescent Psychiatry, 33*(7), 945–953.

23. Renaud, J., Brent, D. A., Baugher, M., Birmaher, B., Kolko, D., & Bridge, J. (1998). Rapid response to psychosocial treatment for adolescent depression: A two-year follow up. *Journal of American Academy of Child and Adolescent Psychiatry, 37*(11), 1184–1190.

24. Sanford, M., Byrne, C., Williams, S., Atley, S., Ridley, T., Miller, J., & Allin, H. (2003). A pilot study of a parent-education group for families affected by depression. *Canadian Journal of Psychiatry, 48*, 78–86.

25. Stein, D., Williamson, D. E., Birmaher, B., Brent, D. A., Kaufman, J., Dahl, R. E., et al. (2000). Parent-child bonding and family functioning in depressed children and children at high risk and low risk for future depression. *Journal of American Academy of Child and Adolescent Psychiatry, 39*(11), 1387–1395.

26. Stern, A. E., Lynch, D. L., Oates, R. K., & O'Toole, B. I. (1995). Self esteem, depression, behavior and family functioning in sexually abused children. *Journal of Psychology and Psychiatry and Allied Disciplines, 36*(6), 1077–1089.

27. Swanston, H. Y., Tebbutt, J. S., O'Toole, B. I., & Oates, R. K. (1997). Sexually abused children 5 years after presentation: A case-control study. *Pediatrics, 100*(4), 600–608.

28. Tamplin, A., Goodyer, I. M., & Herbert, J. (1998). Family functioning and parent general health in families of adolescents with major depressive disorder. *Journal of Affective Disorders, 48,* 1–13.

29. Tamplin, A., & Goodyer, I. M. (2001). Family functioning in adolescents at high and low risk for major depressive disorder. *European Child and Adolescent Psychiatry, 10*(3), 170–179.

30. Tebbutt, J., Swanston, H., Oates, R. K., & O'Toole, B. I. (1997). Five years after child sexual abuse: Persisting dysfunction and problems of prediction. *Journal of American Academy of Child and Adolescent Psychiatry, 36*(3), 330–339.

D. *Studies of Patients with Psychiatric Illnesses—Adults* (D)

1. Akister, J., Meekings, E., & Stevenson-Hinde, J. (1993). The spouse subsystem in the family context: Couples interaction categories. *Journal of Family Therapy, 15,* 1–21.

2. Black, D., Gaffney, G., Schlosser, S., & Gabel, J. (1998). The impact of obsessive–compulsive disorder on the family: Preliminary findings. *Journal of Nervous and Mental Disease, 186*(7), 440–442.

3. Calvocoressi, L., Lewis, B., Harris, M., Trufan, S. J., Goodman, W. K., McDougle, C. J., et al. (1995). Family accommodation in obsessive-compulsive disorder. *American Journal of Psychiatry, 152*(3), 441–443.

4. DeVanna, M., Pascolo, E., Pressi, P., & Aguglia, E. (1996). The depressed patient and his family. *Psichiatria-e-Psicoterapia-Analitica, 15*(1), 87–96.

5. Dickstein, S., Seifer, R., Hayden, L. C., Schiller, M., Sameroff, A. J., Keitner, G., et al. (1998). Levels of family assessment: II. Impact of maternal psychopathology on family functioning. *Journal of Family Psychology, 12*(1), 23–40.

6. Fornari, V., Wlodarczyk-Bisaga, K., Matthews, M., Sandberg, D., Mandel, F. S., & Katz, J. L. (1999). Perception of family functioning and depressive symptomatology in individuals with anorexia nervosa or bulimia nervosa. *Comprehensive Psychiatry, 40*(6), 434–441.

7. Hayden, L. C., Schiller, M., Dickstein, S., Seifer, R., Sameroff, A., Miller, I., et al. (1998). Levels of family assessment: I. family marital and parent-child interaction. *Journal of Family Psychology, 12*(1), 7–22.

8. Krawetz, P., Fleisher, W., Pillay, N., Staley, D., Arnett, J., & Maher, J. (2001). Family functioning in subjects with pseudoseizures and epilepsy. *The Journal of Nervous and Mental Disease, 189*(1), 38–43.

9. Liepman, M. R., Nirenberg, T. D., Doolittle, R. H., Begin, A. M., Broffman, T. E., & Babich, M. E. (1989). Family functioning of male alcoholics and their female partners during periods of drinking and abstinence. *Family Process,* 28, 239–249.

10. Livingston, B., Rasmussen, S. A., Eisen, J., & McCartney, L. (1988). Family function and treatment in OCD. In M. Jenikes (Ed.), *Obsessions and compulsions* (2nd ed.). New York: Yearbook Medical Publishers.

11. Lumley, M. A., Mader, C., Gramzow, J., & Papineau, K. (1996). Family factors related to alexithymia characteristics. *Psychosom - Med, 58*(3), 211–216.

12. McKay, J. R., Maisto, S. A., Bettie, M. C., Longabaugh, R., & Noel, N. E. (1993). Differences between alcoholics and spouses in their perceptions of family functioning. *Journal of Substance Abuse Treatment, 10*(1), 17–21.

13. Murphy, P. N., & Bentall, R. P. (1999). Opiate withdrawal outcome: The predictive ability of admission measures from the Family Assessment Device. *Substance Use and Misuse, 34*(2), 307–316.

14. Priest, P., Wagner, H., & Waller, G. (1991). Psychological characteristics of anorexic and bulimic women who attend self-help groups. *British Review of Bulimia and Anorexia Nervosa, 5*(2), 77–84.

15. Saeki, T., Asukai, N., Miyake, Y., Miguchi, M., & Yamawakin, S. (2002). Characteristics of family functioning in patients with endogenous monopolar depression. *Hiroshima Journal of Medical Science, 51*(2), 55–62.

16. Seifer, R., Sameroff, A. J., Dickstein, S., Keitner, G., & Miller, I. (1996). Parental psychopathology, multiple contextual risks, and one-year outcomes in children. *Journal of Clinical Child Psychology, 25*(4), 423–435.

17. Waller, G., Calam, R., & Slade, P. (1989). Eating disorders and family interaction. *British Journal of Clinical Psychology, 28*(3), 285–286.

18. Waller, G., Slade, P., & Calam, R. (1990). Who Knows Best? Family interaction and eating disorders. *British Journal of Psychiatry, 156,* 546–550.

19. Wood, N., & Wassenaar, D. R. (1989). Family characteristics of Indian parasuicide patients: A controlled study. *South African Journal of Psychology, 19*(3), 172–174. (E)

20. Yu-Kit Sun, S., & Cheung, S. K. (1997). Family functioning, social support to families, and symptom remittance of schizophrenia. *Hong Kong Journal of Psychiatry, 7*(2), 19–25.

E. Cross-Cultural Studies (E)

1. Al-Krenawi, A., Slonim-Nevo, V., Maymon, Y., & Al-Krenawi, S. (2001). Psychological responses to blood vengeance among Arab adolescents. *Child Abuse and Neglect, 25,* 457–472. (7)

2. Al- Krenawi, A., Grahan, J. R., & Slonim-Nevo, V. (2002). Mental health aspects of Arab–Israeli adolescents from polygamous versus monogamous families. *Journal of Social Psychology, 142*(4), 446–460. (C)

3. Ben-David, A., & Jurich, J. (1993). A test of adaptability: Examining the curvilinear assumption. *Journal of Family Psychology, 7*(3), 370–375. (F)

4. Guelerce, A. (1996). A family structure assessment for Turkey. In J. Pandey, D. Sinha & D. P. S. Bhawuk (Eds.), *Asian contributions to cross-cultural psychology* (pp. 108–118). New Dehli: Sage. (F)

5. Hovey, J. D., & King, C. A. (1996). Acculturative stress, depression, and suicidal ideation among immigrant   and second-generation Latino adolescents. *Journal of American Academy of Child and Adolescent Psychiatry, 35*(9), 1183–92. (C)

6. Moretti, M., Kurimay, T., Molnar, Z., & Szerdahelyi, F. (1997). At the price of assimilation. *Psychiatria Hungarica, 12*(1), 5–18.

7. Morris, T. M. (1990). Culturally sensitive family assessment: An evaluation of the Family Assessment Device used with Hawaiian-American and Japanese-American Families. *Family Process, 29,* 105–116.

8. Roncone, R., Rossi, L., Muiere, E., Impallomeni, M., Matteucci, M., Giacomelli, R., et al. (1998). The Italian version of the family assessment device. *Social Psychiatry Epidemiology, 33*(9), 451–461.

9. Shek, D. T. (2001). The general functioning scale of the family assessment device: Does it work with Chinese adolescents? *Journal of Clinical Psychology, 57*(12), 1503–1516

10. Wenniger, W., Hageman, W., & Arrindell, W. (1993). Cross-national validity of dimensions of family functioning: First experiences with the Dutch Version of the McMaster Family Assessment Device (FAD). *Personality and Individual Differences, 14*(6), 769–781. (F)

F. Instrument Development and Methodology (F)

1. Boyle, M. H., & Pickles, A. R. (1998). Strategies to manipulate reliability: Impact on statistical associations. *Journal of the American Academy of Child and Adolescent Psychiatry, 37,* 1077–1084.

2. Byles, J., Byrne, C., Boyle, M., & Offord, D. (1988). Ontario Child Health Study: Reliability and validity of the general functioning subscale of the McMaster Family Assessment Device. *Family Process, 27,* 97–104.

3. Fristad, M. A. (1989). A comparison of the McMaster and Circumplex family assessment instruments. *Journal of Marital and Family Therapy, 15*(3), 259–269.

4. Kaufman, K. L., Tarnowski, K. J., Simonian, S. J., & Graves, K. (1991). Assessing the readability of family assessment self-report measures. *Journal of Consulting and Clinical Psychology, 3*(4), 697–700.

5. Perosa, L. M., & Perosa, S. L. (1990). Convergent and discriminant validity for family self-report measures. *Education and Psychological Measurement, 50,* 855–868.

6. Peterson, R., & Prillaman, J. (2000). Implementation of a web-based, self-scoring version of the family assessment device (FAD) for parent education. *Journal of Extension,38*(6).

7. Portes, P. R., Smith, T. L., & Brown, J. H. (2000). The divorce adjustment inventory revised: Validation of a parental report concerning children's post-custody adjustment. *Journal of Divorce and Remarriage, 33*(3–4), 93–109. (G)

8. Ridenour, T. A., Daley, J. G., & Reich, W. (2000). Further evidence that the Family Assessment Device should be reorganized: Response to Miller and colleagues. *Family Process, 39*, 375–380.

9. Ridenour, T. A., Daley, J. G., & Reich, W. (1999). Factor analyses of the Family Assessment Device. *Family Process, 38*(4), 497–510.

10. Sabatelli, R. M., & Bartle, S. E. (1995). Survey approaches to the assessment of family functioning: Conceptual, operational, and analytical issues. *Journal of Marriage and the Family, 57*(4), 1025–1040. (G)

11. Wamboldt, W. Z., Wambolt, F. S., Gavin, L., & McTaggart, A. S. (2001). A parent-child relationship scale derived from the child and adolescent assessment (CAPA). *Journal of the American Academy of Child and Adolescent Psychiatry, 40*(8), 945–953.

12. Wilhelm, K., Brownhill, S., & Boyce, P. (2000). Marital and family functioning: different measures and viewpoints. *Social Psychiatry and Psychiatric Epidemiology, 35*(8), 358–365.

G. *Normals, Community Samples* (G)

1. Akister, J., & Stevenson-Hinde, J. (1991). Identifying families at risk: exploring the potential of the McMaster Family Assessment Device. *Family Therapy, 13*, 63–73.

2. Akister, J., Meekings, E., & Stevenson-Hinde, J. (1993). The spouse subsystem in the family context: Couples interaction categories. *Journal of Family Therapy, 15*, 1–21.

3. Bagley, C., Bertrand, L., Bolitho, F., & Mallick, K. (2001). Discrepant parent-adolescent views on family functioning: Predictors of poor self-esteem and problems of emotion and behavior in British and Canadian adolescents. *Journal of Comparative Family Studies, 32*(3), 393–403. (3)

4. Bickman, L., Noser, K., & Summerfelt, W. T. (1999). Long-term effects of a system of care on children and adolescents. *Journal of Behavioral Health Services and Research, 26*(2), 158–202.

5. Brown, J. H., Eichenberg, S. A., Portes, P. R., & Christensen, D. N. (1991). Family functioning factors associated with the adjustment of children of divorce. *Journal of Divorce and Remarriage,17*(1–2), 81–95.

6. Clark, A. F., Barrett, L., & Kolvin, I. (2000). Inner city disadvantage and family functioning. *European Child and Adolescent Psychiatry, 9*(2) 77–83.

7. Cohen, J. C., Coyne, J., & Duvall J. (1993). Adopted and biological children in the clinic: Family, parental, and child characteristics. *Journal of Child Psychology and Psychiatry, 34*, 545–562.

8. Corcoran, J. (2001). Multi-systemic influences on the family functioning of teens attending pregnancy prevention programs. *Child and Adolescent Social Work Journal, 18*(1), 37–49.

9. Dundas, S., & Kaufman, M. (2000). The Toronto lesbian family study. *Journal of Homosexuality, 40*(2), 65–79.

10. Dworkin, R. J., Harding, L. T., & Schreiber, N. B. (1993). Parenting or placing: decision making by pregnant teens. *Youth and Society, 25*(1), 75–92.

11. Kinsman, A. M., Wildman, B. G., & Smucker, W. D. (1999). Relationships among parental reports of child, parent, and family functioning. *Family Process, 38*(3), 341–351.

12. Levy, S. Y., Wambolt, F. S., & Fiese, B. H. (1997). Family-of-origin experiences and conflict resolution behaviors of young adult dating couples. *Family Process, 36*(3), 297–310.

13. Lieb, R., Wittchen, H. U., Hofler, M., Fuetsch, M., Stein, M. B., & Merikangas, K. R. (2000). Parental psychopathology, parenting styles, and the risk of social phobia in offspring: a prospective-longitudinal community study. *Archives of General Psychiatry, 57*(9), 859–866. (D)

14. Linker, J. S., Stolberg, A. L., & Green, R. G. (1999). Family communication as a mediator of child adjustment to divorce. *Journal of Divorce and Remarriage, 30*(1–2), 83–97.

15. Maziade, M., Cote, R., Boutin, P., Bernier, H., & Thivierge, J. (1987). Temperament and intellectual development: A longitudinal study from infancy to four years. *American Journal of Psychiatry, 144*(2), 144–150.

16. Maziade, M., Bernier, H., Thivierge, J., & Cote, R. (1987). The relationship between family functioning and demographic characteristics in an epidemiological study. *Canadian Journal of Psychiatry, 32*(7), 526–533. Errata, *Canadian Journal of Psychiatry, 32*(8), 701; *32*(9), 763.

17. Pavuluri, M. N., Luk, S. L., & McGee, R.(1996). Help-seeking for behavior problems by parents of preschool children: a community study. *Journal of American Academy of Child and Adolescent Psychiatry, 35*(2), 215–222.

18. Peek, C. W., Bell, N. J., Waldron, T., & Sorell, G. T. (1988). Patterns of functioning in families of remarried and first-married couples. *Journal of Marriage and Family Therapy, 50*, 699–708.

19. Saayman, G. S., & Saayman, R. V. (1988/89). The Adversarial Legal Process and Divorce: Negative Effects upon the Psychological Adjustment of Children. *Journal of Divorce, 12*, 329–348. (C)

20. Sawyer, M. G., Sarris, A., Baghurst, P. A., Cross, D. G., & Kalucy, R. S. (1988). Family Assessment Device: Reports from mothers, fathers, and adolescents in community and clinic families. *Journal of Marital and Family Therapy, 14*(3), 287–296.

21. Verhulst, F. C., & van der Ende, J. (1997). Factors associated with child mental health service use in the community. *Journal of American Academy of Child and Adolescent Psychiatry, 36*(7), 901–909. (C)

References

1. Epstein, N. B. (1994, May). *Lessons learned: Reflecting on the state of the art.* Paper presented at OAMFT Conference, The Evolution and State of the Art of Marital and Family Therapy in Canada. London, Ontario.
2. Ackerman, N. W. (1966). *Treating the troubled family.* New York: Basic Books.
3. Guttman, H. A. (2002). *Remembering times past.* Personal communication.
4. Kardiner, A., Linton, R., & Dubois, C. (1945). *The psychological frontier of society.* New York: Columbia University Press.
5. Rado, S. (1961).Towards the construction of an organized foundation for clinical psychiatry. *Comprehensive Psychiatry, 2*, 65–73.
6. Levy, D. M. (1943). *Maternal overprotection.* New York: Columbia University Press.
7. Epstein, N. B. (1969). *Family therapy today: An overview.* Paper presented at the International Symposium, Psychiatry over the last decades, Montebello, Quebec.
8. Epstein, N. B., & Bishop, D. S. (1973). Position paper—family therapy, state of the art. *Canadian Association Psychiatric Journal, 18*(3), 175–183.
9. Epstein, N. B., & Bishop, D. S. (1980). Overview of the family therapies. In *The family, Monograph #11.* Ontario Ministry of Community and Social Services, 20th Annual Symposium.
10. Westley, W. A., & Epstein, N. B. (1969). *The silent majority.* San Francisco: Jossey-Bass.
11. Epstein, N. B. (1992, October). *Description of a long time family research program: Integration of qualitative and quantitative research.* Paper presented at the Institute de la Familia, A.C. XX Anniversary International Symposium, New Mexico.
12. Epstein, N. B., & Levin, S. (1973). Training for family therapy within a faculty of medicine. *Canadian Psychiatric Association Journal, 18,* 203–208.
13. Epstein, N. B., Baldwin, L. M., & Bishop, D. S. (1983). The McMaster family assessment device. *Journal of Marital and Family Therapy, 9*(2), 171–180.
14. Epstein, N. B., Bishop, D. S., & Levin, S. (1984). The McMaster model of family functioning. In J. G. Howells (Ed.), *Advances in family psychiatry,* International Universities Press, 1984.
15. Epstein, N. B., Bishop, D. S., and Levin S. (1978). The McMaster model of family functioning. *Journal of Marriage and Family Counseling, 4,* 19–31.
16. Epstein, N. B., Ryan, C. E., Bishop, D. S., Miller, I. W., & Keitner, G. I. (2003). The McMaster model: A view of healthy family functioning. In F. Walsh (Ed.), *Normal family processes* (3rd ed., pp. 581–607). New York: Guilford Press.
17. Lederer, W. J., & Jackson, D. (1968). *The mirages of marriage.* New York: W.W. Norton.
18. Epstein, N. B., Bishop, D. S., Miller, I. W., & Keitner, G. I. (1989). *Problem centered systems therapy of the family: A treatment manual.* Providence, RI: Brown University Family Research Program..

19. Epstein, N. B., & Bishop, D. S. (1981). Problem centered systems therapy of the family. *Journal of Marital and Family Therapy, 7*(1), 23–31.
20. Epstein, N. B., Bishop, D. S., Keitner, G. I., & Miller, I. W. (1990). A systems therapy: Problem-centered systems therapy of the family. In R. A. Wells & V. J. Giannetti (Eds.), *Handbook of the brief psychotherapies* (pp. 405–436). New York: Plenum Press.
21. Cleghorn, J., & Levin, S. (1973). Training family therapists by setting learning objectives. *American Journal of Orthopsychiatry, 43*, 439–448.
22. Tomm, K. M. & Wright, L. M. (1979). Training in family therapy: Perceptual, conceptual, and executive skills. *Family Process, 18*, 227–250.
23. Kaplan, H. I., & Sadock, B. J. (1995b). Typical signs and symptoms of psychiatric illness. In H. I. Kaplan & B. J. Sadock (Eds.), *Comprehensive textbook of psychiatry*. Baltimore: Williams & Wilkins.
24. Kaplan, H. I., & Sadock, B. J. (1995a). Psychiatric report. In H. I. Kaplan & B. J. Sadock (Eds.), *Comprehensive textbook of psychiatry* (6th ed., pp. 531–534). Baltimore: Williams & Wilkins.
25. Strauss, G. D. (1995). The psychiatric interview, history, and mental status examination. In H. I. Kaplan & B. J. Sadock (Eds.), *Comprehensive textbook of psychiatry* (6th ed., pp. 521–530). Baltimore: Williams & Wilkins.
26. Scheiber, S C. (1999). The psychiatric interview, psychiatric history, and mental status examination. In R. E. Hales, S. C. Yudofsky, & J. A. Talbott (Eds.), *The American psychiatric press textbook of psychiatry*. (2nd ed., pp. 187–219). Washington, DC: American Psychiatric Press.
27. Bishop, D. S. (1980). *Questions that might be used in assessing a family*. Providence, RI: Brown University Family Research Program.
28. Group for the Advancement of Psychiatry. (1970). *The Field of Family Therapy, Report No. 78*.
29. Prochaska, J. O., & DiClemente, C. C. (1992). Stages of change in the modification of problem behaviors. *Program in behavior modification*,183–218.
30. Bishop, D. S., Byles, J., & Horn, D. (1984). Family therapy training methods: Minimal contact with an agency. *Journal of Family Therapy, 6*, 323–334.
31. Rubenstein, J. S.(1982). Learning objectives in family therapy training. *Canadian Journal of Psychiatry, 27,* 556–558.
32. Byles, J., Bishop, D. S., & Horn, D. (1983). Evaluation of a family therapy training program. *Journal of Marital and Family Therapy, 9*(3), 299–304.
33. Epstein, N. B., Levin, S., & Bishop, D. S. (1976). The family as a social unit. *Canadian Family Physician, 22*, 1411–1413.
34. Bishop, D. S. (1982). *Evaluation of conceptual skills*. Providence, RI: Brown University Family Research Program.
35. Bishop, D. S. (1982). *Evaluation of perceptual skills*. Providence, RI: Brown University Family Research Program.
36. Epstein, N. B., Baldwin, L. M., & Bishop, D. S. (1982). *Family assessment device*. Providence, RI: Brown University Family Research Program.
37. Epstein, N. B., Baldwin, L. M., & Bishop, D. S. (1982). *The McMaster clinical rating scale*. Providence, RI: Brown University Family Research Program.
38. Bishop, D. S., Epstein, N. B., Keitner, G. I., Miller, I. W., & Zlotnick, C. (1987). *The McMaster structured interview of family functioning*. Providence, RI: Brown University Family Research Program.
39. Miller, I. W., Epstein, N. B., Bishop, D. S., & Keitner, G. I. (1985). The McMaster family assessment device: Reliability and validity. *Journal of Marital and Family Therapy, 11*(4), 345–356.
40. Kabacoff, R. I., Miller, I. W., Bishop, D. S., Epstein, N. B., & Keitner, G. I. (1990). A psychometric study of the McMaster family assessment device in psychiatric, medical and nonclinical samples. *Journal of Family Psychology, 3*(4), 431–439.
41. Ridenour, T. A., Daley, J. G., & Reich, W. (2000). Further evidence that the family assessment device should be reorganized: Response to Miller and colleagues. *Family Process, 39*(3), 375–380.
42. Miller, I. W., Ryan, C. E., Keitner, G. I., Bishop, D. S., & Epstein, N. B. (2000). Why fix what isn't broken? A rejoinder to Ridenour, Daley, and Reich. *Family Process, 39*(3), 381–384.

43. Tasto, D. L. (1986). Self-report schedules and inventories. In A. Ciminero, K. Calhoun, & H. Adams (Eds.), *Handbook of behavioral assessment* (pp. 153–193). New York: Wiley.

44. Miller, I. W., Kabacoff, R. I., Epstein, N. B., Bishop, D. S., Keitner, G. I., Baldwin, L. M., & van der Spuy, H. I. J. (1994). The development of a clinical rating scale for the McMaster model of family functioning. *Family Process, 33*, 53–69.

45. Olson, D. H., McCubbin, H. I., Barnes, H., Larsen, A., Muxen, M., & Wilson. (1983). *Families: What makes them work*. Beverly Hills: Sage.

46. Sigafoos, A., Reiss, D., Rich, J., & Douglas, E. (1985). Pragmatics in the measurement of family functioning: An interpretive framework for methodology. *Family Process, 24*, 189–203.

47. Beavers, W. R., & Hampson, R. B. (1990). *Successful families: Assessment and intervention*. New York: W. W. Norton.

48. Bishop, D. S., Epstein, N. B., Keitner, G. I., Miller, I. W., Zlotnick, C., & Ryan, C. E. *The McMaster structured interview of family functioning (McSiff)*. Providence, RI: Brown University Family Research Program.

49. Bishop, D. S., Epstein, N. B., & Baldwin, L. M. (1980). Structuring a family assessment. *Canadian Family Physician, 26*, 1534–1537.

50. Epstein, N. B., Keitner, G. I., Bishop, D. S., & Miller, I. W. (1988). Combined use of pharmacological and family therapy. In J. Clarkin, G. Haas, & I. Glick (Eds.), *Affective disorders and the family*. New York: Guilford Press.

51. Epstein, N. B. (1958). Concepts of normality or evaluation of emotional health. *Behavioral Science, 3*, 335–343.

52. Walsh, F. (2003). Clinical views of family normality, health, and dysfunction. In F. Walsh (Ed.), *Normal family processes* (pp. 27–57). New York: Guilford Press.

53. Lebow, J. (1992). Continuing the dialog between family therapists and family researchers. *AFTA Newsletter, 47*, 19–21.

54. Epstein, N. B., Bishop, D. S., & Baldwin, L. M. (1982). McMaster model of family functioning: A view of the normal family. In F. Walsh (Ed.), *Normal family processes* (1st ed., pp. 115–141). New York: Guilford Press.

55. Miller, I. W., Kabacoff, R. I., Keitner, G. I., Epstein, N. B., & Bishop, D. S. (1986). Family functioning in the families of psychiatric patients. *Comprehensive Psychiatry, 27*(4), 302–312.

56. Keitner, G. I., Miller, I. W., Epstein, N. B., Bishop, D. S., & Fruzzetti, A. E. (1987). Family functioning and the course of major depression. *Comprehensive Psychiatry, 28*, 54–64.

57. Miller, I. W., Bishop, D. S., Norman, W. H., & Maddever, H. (1985). The modified Hamilton depression rating scale: Reliability and validity. *Psychiatric Research, 14*, 131–142.

58. Keitner, G. I., Miller, I. W., Ryan, C. E., Epstein, N. B., & Bishop, D. S. (1989). Compounded depression and family functioning during the acute episode and 6-month follow-up. *Comprehensive Psychiatry, 30*(6), 512–521.

59. Keitner, G. I., Ryan, C. E., Miller, I. W., Kohn, R., & Epstein, N. B. (1991). 12-month outcome of patients with major depression and comorbid psychiatric or medical illness (compound depression). *American Journal of Psychiatry, 148*(3), 345–350.

60. Keitner, G. I., Ryan, C. E., Miller, I. W., & Norman, W. H. (1992). Recovery and major depression: Factors associated with 12-month outcome. *American Journal of Psychiatry, 149*, 93–99.

61. Keitner, G. I., Ryan, C. E., Miller, I. W., Kohn, R., Bishop, D. S., & Epstein, N. B. (1995). Role of the family in recovery and major depression. *American Journal of Psychiatry, 15*(27), 1002–1008.

62. Keitner, G. I., Ryan, C. E., Miller, I. W., & Zlotnick, C. (1997). Psychosocial factors and the long-term course of major depression. *Journal of Affective Disorders, 44*, 57–67.

63. Miller, I. W., Keitner, G. I., Whisman, M. A., Ryan, C. E., Epstein, N. B., & Bishop, D. S. (1992). Depressed patients with dysfunctional families: Description and course of illness. *Journal of Abnormal Psychology, 101*, 637–646.

64. Keller, M. B., Lavori, P. W., Mueller, T. I., Endicott, J., Coryell, W., Hirschfeld, M. A., & Shea, M. T. (1992). Time to recovery, chronicity, and levels of psychopathology in major depression. *Archives of General Psychiatry, 49*, 809–816.

65. Maj, M., Veltro, F., Pirozzi, R., Lobrace, S., & Maliano, L. (1992). Pattern of recurrence of illness after recovery from an episode of major depression: A prospective study. *American Journal of Psychiatry, 149*, 795–800.

66. Giles, D. E., Jarrett, R. B., Biggs, M. M., Guzick, D. S., & Rush, A. J. (1989). Clinical predictors of recurrence in depression. *American Journal of Psychiatry, 146*(6), 764–767.

67. Keitner, G. I., Miller, I. W., Fruzzetti, A. E., Epstein, N. B., Bishop, D. S., & Norman, W. H. (1987). Family functioning and suicidal behavior in psychiatric inpatients with major depression. *Psychiatry, 50*, 242–255.

68. Keitner, G. I, Ryan, C. E., Miller, I. W., Epstein, N. B., Bishop, D. S., & Norman, W. H. (1990). Family functioning, social adjustment, and recurrence of suicidality. *Psychiatry, 53*, 17–30.

69. Keller, M. B., Lavori, P. W., Lewis, C. E, & Klerman, G. L. (1983). Predictors of relapse in major depressive disorder. *Journal of American Medical Association, 250*(24), 3299–3304.

70. Keitner, G. I., Ryan, C. E., Miller, I. W., & Keller, M. B. (1996). *Family functioning of chronically depressed patients.* Presented at American Psychiatric Association, New York.

71. Friedmann, M. S., McDermut, W. H., Solomon, D. A., Ryan, C. E., Keitner, G. I., & Miller, I. W. (1997). Family functioning and mental illness: A comparison of psychiatric and nonclinical families. *Family Process, 36*, 357–367.

72. Keitner, G. I., Ryan, C. E., Fodor, J. Miller, I. W., Epstein, N. B., & Bishop, D. S. (1990). A cross-cultural study of family functioning. *Contemporary Family Therapy, 12*(5), 439–454.

73. Keitner, G. I., Fodor, J., Ryan, C. E., Miller, I. W., Bishop, D. S., & Epstein, N. B. (1991). A cross-cultural study of major depression and family functioning. *Canadian Journal of Psychiatry, 36*, 254–259.

74. Saeki, T., Asukai, N., Miyake, Y., Miguchi, M., & Yamawaki, S. (1997). Reliability and validity of the Japanese family assessment device (FAD). *Archives of Psychiatric Diagnostics and Clinical Evaluation* (in Japanese with an English abstract), *8*, 181–192.

75. Keitner, G. I., Ryan, C. E., Saeki, T., & Miller, I. W. (2001). *Cross-cultural studies of family functioning in depressed patients.* Presented at European Family Therapy Association IV European Conference, Budapest, Hungary.

76. Bishop, D. S., Evans, R. L., Minden, S., McGowen, M., Marlowe, S., Amdreoli, N., Trotter, J., & Williams, C. (1987). Family functioning across different chronic illness/disability groups. *Archives of Physical Medicine and Rehabilitation, 69*, 610.

77. Bishop, D. S., & Miller, I. W. (1988). Traumatic brain injury: Empirical family assessment techniques. *Journal of Head Trauma Rehabilitation, 3*(4), 16–30.

78. Bishop, D. S., Epstein, N. B., Keitner, G. I., Miller, I. W., & Srinivasan, S. V. (1986). Stroke: Morale, family functioning, health status and functional capacity. *Archives of Physical Medicine and Rehabilitation, 67*, 84–87.

79. Evans, R. L., Bishop, D. S., & Ousley, R. (1992). Providing care to persons with physical disability: Effect of family caregivers. *American Journal of Physical Medicine Rehabilitation, 71*(3), 140–144.

80. Evans, R. L., Bishop, D. S., Halar, E., Matlock, A., Stranahan, S., & Smith, G. G. (1987). Family interaction & treatment adherence after stroke. *Archives of Physical Medicine and Rehabilitation, 68*, 513–517.

81. Evans, R. L., Bishop, D. S., Haselkorn, J. K., Hendricks, R. D., Baldwin, D., & Connis, R. T. (1991). From crisis to recovery: The family's role in stroke rehabilitation. *NeuroRehabilitation, 1*(2), 69–77.

82. Evans, R. L., Matlock, A. L., Bishop, D. S., Stranahan, S., & Pederson, C. (1988). Family intervention after stroke: Does counseling or education help? *Stroke, 19*(10), 1243–1247.

83. Miller, I. W., Keitner, G. I., Ryan, C. E., Solomon, D. A., & Gollan, J. (2000). *Measurement of long-term outcome in depression.* Presented at AABT Annual Meeting.

84. Keitner, G. I., Drury, L. M., Ryan, C. E., Miller, I. W., Norman, W. H., & Solomon, D. A. (2002). Multi-family group treatment for major depressive disorder. In W. McFarlane (Ed.), *Multi-family groups in the treatment of severe psychiatric disorders* (pp. 244–267). New York: Guilford Press.

85. Bech, P., Bolwig, T. G., Kramp, P., & Rafaelsen, O. J. (1979). The Bech-Rafaelsen mania scale and the Hamilton depression scale. *Acta Psychiatica Scandinavia, 59*, 420–430.

86. Solomon, D. A., Miller, I. W., Ryan, C. E., Keitner, G. I., & Kelley, J. (2002). *Recovery from acute mood episodes of bipolar I disorder.* Presented at NCDEU Annual Meeting, Boca Raton, Florida.

87. Ryan, C. E., Keitner, G. I., Solomon, D. A., Kelley, J., & Miller, I. W. (2003). *Factors related to a good, poor, or fluctuating course of illness.* Presented at 156th Annual American Psychiatric Association meeting, San Francisco.

88. Keitner, G. I., Ryan, C. E., Kelley, J., Solomon, D. A., & Miller, I. W. (2002). *Response to treatment in patients with severe bipolar disorder: Gender, polarity and social support.* Presented at First Biennial Conference, International Society for Affective Disorders, Taormina, Sicily.

89. Miller, I. W., Keitner, G. I., Ryan, C. E., Solomon, D. A., Cardemil, E. V., & Beevers, C. G. (in press). Treatment matching in the post-hospital care of depression. *American Journal of Psychiatry.*

90. Bishop, D. S., Evans, R. L., Miller, I. W., Epstein, N. B., Keitner, G. I., & Ryan, C. E. (1998). *Family intervention telephone tracking: A treatment manual for acute stroke patients.* Providence, RI: Brown University Family Research Program.

91. Miller, I. W., Weiner, D., Bishop, D. S., Johnson, B., & Albro, J. (1998). Telephone administered family intervention following stroke. *Rehabilitation Psychology, 43,* 323–324.

92. Bishop, D. S., Miller, I. W., Johnson, B., Weiner, D., & Albro, J. (1998). *FITT therapist guide: Topics definitions, conceptual background, intervention descriptions, and dialogue examples.* Providence, RI: Brown University Family Therapy Program.

93. Bishop, D. S., Miller, I. W., Johnson, B., Weiner, D. N., Guilmette, T. J., Mukand, J. A., Statson, W. B., Keitner, G. I., Ryan, C. E., & Epstein, N. B. (2002). *Family intervention telephone tracking (FITT): A preliminary stroke outcome study.* Providence, RI: Brown University Family Research Program.

94. Heru, A. M., Ryan, C. E., & Vlastos, K. (2004). Quality of life and family functioning in caregivers of patients with mood disorders. *Psychiatric Rehabilitation Journal, 28,* 67–71.

95. Heru, A. M., & Ryan, C. E. (2002). Depressive symptoms and family functioning in the caregivers of recently hospitalized patients with chronic/recurrent mood disorders. *International Journal of Psychosocial Rehabilitation, 7*(53), 53–60.

96. Byles, J., Byrne, C., Boyle, M., & Offord, D. (1988). Ontario child health study: Reliability and validity of the general functioning subscale of the McMaster family assessment device. *Family Process, 27,* 97–104.

97. Keitner, G. I., Ryan, C. E., Solomon, D. A., Kelley, J., & Miller, I. W. (2003). *Family therapy and family functioning in patients with mood disorders.* Presented at Annual Meeting American Psychiatric Association. San Francisco.

Index

Numbers in italic refer to tables and figures.